HISTORY
AND POPULAR
MEMORY

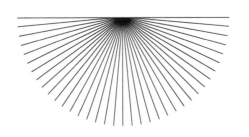

HISTORY
AND POPULAR
MEMORY

THE POWER OF STORY
IN MOMENTS
OF CRISIS

PAUL A. COHEN

COLUMBIA UNIVERSITY PRESS
NEW YORK

Columbia University Press
Publishers Since 1893
New York   Chichester, West Sussex
cup.columbia.edu

Copyright © 2014 Columbia University Press
Paperback edition, 2017

Library of Congress Cataloging-in-Publication Data

Cohen, Paul A.
History and popular memory : the power of story in moments of crisis /
Paul A. Cohen.
pages cm
Includes bibliographical references and index.
ISBN 978-0-231-16636-2 (cloth : alk. paper)—
ISBN 978-0-231-16637-9 (pbk. : alk. paper)—
ISBN 978-0-231-53729-2 (e-book)
1. Historiography—Social aspects—Case studies.   2. Collective memory—
Case studies.   3. Crises—History—Case studies.   4. Kosovo, Battle of,
Kosovo, 1389—Influence.   5. Masada Site (Israel)—Siege, 72–73—
Influence.   6. Goujian, –465 B.C.—Influence.   7. Joan, of Arc, Saint,
1412–1431—Influence.   8. Aleksandr Nevskii (Motion picture)—Influence.
9. Henry V (Motion picture : 1944)—Influence.   I. Title.

D13. C589 2014
907.2—dc23

2013032842

Cover design: Lisa Hamm

FOR JESSE, JULIA, AND TALYA

CONTENTS

ILLUSTRATIONS

MAPS

FIGURES

PREFACE

I n a recent book, *Speaking to History: The Story of King Goujian in Twentieth-Century China,*[1] I examined in some detail the power that an ancient Chinese story had at a number of key junctures in the history of China in the twentieth century. During that span of time, the story's impact was greatest at moments of protracted crisis, such as the mounting tension with Japan in the years leading up to the Sino-Japanese War of 1937–1945 and the predicament of Chiang Kai-shek's beleaguered Nationalists on Taiwan after 1949. By presenting a model of the world that incorporated a favorable outcome for the crisis, the right story in these circumstances pointed to a more hopeful future. What especially intrigued me about this process was the resonance or reverberation between story and situation, between a narrative and a contemporary historical condition that prompted those living in it to attach special meaning to that narrative.

Such narratives can in theory be ancient or modern, fictional or factual, religious or secular, indigenous or foreign. On the eve of the 2008 presidential election campaign in the United States, to cite one particularly arresting example of a religious nature, Barack Obama consciously inserted himself into a biblically structured history of the American civil rights movement in which (as he put it in a talk in Selma, Alabama, in March 2007) Martin Luther King Jr. and others represented "the Moses generation"—"the men and women of the movement, who marched and suffered but who, in many cases, 'didn't cross over the river to see the Promised Land'—and his own generation, 'the Joshua generation.'"[2]

Obama here tapped into a pervasive tendency among African Americans to frame the trajectory of their history through the prism of biblical prophesy. For many who decades earlier had marched and sung in the movement to extend voting rights to black people, exercising the right to vote in the presidential election of 2008, when a black candidate was given a better than even chance of winning, can only be described as a magical moment. "King made the statement that he viewed the Promised Land, won't get there, but somebody will get there, and that day has dawned," said the eighty-one-year-old pastor of the Shiloh Baptist Church in Albany, Georgia, as he pushed his wife in a wheelchair to the polls on Tuesday morning.[3] Apart from the resonance between Moses/ Joshua and King/Obama, there was an additional layer of meaning in the biblical story because although Moses himself didn't make it to the Promised Land, he was instrumental in freeing the Jews from bondage in Egypt and thus served as a powerful metaphor for the eventual realization of African American liberation—a dream that in American history Martin Luther King Jr. articulated and Barack Obama finally exemplified.

There are many other human communities as well in which stories of a religious character have taken an important part in the lived experience of the community's members, often serving as a template for this experience. But equally common are instances in which communities have looked for such sustenance to narratives from their own pasts, stories that, although undergoing a greater or lesser degree of reworking over time, had real historical origins. This process has perhaps been unusually prevalent in China, where since time immemorial people have demonstrated a strong affinity for stories dressed in historical garb, but the part taken by such stories—we might call them "history stories" as opposed to stories grounded in religion or myth—has been compellingly demonstrated in many other societies also.

In the process of writing the Goujian book, I became sensitized to the overall pattern of how the interplay between past story and present history functioned, and so I thought it might be interesting to see what happened if, from the multitude of possible examples, I selected a finite number, all relating to a specific set of issues, and looked at them in some depth. In this book, I focus on six countries—Serbia, Palestine/ Israel, China, France, the Soviet Union, and Great Britain—all of which faced severe crises in the course of the twentieth century. The crises I have singled out to deal with in every instance involved war or the threat of war, in response to which the populations and states affected drew upon older historical narratives that embodied themes broadly analogous to what was taking place in the historical present. Creative works—plays, poems, films, operas, and the like—often played an important role in the recovery and revitalization of these narratives, and as we would expect in the twentieth century, nationalism took a vital part in each case.

This reverberation between story and history is a phenomenon of no little historical interest. It is, however, exceedingly complex, reflecting deeply on how individual leaders or entire peoples or subgroups within a society position themselves in the space of historical memory. The manner of this positioning varies significantly from instance to instance. Yet running through them all is a constant: the mysterious power that people in the present draw from stories that sometimes derive from remotest antiquity and that, more often than not, recount events that, although making claims to historical accuracy, have been substantially reworked over time and have only the thinnest basis in an actual historical past. The question the eminent psychologist Jerome Bruner poses in reference to this storytelling phenomenon, although not referring explicitly to history, is central. "Why," he asks, "do we use story as the form for telling about what happens in life and in our own lives? Why not images, or lists of dates and places and the names and qualities of our friends and enemies? Why this seemingly innate addiction to story?"[4]

The power of story, so common and yet so poorly understood, merits far more scrutiny than it has generally received from historians.[5] Bruner, in response to his own question, cautions "Beware an easy answer!"[6] My hope is that the multifaceted connections developed in this book between story and history in a range of cultural settings and historical circumstances may serve to illuminate the problem he raises.

Because the older stories never supplied an exact match to what was currently transpiring in history, they were regularly modified to a greater or lesser degree to make the fit closer. This is where popular memory became important. Popular memory—what people in general *believe* took place in the past—is often a quite different animal from what serious historians, after carefully sifting through the available evidence, judge to have *actually* taken place. This distinction between memory and history, vitally important to historians, is often blurred in the minds of ordinary folks (that is, nonhistorians), who are likely to be more emotionally drawn to a past that fits their preconceptions—a past they feel comfortable and identify with—than to a past that is "true" in some more objective sense. This blurring is of course greatly facilitated when, as a result of a dearth of historical evidence or the unreliability of such evidence as has survived, even professional historians cannot know with absolute confidence what occurred in the past. Such is the case with each of the examples dealt with in the following pages. But, as we shall see again and again, even when there exists a minimum core of certainty about what happened in the past—that Joan of Arc, for instance, was burned at the stake in 1431 or that the forces of the Roman Empire besieged Jerusalem and destroyed the Second Temple of the Jews in 70 C.E.—the power of the historian's truth often has a difficult time competing with the power of the right story, even though (or perhaps precisely because) the latter has been hopelessly adulterated with myth and legend. A major objective of the present book is to seek a deeper understanding of why this is so.

Let me say a word or two, finally, about the book's larger import. As a lifelong historian of China, my work has centered on a single country and culture. I have, of course, drawn comparisons from time to time with other countries and cultures, but mainly for the purpose of deepening and enriching my own and my readers' understanding of Chinese history. In this book, although there is a chapter drawn from Chinese history, it is just one case among several, having neither more nor less weight than the chapters devoted to France, Serbia, England, Palestine/Israel, and the Soviet Union. The focus of the book, rather than being on a particular country or culture, is on a transcultural phenomenon—the part taken by story in popular memory—that, if not universal, is certainly encountered in a vast array of places around the world, regardless of the linguistic, religious, social, cultural, and other differences that pertain among the peoples inhabiting these places. What we have, in short, is a different sort of world history, one that instead of being based on conjunctures and influences is manifested in analogous patterns, independently arrived at and very possibly rooted in certain human propensities that transcend the specificities of culture. I will have more to say on this type of history in the conclusion.

ACKNOWLEDGMENTS

Since my career up to now has been spent entirely in the field of Chinese history, focusing mainly on the nineteenth and twentieth centuries, almost everything I have previously written has relied extensively on sources in the Chinese language, the main exception being an interpretive account of American writing on recent Chinese history that I published more than a quarter-century ago. What this means is that for several parts of the present work (above all, the sections dealing with Serbia, Palestine/Israel, and the Soviet Union), where I do not read the original languages of the countries concerned, I have leaned heavily on translated primary materials and an array of excellent secondary scholarship in English. It also means that I am more than habitually grateful to those individuals who have generously responded to my requests for bibliographical guidance or for comment on parts of the book regarding which their expertise is far greater than my own.

First, let me extend loving thanks to my longtime comrade-in-arms, Elizabeth Sinn, who for many years now has been my first reader and most dependable critic. Thanks also to several individuals—Alan Lebowitz (a specialist in American and English literature), Jeff Wasserstrom (a fellow China historian), and an anonymous reviewer for Columbia University Press—who went over different versions of the manuscript and, aside from offering much encouragement, pointed out areas in need of clarification or strengthening. I benefited greatly from their suggestions. My gratitude goes as well to Omer Bartov and to an anonymous reader, both of whom went through the chapter on Masada and made a host of useful comments; Nina Tumarkin, a former colleague at Wellesley College, for her helpful ideas relating to Alexander Nevsky and her immensely intelligent reading of chapter 5, which deals with the *Alexander Nevsky* and *Henry V* films together; Don Ostrowski, whose heroic efforts to strip away the accretion of legend surrounding the historical Nevsky are contained in a number of illuminating articles, which he was kind enough to send me; Peter Cunich for heeding my cry for help upon encountering some phrases in medieval Latin that needed decoding; Larissa Taylor for her advice on Joan of Arc images; Lisa Cohen for her excellent work preparing the book's illustrations for publication; and Martin Hinze for his equally skillful drawing of the maps.

When I was just getting into this project and described the themes I was working with to the Hong Kong historian Chris Munn, his eyes brightened as he urged me to include Laurence Olivier's *Henry V* in the book; much the same thing happened again some months later when, over lunch at Harvard's Fairbank Center for Chinese Studies, Steve Goldstein said that if I were going to include *Henry V*, I really needed to consider adding Sergei Eisenstein's *Alexander Nevsky* as well. I am indebted to both Chris and Steve for these suggestions and to Chris also for his immensely helpful reading of an early version of the films chapter.

At Columbia University Press, I thank Anne Routon for her keen interest and encouragement when I first told her about the book and her helpful advice later on in regard to the title; Whitney Johnson for her able handling of the early phases of the production process; copy editor Annie Barva for the meticulous care and consummate skill with which she edited the manuscript, Anne McCoy and Kathryn Jorge for their expert guidance in the later phases of the manuscript preparation; and Lisa Hamm for her imaginative design of the book cover.

I thank the staffs of the Harvard University and University of Hong Kong libraries, where I carried on most of the research for this book. It is a blessing for a scholar to have access to such fine collections. As a retired academic, I also thank the Fairbank Center for Chinese Studies for the supportive and stimulating intellectual environment that it has been my privilege to enjoy for close to half a century and the Hong Kong Institute for the Humanities and Social Sciences at the University of Hong Kong, which has graciously provided me with office space, administrative assistance, and, not least, a wonderful group of interesting colleagues during my frequent visits to Hong Kong.

A generation ago I published a book with Columbia University Press that I dedicated to my children. Now, almost exactly thirty years later, it gives me a very special pleasure to dedicate this book to my grandchildren, who despite all the changes that have taken place over the past thirty years still inhabit a world defined in the most profound ways by the power of story.

HISTORY
AND POPULAR
MEMORY

1

THE BATTLE OF KOSOVO OF 1389
AND SERBIAN NATIONALISM

I n his defense of the notion of collective memory, the Israeli philosopher Avishai Margalit includes an interesting discussion of
why the Battle of Kosovo still carries such emotional power for
the Serbs, whereas the Battle of Hastings is all but forgotten by the English.[1]
This is a good question, and answering it suggests something about the
range of possible ways in which people in the present day may relate to
past events. Both battles, after all, signaled vital turning points in the
histories of their respective countries. How is it that the alleged defeat
of the Serbs at the hands of the Ottoman Turks in the Battle of Kosovo
continues to be so deeply and passionately felt more than six centuries
after its occurrence, but the French defeat of the English at Hastings has
been relegated to the history books?

THE KOSOVO MYTH

The first thing we learn when we look into this question more carefully—
and it is telling—is that in fact very little is known about what actually
happened in the Battle of Kosovo. There is a widely held view among
historians today that an earlier Ottoman defeat of the Serbian army in
1371—an encounter that took place in the Maritsa (Marica) River valley
in what is now Bulgaria and resulted in the slaughter of large numbers of
Serbs—was of far greater consequence militarily, permitting the Turks to

extend their control over southern Serbia and Macedonia. By 1389, the Serbs were plagued by low morale and disunity, with numerous noblemen alternately fighting against and forming alliances with one another. When the Ottomans threatened, Lazar Hrebeljanović, a noble who had extended his territorial control after the battle of 1371 and become one of the more powerful Serb leaders (he is often referred to as "Prince Lazar" owing to a title conferred on him years earlier), chose not to submit. The battle that resulted was fought on June 28, 1389, on Kosovo Polje (Field of Blackbirds), a few kilometers distance from Priština. Both Lazar, who headed the Serbian force, and the Ottoman Turk leader Sultan Murad were killed. The battle itself, although remembered by the Serbs ever since as a calamitous Serbian defeat, seems in fact to have been somewhat inconclusive. Indeed, it was not until 1459, some seventy years later, that Serbia finally succumbed to the Turks.[2]

How, then, did the Battle of Kosovo become, in the words of one Serbian scholar, "the central event" in the entire history of the Serbian people?[3] Two factors were of key importance. One was the emergence in the years immediately following the battle of a flurry of epic poems and folk ballads that dealt in heavily mythologized fashion with the fall of the Serbian state and the inception of a condition of vassalship under the Ottomans, an alien society with an alien religion. The other consisted in the Serbian Orthodox Church's energetic promotion of a Christianized reading of what had transpired. The two together, focusing on a number of prominent participants and substantive themes, produced in embryonic form the myth or legend of Kosovo.

The core of the myth, which reached its culminating shape in the nineteenth century, was the "Kosovo covenant," according to which Lazar was said to have been invested with Christ-like characteristics already on the eve of the Battle of Kosovo. Presented with the choice between a kingdom in heaven or a kingdom on earth, he opted for the former, exclaiming that "it is better for us to die by a heroic act than to live in shame." The Serbian scholar Olga Zirojević elaborates: "Lazar's words are accepted by his warriors[,] who reply in the form of a chorus; the idea of death is elevated to a heroic feat through which they will pass to eternal life. Through their sacrifice, the Serbs earned freedom . . . in the heavenly kingdom, . . . out of the reach of any conqueror. Although defeated, they were never enslaved."[4] Soon after the battle, Lazar was canonized by the church. The cult of the dead leader was preserved in ten cycles of

folk ballads created between 1390 and 1419. His bones were also preserved and, as late as 1988, were carried in a religious procession from
one holy site to another in Serbia before being deposited, in time for the
six hundredth anniversary of the Battle of Kosovo, in the great Gračanica
monastery adjacent to the plain where the battle was fought.[5]

A major theme of the Kosovo legend is the tension between loyalty
and betrayal, as represented primarily in the figures of Miloš Obilić (or

FIGURE 1.1 Prince Lazar, late seventeenth-century image, in the Museum of the Ser-
bian Orthodox Church, Belgrade. (From Thomas A. Emmert, *Serbian Golgotha:
Kosovo, 1389*, East European Monographs no. 278 [New York: Columbia University
Press, 1990]. By permission of Thomas A. Emmert.)

Kobilić) and Vuk Branković. This tension reflected the historical reality that after the devastating defeat of 1371, which accelerated the collapse of the great medieval Serbian Empire built by Stefan Dusan (who reigned as king from 1331 to 1346 and as emperor from 1346 until his death in 1355), numbers of Serbian warriors did in fact go over to the Ottoman side,[6] some of them, in dramatic subversion of what the legend tells us, very probably fighting alongside the Turks in the Battle of Kosovo.[7] A key episode in many renderings of the Lazar story is the dinner the prince gives on the eve of the battle. In one version—the version first set down in writing and published in the nineteenth century by Vuk Karadžić—Lazar drinks a toast to his knights. When he gets to Miloš Obilić, he refers to him as a "faithful traitor": "first faithful, then a traitor! At Kosovo tomorrow you will desert me, you will run to Murad, the Emperor." In anger, Obilić jumps to his feet to defend himself and identify the real traitor:

I have never been any traitor,
never shall be one,
at Kosovo tomorrow I intend
to die for the Christian faith.
The traitor is sitting at your knee
drinking cold wine under your skirts:
Vuk Branković, I curse him.
Tomorrow is lovely St Vitus day
and we shall see in Kosovo field
who is faithful, who is the traitor.
The great God is my witness!
Tomorrow I shall march on Kosovo,
and I shall stab Murad, Tsar of Turkey,
and stand up with his throat under my foot.
And if God grants and my luck grants
that I shall come home to Krushevats*
I shall take hold of Vuk Branković,
and I shall tie him on my battle-lance
like a woman's raw wool on a distaff,
and carry him to Kosovo field.[8]

---

*Or "Kruševac"; the central Serbian town that was the base of Lazar's domain.

FIGURE 1.2 Fresco of Miloš Obilić, with the halo of a saint. Serbian Monastery of Hilendar on Mount Athos, first decade of nineteenth century. (From Thomas A. Emmert, *Serbian Golgotha: Kosovo, 1389*, East European Monographs, no. 278 [New York: Columbia University Press, 1990]. By permission of Thomas A. Emmert.)

Luck, according to the legend, did not grant Obilić's wish. On the pretext that he wanted to join the Turkish side, he is said to have entered Murad's tent and killed him with a dagger that he had concealed under his clothing, after which he himself was promptly slain. This act proved beyond any doubt Obilić's heroism and loyalty to Lazar and the Serbian cause, and the real traitor, Vuk Branković, became "the ancestral curse of all Slavic Muslims."[9] Although scholars have questioned whether the historical Branković actually betrayed the Serbian side and whether Obilić even existed historically,[10] the metaphoric power of these two individuals in Serbian national consciousness was (and remains to this day) immense,

Branković being represented as the archetypical "negative character, a slanderer, defiler and traitor," in contrast to the "proud and . . . just hero and loyal vassal, Miloš Obilić."[11]

The Christianization of the legend of Kosovo was in some respects present from the start, but it evolved over time, becoming especially pronounced in the nineteenth century. At that time, a cult grew up around Miloš Obilić that the Serbian Orthodox Church officially recognized.[12] Also, the supper hosted by Lazar on the eve of the battle took on more and more of the attributes of the biblical Last Supper, with Lazar portrayed as Christ surrounded by his disciples (in some renderings explicitly numbering twelve), among whom one, Vuk Branković, was a Judas figure.[13]

Another aspect of the legend's Christianization was its close association with St. Vitus's Day. This holiday, also known as "Vidovdan," was celebrated on June 28, the same date as that on which the Battle of Kosovo was fought. On the eve of St. Vitus's Day, it is said, Serbian family heads would give each household member a peony as he or she left to take part in the festivities, saying, "I want you to be as red and strong as this flower," in reply to which the recipient would say, "I shall be as those who shed their blood on the Field of Kosovo." In the late nineteenth century, when St. Vitus's Day became an important day in the church calendar and for the first time a Serbian national holiday, stories circulated in Kosovo "about the rivers Sitnica, Morava and Drim, which would turn red as blood on St. Vitus's Day"—a phenomenon that would be repeated until "the revenge of Kosovo and its complete liberation from the Turkish yoke."[14]

KOSOVO: HISTORICAL BACKGROUND

But we are getting ahead of ourselves. Before discussing the full maturation and crystallization of the Kosovo myth in the nineteenth century, both in response to and as a shaper of modern Serbian nationalism, we need to sketch the history of Kosovo over the previous half-millennium or at least to identify some of its more salient themes. The traditional Serbian view is that the Kosovo region, from the Slav invasions of the fifth and sixth centuries until fairly recently, was predominantly Serb.

Albanians, however, claiming descent from the ancient Illyrians, who inhabited the area long before the arrival of the Slavs, argue that Kosovo is *their* ancestral home, not that of the Serbs. Likening the debate to that surrounding the Palestinian issue in recent times, Julie Mertus suggests that, in truth, Kosovo is integral to the "competing national identities" of both peoples.[15]

Up until the late twelfth century, Kosovo was part of the Byzantine Empire. In the 1180s, however, Serbia, under the new Nemanjic dynasty, was able to conquer the Kosovo region and penetrate into northern Macedonia, gaining control over a substantial stretch of territory. Soon thereafter (in 1219), an event of enormous importance for subsequent Serbian history took place with Byzantium's acquiescence in the establishment of an autonomous Serbian Orthodox Church. The national church, which achieved full independence in 1346, became a staunch supporter of the Serbian state in the years prior to the Ottoman conquest and during the centuries of Turkish rule was an energetic proponent of the idea that Serbia—like Christ—would be resurrected. Most of the Serbian monarchs were canonized, their images incorporated in late Byzantine frescoes (often of exceptional quality) on the walls of Serbian churches and monasteries. "So, for hundreds of years," Tim Judah observes, "the Serbian peasant went to church and in his mind the very idea of Christianity, resurrection and 'Serbdom' blended together."[16] In the mid-fourteenth century, Stefan Dusan took advantage of the straitened circumstances that had befallen the European areas of Byzantium to overpower the Albanian-speaking lands (including the territory now known as Albania). The evidence suggests, however, that at least up to the time of Lazar and probably beyond Albanians constituted only a minor part of the population of Kosovo.[17]

During the four and a half centuries of Ottoman rule (1455–1912), a number of important changes took place in Kosovo. One was a shift in the ratio of Serbian to Albanian inhabitants of the area. Given the unrelenting tug-of-war in modern times between Serbian and Albanian nationalists over the question of who the rightful "owner" of Kosovo is, it is no surprise to find that each side has gone to great lengths (including in some cases flagrant manipulation of the evidence) to justify its position. The actual situation has been more complex than either side has portrayed it, but the overall trend is fairly clear. At the outset, the Ottoman register of landed property of 1455, which covered an area roughly corresponding to the larger part of late-twentieth-century Kosovo, recorded

"an overwhelming Slavic (Serb) majority."[18] There was significant migration of Albanians into Kosovo in the early sixteenth century, resulting
by midcentury in a sizable ethnic Albanian presence in parts of western
Kosovo. The movement of Albanians into Kosovo continued in the following century. As a result of the Hapsburg–Ottoman wars of the late
seventeenth and early eighteenth centuries, substantial numbers of Serbs
fled northward to the safety of Hungary, opening the way for resettle-
ment of Kosovo by Albanians (some of whom had also fled the wars).[19]
By the middle of the nineteenth century, according to Noel Malcolm's
estimate, it seems reasonably certain that there was an absolute majority
of Albanian speakers over Slav speakers in the Kosovo population. During
the Serbian–Ottoman wars of the late 1870s, the proportion of Albanians
became greater still when the mass expulsion of Muslims (many of them
ethnic Albanians) from Serbia resulted in some sixty to seventy thousand
Albanian refugees streaming southward into Kosovo. As a result of these
population shifts, according to an Austrian study published in the 1890s
and based on close analysis of Ottoman statistics, the Kosovo population consisted of a little more than 70 percent Muslims (mostly, if not
all, of Albanian descent) and slightly less than 30 percent non-Muslims
(mostly Serbs).[20]

Another important change that took place in Kosovo during the Ottoman period was the increasing Islamization of the populace. As suggested
in the account given earlier, the great majority (although by no means
all) of the converts to Islam were ethnic Albanians. During the fifteenth
century, the Albanian inhabitants of Kosovo had been for the most part
Christian, and Albanians and Serbs in general lived together peacefully.[21]
By the mid-seventeenth century, however, this situation had begun to
change. Although the Ottomans' stance toward the Serbian Orthodox
Church was reasonably tolerant, it viewed the Catholic Church in more
adversarial terms, in part because of the latter's allegiance to a foreign
power (Rome). As a result, there appears to have been a deliberate Ottoman policy of pressuring Roman Catholics (most of whom were ethnic
Albanians) to convert to Islam. To this end, a poll tax on Christians in the
western edges of the Ottoman Empire was sharply increased. Also, as the
Ottomans became involved in conflicts with the powers of Europe, who
fought in the name of the Roman Church, Kosovo Catholics, because of
their identification with that church, increasingly became targets of forced
conversion. Although, generally speaking, most of the converts to Islam

in Kosovo continued to come from the ethnic Albanian population—a pattern that became stronger still in the eighteenth century—Serbs also were under pressure to convert, both in order to avoid Ottoman financial levies and (owing to the periodic wars fought by the Turks against the Hapsburgs) to escape the mounting military obligations imposed upon Christian men.[22]

Prior to the nineteenth century, when modern nationalism swept across much of Europe, including the Balkan Peninsula, the relationship between the Serbian and Albanian inhabitants of Kosovo was far more complex and nuanced than one would ever guess from the starkly over-simplified picture later constructed by Serbian and Albanian nationalists. Serbs and Albanians fought side by side in the Battle of Kosovo in 1389, and several centuries later, during the Austrian (Hapsburg) invasions of Kosovo (1689–1690), both Kosovo Albanians and Serbs seized the oppor-tunity to rebel against Ottoman rule. Serbs who under Ottoman pressure had converted to Islam at the turn of the nineteenth century gradually adopted Albanian dress and language, many of them also taking Albanian Muslim wives. In addition, according to Serbian accounts, Albanians not infrequently protected Orthodox cemeteries from desecration, know-ing that their own forebears might well have been laid to rest in them. In short, without suggesting that there was never friction or hostility between Serb and Albanian over the long centuries of Ottoman rule, such conflict as from time to time emerged was not the product of an unbridgeable sense of ethnic difference.[23] This situation underwent a pro-found transformation in the course of the nineteenth century, however, as relations between the two peoples became increasingly politicized, and mutual distrust deepened.

THE NINETEENTH CENTURY AND THE BLOSSOMING OF SERBIAN NATIONALISM

One of the key arguments made in this book is that at certain junctures in the history of each country dealt with, a particular story, in each instance derived from that country's past, becomes energized and takes on fresh life. The primary reason for this revival is that the story's thematic content—invariably, to be sure, after it has undergone a degree of reshaping—serves as a metaphor for what is happening historically in the country at the time. The story, as adapted, becomes keyed to a particular historical moment. Vasa Mihailovich, a prolific scholar of Serbian literature, makes the case for this process in regard to the Kosovo story, contending that the Serbs, whenever faced with critical junctures in their history, have invariably turned to this story—he calls it the "Kosovo mystique"—as a source of strength and inspiration.[24] (Another Serbian scholar, Radmila Gorup, makes essentially the same point in her assertion that "whenever the nation is threatened, Kosovo matters again."[25]) Mihailovich identifies four specific moments when this turn to the story occurred, each embodying its own distinctive characteristics and emphasis. The first was the period of several decades immediately following the Battle of Kosovo. Fewer than a dozen writings from this early period survive. Composed by both ecclesiastics and laypersons and filled with religious zeal and a spirit of sadness and mourning, they focus reverently on Prince Lazar, the only major Serbian leader to die in the battle. An encomium written by Lazar's widow, Princess Milica, is illustrative:

> Rejoice, O lily which sprang from the thorn-bush,
> Perfect armament for soldiers.
> Rejoice, O teacher to the hermits.
> Rejoice, O Lazar,
> O rudder and calm port for sailors.
> Rejoice, avenger of the wronged,
> O reprimander of liars.
> Rejoice, O comforter of mourners,
> The poor's defendant, the naked's raiment.
> Rejoice, O beauty of the strong ones,
> O firm protector of the widows. . . .
> There is no praise of which you are unworthy.[26]

During the centuries of Ottoman rule, not much new was written about the Battle of Kosovo, though key elements of the legends surrounding it were retained in popular memory, in part by the Serbian Orthodox Church and in part by folk songs and tales that over time developed into oral epic chronicles. The latter, sung to the accompaniment of the *gusle* (a single-stringed instrument played with a bow) and easily memorized by a largely illiterate population (as late as 1866, only 4.2 percent of

Serbs could read and write), played an important part in the preservation of Serbian cultural and ethnic identity. Thus, although during the long Ottoman period "the glow of the Kosovo flame" dimmed in Serbian consciousness, it never disappeared entirely "and was always ready to flare up at a propitious moment."[27]

Such a moment (the second in Mihailovich's periodization) came in the early nineteenth century. It began with the first Serbian uprising against the Turks (1804–1813, led by Karadjordje, "Black George") and continued sporadically as the century unfolded and Serbs gravitated in the direction of full independence. During this period, developments in the realm of literature played a major role in stimulating Serbian nationalism and articulating its agenda. Although the Kosovo legend remained the underlying theme, the difference in tone and content between the Serbian literature of the nineteenth century, with its robust nationalistic stamp, and the more spiritually oriented writings of the immediate post-1389 decades is striking.[28] For example, Jovan Sterija Popović (1806–1856) wrote in the foreword to his first play in 1827 that

[e]very nation has a pivotal point, fortunate or unfortunate, to which the descendants always look up. The Romans could not easily forget Cannae; they often mentioned it even though it was a disaster for them. When the Serbs hear about the Battle of Kosovo, they find themselves unusually agitated. Their inflamed imagination reaches all the way to Kruševac, they defend the unjustly accused Miloš [Obilić] before Lazar, they help him kill Murad, they return to the battle and fight it over and over again, they damn Vuk [Branković], and they shed tears seeing the final downfall of the Serbian lands. What is this but a sacred love for fatherland?[29]

In the course of the nineteenth century, the development of Serbian nationalism was profoundly shaped by two giants in the world of literature. One was Vuk Karadžić (1787–1864), a reformer of the Serbian language and tireless publicizer of Serbian folk tales, songs, and poems. Karadžić pioneered in the compilation and publication of Serbian epic ballads (his first collection appeared in Vienna in 1814), melding them into coherent narratives that "canonized" the story of Lazar and the Battle of Kosovo and "provided Serbian national ideology with its mythical cornerstone."[30] His collections were widely influential in Europe, thriving on the lively contemporary curiosity concerning national folk traditions; they also owed much of their European success to the ardent interest the eminent scholar-critic Jakob Grimm showed in the Serb anthologist's work. But Karadžić's greatest achievement in the folk literature realm, at least for our purposes, was to render Serbian epic traditions immediately accessible to the newly literate classes among the Serbs themselves, arming them with the core ingredients of a new nationalist faith.[31]

Karadžić's other great contribution to the flowering of Serbian nationalism lay in his reform of the Serbian language and writing system. Coming from a poor peasant background, he strove to modernize the Serbian literary language, to distance it from the liturgical language of the Serbian Orthodox Church and bring it closer to the speech of ordinary Serbs. His efforts in language led him to develop certain ideas about the nature and identity of the peoples of the southern Balkans—most importantly that the Slavs inhabiting this region, although divided along religious lines among Orthodox, Catholic, and Muslim, were all at bottom Serbs. Although there were those who took issue with some of his theorizing, the effect of Karadžić's ideas was "to give intellectual backbone to Serbian or more particularly Greater Serbian nationalism."[32]

Just prior to the middle of the nineteenth century, a strain of Serbian nationalism notable for the uncompromising violence of its rhetoric made its appearance in a poetic drama by the Montenegrin bishop-prince Petar Petrović Njegoš (1813–1851). Njegoš's play, which many view as a masterpiece and some as the finest work in all of Serbian literature,[33] is titled *Gorski vijenac* (*The Mountain Wreath*). It is based on an event of dubious historicity known as "the extermination of the Turkish converts" that was said to have taken place in Montenegro, an ethnically Serbian region in the western part of the Balkan Peninsula, on a Christmas Eve toward the end of the seventeenth century. The play's overriding theme is the fight against those Montenegrins who had converted to Islam and gone over to the Turkish occupiers' side. The plot focuses on the annihilation of those Muslim converts (some of whom are identified in the play as being of Albanian ethnicity) who refuse to return to the Christian fold. The drama thus gives expression to Njegoš's paramount goal, as the ruler of Montenegro from 1830 to 1851, of freeing his land from Turkish domination[34]—a goal also reflected in his decision to dedicate *The Mountain Wreath* to the leader of the 1804 uprising, "the great, immortal Karadjordje," who "roused [the] people, christened the land, and broke the

FIGURE 1.3 Drawing of Petar Petrović Njegoš (1813–1851), artist unknown. (From P. P. Njegoš, *The Mountain Wreath*, trans. and ed. Vasa D. Mihailovich [Irvine, Calif.: Schlacks, 1986]. By permission of Vasa D. Mihailovich.)

barbarous fetters, summoned the Serbs back from the dead, and breathed life into their souls."[35]

The Mountain Wreath is saturated with the mythology of Kosovo, above all the saintly and heroic Miloš Obilić, on the one hand, and the iconically traitorous Vuk Branković, on the other. Early in the play, the disunity and treachery that so bedeviled the Serbs at the time of the Battle of Kosovo are alluded to, as if they had happened only yesterday, in a folk dance (*kolo*) performed and sung by the people:

God is angry at the Serbian people
because of their many mortal sins. . . .
Our own leaders, may all their trace vanish,
sowed the bitter seed of disharmony
and thus poisoned the entire Serbian tribe.
Our own leaders, miserable cowards,
thus became the traitors of our nation.

O that accursed supper of Kosovo!
It would be good fortune had you poisoned
all our chieftains and wiped out their traces,
had only Miloš remained on the field,
along with both of his true sworn brothers;
then would the Serb have remained a true Serb!
Vuk Branković, o you shameful scoundrel,
was that a way to serve your fatherland?[36]

A central theme in Njegoš's play is the irreconcilability of Serbs and Turks. At one point, a Montenegrin guest at a wedding (at which Turks are also present) dilates upon this theme in his account of Obilić's killing of Murad:

Our Obilić, you fiery dragon,
the eyes of those who look at you go blind.
All brave men will always honor your name!
You did not fail our crown like a coward
when you set your foot on the Sultan's throat
and stepped into the Sultan's torn belly.
Now I see you riding your stallion, Ždral,
and dispersing the Turks around the tent.
What will happen? Who will do the right thing?
Serb and Turk can never get together.
The salty sea will sooner change to sweet.[37]

The apotheosis of Miloš Obilić in *The Mountain Wreath* is suggested in other ways as well. One of the Montenegrin warriors, Voivode Batrić, in attempting to persuade a Muslim convert to return to the Christian religion, says he does "swear by the faith of Obilić" that if the convert rejects his plea, both of their faiths "will be swimming in blood."[38] At a later stage in the drama, after the warriors arise from their sleep and gird their arms to start for home, Batrić says to his comrades:

Let's tell our dreams before we all depart!
I had a dream I've never had before
(a good omen it must be for my arms):
Last night in dream I saw Obilić fly

over the plain Field of Cetinje there,
on a white steed as if on a *vila*.*
Oh my dear God, how resplendent he was!

Thirty to forty of Batrić's fellow warriors tell their dreams, and, lo and
behold, each one has had the same dream as Batrić. They all have seen
Obilić. Their collective spirit aroused, they repair to the church joyfully
to swear an oath to fight the Turks together.[39]

After they have entered the church, the political and religious leader
of Montenegro at the turn of the eighteenth century, Vladika (Bishop)
Danilo,[40] who is present throughout Njegoš's drama and is torn over how
to deal with those of his compatriots who have embraced Islam, cautions
the warriors against being too quick to challenge the powerful Turks. To
one of them in particular he says (referring to the warrior's home place):
"You aren't that strong in Crmnica, you know, and Crmnica lies at the
Turks' doorstep. Do not take home a spurious oath with you, for it is hard
to struggle against God!" But the warriors are insistent, and one of their
number confirms their collective intention to fight the Turks by reciting
an oath, the emphasis of which is entirely on the ill fate that will befall
any who betray the Serbian cause:

Keep this in mind firmly, Montenegrins!

He who begins this fight will be the best!
But who betrays those brave ones that begin,
may all he has turn to stone and ashes!
May the Great Lord with His awesome power
change all the seeds in his fields to pebbles
and the children in his wife's womb to stone!
May his offspring all turn into lepers,
and may people point their finger at them! . . .

He who betrays, brothers, all these heroes
who will begin to fight our enemies,
may the shame of Branković fall on him,

---

*Cetinje is a municipality in southern Montenegro rich in historical and religious associa-
tions. A *vila* is a fairy in Serbian folklore.

and for the dogs be his holy Lenten!
May his grave reach all the way to deep hell!

He who betrays, brothers, all these heroes,
neither wine nor bread may he take to church,
but may he take the faith of dogs instead.
May blood be poured over his Christmas log.
May he observe his *slava* day* in blood
and eat that day his own children roasted![41]

After saying "Amen!" in chorus, the warriors leave the church and go to their homes. Early on Christmas Day, Voivode Batrić reports to Bishop Danilo about "a skirmish with the Turks" the previous evening:

We put under our sharp sabers all those
who did not want to be baptized by us.
But all those who bowed to the Holy Child
and crossed themselves with the sign of [the] Christian cross,
we accepted and hailed as our brothers.
We set on fire all the Turkish houses,†
that there might be not a single trace left
of our faithless domestic enemy.

Over the next few days, more reports come in of the despised turn-coats in flight, houses set ablaze, mosques reduced to ruins, rivers filled with slaughtered Turks. To the heroic warriors, Bishop Danilo exclaims:

"You have brought me great gladness, my falcons,‡
great joy for me. Heroic liberty!
This bright morning you've been resurrected
from every tomb of our dear forefathers!"

---

*A *slava* is the ritual celebration of a family's patron saint, observed annually on that saint's feast day.
†"Turkish" here clearly refers to Montenegrins (and perhaps some Albanians) who have converted to Islam.
‡In Serbian epic poetry, the falcon symbolizes a brave young man.

Abbot Stefan, an old Orthodox monk who is present, says he wishes to hold a memorial service dedicated to the souls of the nation's great heroes: "This day will be the most priceless to them. / Since Kosovo there's never been such [a] day."[42]

Mark Mazower comments usefully on the rampant distortion of historical reality characterizing Njegoš's play. "On the lookout for evidence of Balkan bloodthirstiness," he writes in his short but insightful book *The Balkans*,

> Western observers have often mistaken the myths spun by nineteenth-century romantic nationalists for eternal truths. Across Europe, from Ireland to Poland, poetic visionaries dreamed of resurrection, sacrifice and blood spilled for the sake of the nation's future. To take but the best-known Balkan exemplar of this genre, *The Mountain Wreath*'s glorification of the supposed extermination of Muslims in Montenegro a century and a half earlier was the product of . . . Njegoš's poetic imagination, not of historical fact: it lauded as heroic atrocity the much less bloody real story of the gradual departure of Muslims from Montenegrin land over more than a century.

Mazower goes on to suggest that "the rise of the Kosovo legend during the twentieth century was similarly misleading—an indication of modern not medieval prejudices. In both cases, the emergence of Balkan epics of bloodshed and national unity was not fortuitous; they emerged at points in the nineteenth century when the nation-building process was coming under particular strain. This, not the primeval past, was the origin of their ethnically polarized sentiments."[43]

It is worthy of note that in 1836 Njegoš's brother and cousins had been decapitated by Turks, an action that he avenged in like fashion four years later.[44] There manifestly was no turning of the other cheek in the bishop's vision of Christianity: vengeance was holy. Tim Judah, in his 1997 book *The Serbs*, has this to say about the significance of Njegoš's play: "It is hard to underestimate the influence of *The Mountain Wreath*. Today it is still celebrated as one of the pinnacles of Serbian literary achievement. But, in the wake of another Balkan war, its significance is that of a missing link. It helps explain how the Serbian national consciousness has been moulded and how ideas of national liberation became inextricably intertwined with the act of killing your neighbour and burning his village."[45]

Ger Duijzings, however, calls for caution "in drawing a straight line of causation from a literary text to the occurrence of genocidal practices," something he charges Judah and others with having done.[46] Whatever the case—and it is not an easy one to determine—we must not ignore the important developments in Serbia's political evolution that took place in the century and a half between the publication of Njegoš's play (1847) and the late-twentieth-century Balkan war Judah alludes to. After the Turks crushed the first uprising against them in 1813, a second revolt took place in 1815 (this one led by Miloš Obrenović) that succeeded in gaining autonomy for a small piece of Serbia. Over the ensuing decades, the territorial extent of the fledgling state expanded in size, most dramatically as a result of the Serbian–Montenegrin victory in the wars of 1877–1878 against the Ottomans, which gained for Serbia recognition as an independent state with its capital in Belgrade. The expulsion en masse of Albanians and other Muslims from the newly conquered areas (and the resulting flood of refugees into Kosovo, which remained under Ottoman control) convinced the Albanians of Kosovo that Serbia constituted a serious menace to their existence.[47] Such apprehension can only have been exacerbated over the next few decades by the heightened attention Serbs paid to the spirit of Kosovo and the unfinished business of unification. This attention reached peak intensity in 1889 with the elaborate celebrations marking the five hundredth anniversary of the Battle of Kosovo, after which the government dedicated St. Vitus's Day to all Serbs who had "died in wars for the Faith and the Fatherland," and the annual anniversaries became a popular symbol in the struggle for the complete freeing of Serbian lands from foreign rule.[48]

THE KOSOVO STORY IN THE TWENTIETH CENTURY: RACIAL NATIONALISM AND DEMAGOGUERY

For years, the moment Serbs and Montenegrins had been yearning for was frustrated by the actions of the Great Powers. But it finally arrived in October 1912 when the recently formed Balkan League, consisting of Serbia, Montenegro, Greece, and Bulgaria, declared war against the Turks and within weeks finally drove them from Kosovo and the rest of the Balkan Peninsula, thus ending Ottoman power in Europe. The predictable impact of this event on the emotions of Serbs, for whom the conflict bore "the character of a holy war,"[49] was captured in a young Serbian soldier's recollections:

> The single sound of that word—Kosovo—caused an indescribable excitement. . . . Each of us created for himself a picture of Kosovo while we were still in the cradle. Our mothers lulled us to sleep with the songs of Kosovo, and in our schools our teachers never ceased in their stories of Lazar and Miloš. . . . When we arrived on Kosovo and the battalions were placed in order, our commander spoke: "Brothers, my children, my sons!" His voice breaks. "This place on which we stand is the graveyard of our glory. We bow to the shadows of fallen ancestors and pray God for the salvation of their souls." His voice gives out and tears flow in streams down his cheeks and grey beard and fall to the ground. He actually shakes from some kind of inner pain and excitement. The spirits of Lazar, Miloš, and all the Kosovo martyrs gaze on us. We feel strong and proud, for we are the generation which will realize the centuries-old dream of the whole nation: that we with the sword will regain the freedom that was lost with the sword.[50]

The recovery of Kosovo at an early juncture in the Balkan Wars of 1912–1913 electrified Serbs throughout Europe and brought to a high point the third great moment in Serbian cultural history in which extraordinary interest in Kosovo themes was displayed.[51] In 1914, Serbian national societies and secondary-school teachers organized tours of Kosovo. St. Vitus's Day visits were arranged so that people could attend services at the famed Gračanica monastery. Serbian travelers to the "Holy Land" collected soil from Kosovo to take home as souvenirs.[52]

Although for Kosovo's Serbs, who now constituted some 30 to 40 percent of the population, the Serbian victory was experienced as a liberation, it was an unmitigated disaster for the Albanians there, with as many as twenty thousand of them being killed and tens of thousands more taking flight. Entire villages were transformed into rubble, innocent noncombatants were massacred, and the Serbian and Montenegrin troops committed every kind of violence and brutality. Albanians got their revenge in the early part of World War I, however, when the Serbian army was defeated by the Austro-Hungarians, Germans, and Bulgarians, who now occupied Serbian territory. But then in the last year of the war the Serbian side reoccupied Kosovo, and with the birth of the new Yugoslav state on December 1, 1918, thousands of Albanians and other Muslims left Kosovo, many of them going to Turkey, and seventy thousand colonists (mostly, one assumes, Serbs) were brought in.[53]

The Yugoslav state that came into being in 1918 was an ethnically mixed kingdom of Serbs, Croats, and Slovenes, with the Serbs by far the most numerous of the three. From the outset, the government adopted an adversarial stance toward Albanian culture and the Albanian population in Kosovo. Albanian-language schools were shut down, and Kosovo Albanians were pressured either to assimilate or to emigrate. As a result, tens of thousands of ethnic Albanians—some say as many as half a million— left Yugoslavia during the interwar years, to be quickly replaced by Serb and Montenegrin settlers who were granted special economic privileges. This phase in the history of Yugoslavia ended in 1941 with the invasion and subsequent occupation of the country by Germany and its allies.

It is significant that for some years after 1918, according to Vasa Mihailovich, there was a sharp diminution of Kosovo motifs in Serbian literature, mainly, in his view, because "the centuries-old dream of the liberation of all Serbian lands had been realized and Kosovo . . . avenged."[54] The flip side, of course, was that the allure of Kosovo traditions and stories might be expected to return the moment the Serbs as a people again felt humiliated, victimized, and oppressed, which is exactly what happened in the latter decades of the twentieth century, the fourth period in which Kosovo themes dominated Serbian cultural and political consciousness.[55]

During World War II, although some Kosovo Albanians joined forces with the Partisans led by Josip Broz Tito, a majority experienced the German occupation as a liberation, not so much out of love of the Axis as out of hatred for the Serbs, against whom they now took revenge, driving thousands from the area. The Socialist Yugoslavia created by Tito in 1945 dealt with the national aspirations of the country's competing ethnic constituencies by dividing it into six nominally sovereign republics: Croatia, Serbia, Montenegro, Slovenia, Bosnia-Herzegovina, and Macedonia. Two "provinces" attached to the Republic of Serbia—Vojvodina (nestled between the northern border of Serbia and Hungary and containing a sizable Hungarian minority) and Kosovo (now predominantly Albanian in ethnicity and sandwiched between the southern rim of Serbia and Albania and Macedonia farther to the south)—were given varying degrees

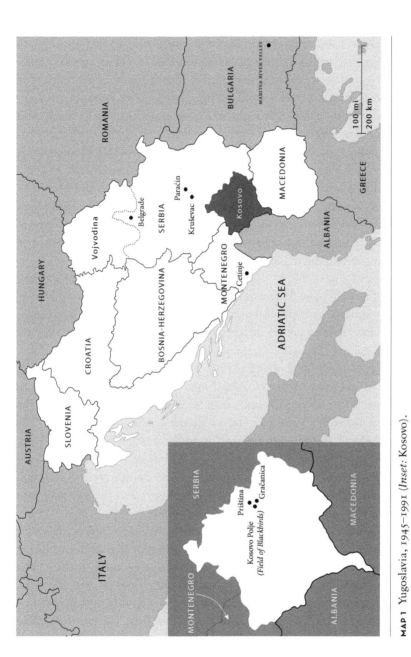

MAP 1 Yugoslavia, 1945–1991 (*Inset: Kosovo*).

of autonomy. Communist rule initially brought a measure of stability to Yugoslavia, but over time ethnic tensions grew once again, including Albanian restiveness in Kosovo, which erupted in rioting in November 1968. In part owing to these tensions but also at times for economic and other reasons, there was a steady emigration of Serbs from the province beginning in the late 1940s and continuing in the ensuing decades. As a result of this emigration and of the extremely high birthrate of the Albanian inhabitants of Kosovo, the proportion of Serbs and Montenegrins in the area slid from 27.5 percent in 1948 to 14.9 percent in 1981 and 10.9 percent in 1991. During the 1970s, a new Yugoslav constitution (1974) granted increased (but not full) autonomy to Kosovo and Vojvodina. Although Kosovo Albanians now made substantial cultural and educational strides, there was a growing sense of grievance among them over their failure to achieve the status of a fully sovereign republic.[56]

Marshal Tito died in 1980, after which an explosive mix of circumstances rapidly gained ground in Yugoslavia. Ethnic Albanian demands (which started with pro-Albanian student demonstrations in March–April 1981, flaunting such slogans as "Kosovo-Republic!" and "We are Albanians, not Yugoslavs!") became progressively more adamant;[57] Serbian nationalism (articulated mainly by the media and intellectuals in Belgrade and increasingly racialized in content) reached a new pitch in intensity; and an especially toxic form of demagoguery, centering on the figure of Slobodan Milošević, burst onto the Serbian political scene. The main focus of the Serbian nationalism of the 1980s was the alleged victimization of the Serbs of Kosovo, which Milošević and other Serb leaders played for all it was worth, injecting the myths and legends that had surrounded the subject of Kosovo since the fourteenth century with new emotional power and fresh potential for violence.

In January 1986, two hundred prominent Belgrade intellectuals submitted a petition to the Yugoslav and Serbian national assemblies bitterly complaining about the treatment Serbs were receiving in Kosovo. The charges leveled against Kosovo Albanians were extreme, ranging from the rape of old women and nuns to the roughing up of young people, the blinding of cattle, and the desecration of churches. The petition called for "decisive measures . . . to halt Albanian aggression in Kosovo and Metohija [the southwestern part of Kosovo]." In September, a draft of a document emanating from the Serbian Academy of Sciences and Arts and generally referred to simply as "the Memorandum" was leaked in a

Belgrade newspaper. The Memorandum questioned whether Serbs could ever be dealt with fairly within the Yugoslav system. The strong reaction the document provoked was owing to the extreme language it employed, an especially striking example of which was its reference to the "physical, political, legal, and cultural genocide of the Serbian population of Kosovo and Metohija." The Memorandum took Serbia's politicians to task for allowing such a situation to come about and, not surprisingly, was widely attacked by officials throughout Yugoslavia. In contrast to the public outcry, however, many Serbs quietly endorsed the document, seeing it as confirmation of their deepest beliefs. For them, Mertus suggests, the message, stripped down to its essence, was: "Albanians (or someone else) have always been the evil Other; Serbs have always been the victims."[58]

One Serb who was less than quiet in his endorsement of the thrust of the Memorandum was Slobodan Milošević, who built a career around the issue of Kosovo. A key step in this direction came on April 25, 1987. Head of the Serbian Communist Party at the time, Milošević had been asked by the president of Serbia to go to Kosovo Polje to attend a meeting at which Kosovo Serbs were to present their grievances to Albanian representatives. Serbs and Montenegrins had planned a public protest outside the building where the meeting was to take place, and when Milošević arrived, thousands of angry demonstrators, who had been waiting for him, began shouting, "We want freedom! We want freedom!"—a play on the name "Slobodan," which means "free." The Albanian police on the scene attempted to restrain the crowd, which responded by throwing rocks at them. Shortly after being ushered into the building, Milošević came out to speak to the protesters:

Comrades . . . you should stay here. This is your country, these are your houses, your fields and gardens, your memories. You are not going to abandon your lands because life is hard, because you are oppressed by injustice and humiliation. . . . You should stay here, both for your ancestors and your descendants. Otherwise you would shame your ancestors and disappoint your descendants. But I do not suggest you stay here suffering and enduring a situation with which you are not satisfied. On the contrary! It should be changed. . . . Yugoslavia does not exist without Kosovo! Yugoslavia would disintegrate without Kosovo! Yugoslavia and Serbia are not going to give up Kosovo.[59]

There are various versions of an iconic phrase Milošević is said to have uttered at one point to the protesters. It went something like "No one should dare to beat you!"—words that defined Milošević as a protector of the Serbs and, according to a later remark by one of the Kosovo Serb leaders, "enthroned him as a Tsar."[60]

The event lasted until dawn, with disgruntled Serbs, one after another, stepping forward to voice their complaints. On Milošević's return to Belgrade, one of his friends reported, "[H]e was like a heated stove. He was full of emotions. He could not control his feelings. He could not calm down." Clearly, as Gale Stokes has observed, the Serbian politician "had discovered he possessed the heady power to move people."[61]

From this point forward, Milošević would make full use of his new-found power. In the remaining months of 1987 and on into the following year, he took advantage of every opportunity to stoke the fires of anti-Albanian sentiment, ousting political figures who did not fully subscribe to his agenda, gaining effective control over the media in Belgrade, and organizing mass rallies of supporters to intimidate officials and Communist Party members into adopting pro-Serbian (anti-Albanian) political positions. Milošević's political ambitions were given an unexpected assist by the Paraćin massacre of September 3, 1987, in which an Albanian soldier in the Yugoslav army opened fire in his army barracks in the Serbian town of Paraćin, killing four soldiers before turning the gun on himself. Although only one of the victims was a Serb, the Serbian media responded with an outpouring of anti-Albanian abuse, reporting the incident as an attack on Yugoslavia as a whole.[62] By 1988, Milošević had become "the most dynamic, visible, and frightening politician in Yugoslavia." Kosovo had moved from being a narrow Serbian problem to a problem for Yugoslavia as a whole, and the stage was set for new constitutional arrangements that in March 1989 placed the autonomous regions of Kosovo and Vojvodina under the firm control of the Serbian central government.[63]

Other developments in 1989 also played into Milošević's hands. Nationalist hysteria peaked in the early summer as the country was deluged with books, films, and plays commemorating the Battle of Kosovo, the six hundredth anniversary of which was celebrated on June 28 that year. This event, attended by a million Serbs from all over Yugoslavia (as well as by thousands of Serbs from abroad), took place on Kosovo Polje, near the spot where Lazar was said to have been slain and where there now stood a monument conveying the prince's admonition to all Serbs:

Let him who fails to join the battle of Kosovo
Fail in all he undertakes in his fields.
Let his fields go barren of the good golden wheat,
Let his vineyards remain without vines or grapes.[64]

These words of warning inscribed on the monument, calling to mind the rhetoric employed by Njegoš in *The Mountain Wreath*, supplied the text for the speech Milošević delivered at the anniversary ceremonies, which probed the lessons of Kosovo mythology for the Serbia of his own day, above all the dangers posed by disunity and betrayal:

At the time when this famous historical battle was fought in Kosovo, the people . . . could allow themselves to be disunited and to have hatred and treason because they lived in smaller, weakly interlinked worlds. . . . Therefore, words devoted to unity, solidarity, and cooperation among people have no greater significance anywhere on the soil of our motherland than they have here in the field of Kosovo, which is a symbol of disunity and treason. In the memory of the Serbian people, this disunity was decisive in causing the loss of the battle and in bringing about the fate which Serbia suffered for a full six centuries. . . . The Kosovo heroism has been inspiring our creativity for six centuries, and has been feeding our pride and does not allow us to forget that at one time we were an army great, brave, and proud, one of the few that remained undefeated when losing. Six centuries later, now, we are being again engaged in battles and are facing battles. They are not armed battles, although such things cannot be excluded yet. However, regardless of what kind of battles they are, they cannot be won without resolve, bravery, and sacrifice, without the noble qualities that were present here in the field of Kosovo in the days past.[65]

Milošević had recently been elected president of Serbia, and the entire federal leadership of Yugoslavia turned out to hear his speech. It was a media event from which he was sure to derive maximum advantage. Already venerated by the Serbian populace—his portrait was plastered on thousands of buses, alongside the images of such heroes of the past as

Karadjordje and Lazar—he flew to Kosovo Polje by helicopter, making a dramatic descent from heaven, as befit a modern-day savior. During the ceremony, moreover, the stage on which the president was seated in the place of honor was festooned with the symbols of Serbian nationalism, including a huge Orthodox Cross encircled by four Cyrillic C's, standing for the slogan "Only Unity/Harmony Saves the Serbs."[66] The June 28 issue of the Belgrade daily *Politika* was devoted entirely to the Kosovo story. The main editorial, although noting that there was some controversy concerning Branković's betrayal, baldly dismissed this possibility as of negligible importance: "Regardless of the historical facts, the Serbian people, from time immemorial . . . , has been cursed by some Branković or other, as an unavoidable destiny. . . . We are once more living in the times of Kosovo, as it is in Kosovo and around Kosovo that the destiny of Yugoslavia and the destiny of socialism are being determined. They want to take away from us the Serbian and the Yugoslav Kosovo, yes, they want to, but they will not be allowed to."[67]

A number of writers have suggested that by successfully asserting Serbian control over Kosovo in the late 1980s, Slobodan Milošević paved the way for the destruction of the Yugoslav Federation in the following decade.[68] Although the inevitable war, when it came, did not break out in Kosovo, as most had predicted it would, it was the dynamics of the political conflict in Kosovo that had precipitated war, first in Slovenia, then in Croatia, and then in Bosnia-Herzegovina.[69] When fighting finally erupted in Kosovo itself in the late 1990s, it was brutal (more than one million ethnic Albanians fled the conflict) and only ended with the controversial North Atlantic Treaty Organization (NATO) bombing of Yugoslavia, which began on March 24, 1999, and was suspended on June 10, a day following the Serbian side's capitulation. On the same date that the bombing ended, a United Nations (UN) Security Council resolution placed Kosovo under transitional UN administration and authorized a NATO-led peacekeeping force. Over the next several weeks, half a million Albanian refugees returned to their homes; it was now the turn of the Serbian inhabitants of Kosovo to get out fast, before Albanian revenge was vented against them.[70]

While the NATO bombing was still in progress, Milošević, who as president of Yugoslavia (an office he held from 1997 to 2000) bore ultimate responsibility for the devastation the Yugoslavian army had wrought in Kosovo, was indicted by the International Criminal Tribunal for the Former

Yugoslavia in The Hague for war crimes committed in the province. In 2001, a year after a popular revolt in early October 2000 forced him to resign the Yugoslav presidency, effectively ending his political career, the Serbian leader was arrested and transported to The Hague to stand trial; he died in his cell on March 11, 2006, before the trial was concluded. The status of Kosovo remains in dispute. The Albanian-dominated Parliament governing the territory (which is now more than 90 percent ethnic Albanian) unanimously declared its independence from Serbia on February 17, 2008, marking the final stage in the dismemberment of the former Yugoslavia. Although Kosovo's independent status has been recognized (as of March 16, 2013) by ninety-nine UN member states (including the United States and most of the European Union countries), it has also been opposed by many others (among them Russia and, of course, Serbia).[71]

THE KOSOVO CASE: DISTINCTIVE FEATURES

In his groundbreaking work *Zakhor: Jewish History and Jewish Memory*, Yosef Hayim Yerushalmi includes a postscript entitled "Reflections on Forgetting," in which he suggests that at certain historical junctures peoples are capable of anamnesis, of reaching "back into an often distant past to recover forgotten or neglected elements with which there is a sudden sympathetic vibration, a sense of empathy, of recognition."[72] This description captures in part the way in which Serbs have related to the Kosovo story. It is certainly true, as we have seen, that the mythology surrounding the Battle of Kosovo attracted unusual notice at specific historical points, especially ones marked by strong nationalist sentiment.

But was this the only way in which Serbs related to their medieval past? Was the Kosovo myth simply a narrative that resonated with memories and responses that Serbs would likely have had anyway? Or was something else, something far deeper, also at work? Yerushalmi, in the main body of his book, asserts that "medieval Jewish chronicles tend to assimilate events to old and established conceptual frameworks. . . . There is a pronounced tendency to subsume even major new events to familiar archetypes, for even the most terrible events are somehow less terrifying when viewed within old patterns rather than in their bewildering specificity.

Thus the latest oppressor is Haman, and the court-Jew who tries to avoid disaster is Mordecai. Christendom is 'Edom' or 'Esau,' and Islam is 'Ishmael.' "[73] In a similar vein, Gabrielle Spiegel maintains that, "for Jews, historical experience is incorporated into the cyclical reenactment of paradigmatic events in Jewish sacred ritual," recent or contemporary experiences acquiring "meaning only insofar as they can be subsumed within Biblical categories of events." She adds that "in such liturgical commemoration, the past exists only by means of recitation; the fundamental goal of such recitation is to make it live again in the present, to fuse past and present, chanter and hearer, into a single collective entity."[74] The situation Yerushalmi and Spiegel describe seems to me very close to what we find in the Serbian case, where the Kosovo myth doesn't simply *resonate* with contemporary historical circumstances but also *shapes* them, defining Serbian memory of past humiliations and how these humiliations should be responded to and in the process supplying the humiliations with meanings they otherwise might not have had.

In the course of so doing, the Kosovo story, like so many mythic constructions, is removed from history and transposed into a realm of timelessness—a phenomenon that one writer after another has taken note of in dealing with the subject.[75] Gale Stokes writes that the importance of the Kosovo myth in Serbian politics lies not in its "actual historical qualities but in its selection by . . . nationalists as the appropriate symbolic universe of Serbianness." The myth, he adds, "provides a vocabulary of experiences outside of time, so to speak." In the war in Bosnia-Herzegovina, according to Olga Zirojević (illustrating a point made by Yerushalmi), "the opponents were not the Bosnian Muslims, but the Turks, that is, the mythical enemy." (This was of course also true of Njegoš's *The Mountain Wreath*, where Montenegrin converts to Islam were regularly referred to as "Turks.") The shrewdness of Serbian "war-propaganda folklore," the respected political anthropologist and cultural critic Ivan Čolović suggests, was "embodied in the presentation of war under the guise of eternity, that is, in transferring the conflicts from the sphere of politics, economy and history into the extrapolated sphere of myth." And, as a result, he continues (writing in 1994), "today we are in danger of answering the call of demagogues, false prophets and politically ambitious and crazy priests, and of succumbing to myth and religion as the only plane of our existence, as the measure and the content of life in its entirety."[76]

There is no better example of the pattern Čolović describes than the Bosnian Serb leader Radovan Karadžić, who like Milošević was indicted for war crimes and, after thirteen years in hiding, was arrested in 2008 and is now standing trial in The Hague.[77] A skillful player of the *gusle* and of course intimately familiar with *The Mountain Wreath*, Karadžić, the Bosnian American novelist Aleksandar Hemon tells us, "clearly understood his role in the light cast by [the Montenegrin ruler] Vladika Danilo. He recognized himself in the martyrdom of leadership; he believed that he was the one to finish the job [of exterminating the Turks] that Vladika Danilo started; he saw himself as the hero in an epic poem that would be sung by a distant future generation."[78]

So where does this latest chapter in the story leave us? After the demise of Milošević, Karadžić, and other indicted war leaders, have the Serbs turned their backs on the mythic constructions that have exercised such a tight grip on Serbian national memory for at least a century and a half and wreaked so much tragedy and suffering in recent Balkan history? Does the fact that Serbia now has a democratically elected government and seeks membership in the European Union mean that the Serbs as a people are prepared to let go of Kosovo—the place Milošević once described as the "love which eternally warms [Serbia's] heart"?[79] On July 22, 2010, the UN's highest court, the International Court of Justice, issued its legally nonbinding ruling that Kosovo's declaration of independence "did not violate international law." The ruling was warmly applauded by Kosovo and, as could have been predicted, adamantly opposed by Serbia, Russia, and many other countries (such as Spain and China) that face secessionist movements within their own borders.[80] The issue of Kosovo and its relationship to Serbia thus remains unresolved,[81] although the relationship recently underwent a potentially groundbreaking change, to be discussed presently.

Žarko Korać, a professor of psychology at Belgrade University, has commented insightfully on the meaning of the hallowed Serbian notion, embodied in the Kosovo covenant, that it is better to fight honorably and die than to live as slaves. "It means," he says, "that because we opted for the kingdom of heaven we cannot lose, and that is what people mean when they talk about the Serbs as a 'heavenly people.' In this way the Serbs identify themselves with the Jews. As victims, yes, but also with the idea of 'sacred soil.' The Jews said 'Next year in Jerusalem' and after 2000 years they recreated their state. The message is 'We are victims, but we are going to survive.'"[82]

Against a background of unusual tension between the Israeli and American governments, Elie Wiesel published a full-page ad titled "For Jerusalem" in the *New York Times* on April 18, 2010. It would be hard to find a clearer statement of the "sacred soil" notion as many Jews see it. "For me, the Jew that I am," Wiesel wrote,

> **Jerusalem is above politics.** It is mentioned more than six hundred times in Scripture—and not a single time in the Koran. **Its presence in Jewish history is overwhelming.** There is no more moving prayer in Jewish history than the one expressing our yearning to return to Jerusalem. To many theologians, it IS Jewish history, to many poets, a source of inspiration. It belongs to the Jewish people and is much more than a city, it is what binds one Jew to another in a way that remains hard to explain. When a Jew visits Jerusalem for the first time, it is not the first time; it is a homecoming. The first song I heard was my mother's lullaby about and for Jerusalem. Its sadness and its joy are part of our collective memory.[83]

Although I do not mean to suggest that all Serbs necessarily subscribe to Korać's analysis in its totality (any more than that all Jews, including Jews currently living in Jerusalem, share Wiesel's uncompromising vision[84]), the notion of "sacred soil," as applied above all to Kosovo, is one that has remained widely held. Vuk Jeremić, Serbia's energetic young foreign minister from May 2007 to July 2012 (he was elected president of the sixty-seventh session of the UN General Assembly and assumed that office in September 2012),[85] is fluent in English, with one degree in theoretical physics from the University of Cambridge and another from Harvard's Kennedy School of Government in public administration in international development. As a student in the late 1990s, Jeremić opposed the Milošević regime. He has been described as a liberal and claims not to be a nationalist. Yet it is a measure of the discouraging intractability of Balkan politics, its stubborn resistance to the peaceful resolution of entrenched differences, that after becoming foreign minister Jeremić spent many months frenetically circling the globe to lobby governments against recognizing Kosovo's independence. His justification for this stance, "This place, Kosovo, is our Jerusalem; you just can't treat it any other way than our Jerusalem,"[86] mirrored longstanding Serbian views of Kosovo and played well among his fellow countrymen. So framed, however, it was hardly a recipe for solving the problem of Kosovo.

The fact is, the mythology surrounding Kosovo—the notion of Kosovo as sacred soil—was likely to remain compelling for Serbs as long as the situation relating to the former Serbian province continued unresolved. Myths tend to flourish in intractable situations in which conflict and tension persist. If, however, a way could be found to reach closure on the core issues dividing Serbia and Kosovo, if the two states, taking into account the interests each views as important, were to arrive at the point where both recognized the need for compromise, there was a slim possibility that, as has happened in other contested historical settings,[87] the Kosovo story and the mythology infusing it, although certainly not disappearing from Serbian memory, might weaken as a driving force behind Serbian nationalism and gradually recede into a more peripheral spot in Serbian national consciousness.

Such a possibility presented itself on April 19, 2013, when the prime ministers of Serbia and Kosovo, after six months of difficult talks (skillfully brokered by Catherine Ashton, the European Union's foreign-policy chief), reached agreement in Brussels on arrangements pertaining to the ethnic Serbian enclave in northern Kosovo. The enclave—which although part of Kosovo had from the time of the 1999 war operated under its own institutions, financed and controlled by Serbia—had long been the main point of contention between Serbia and Kosovo. Resolution of the dispute and consequent normalization of relations between Serbia and Kosovo, the European Union made plain, was an essential precondition for either country to join it.[88] The new agreement, which was ratified within days by the governments of Serbia and Kosovo and welcomed across the political spectrum in both Belgrade and Pristina, specified the nature and degree of local autonomy Kosovo was willing to cede to Serb-majority municipalities in the North, in return for which Serbia recognized Kosovo's overall authority within the disputed area.[89]

Belgrade's main incentive for agreeing to the deal was its desire for membership in the European Union, which would bring substantial benefits to the troubled Serbian economy. The inducement to Kosovo, an impoverished area with large-scale unemployment, was also in part economic. But more important, in the final analysis, was the promise that the agreement, once implemented, would cement Kosovo's standing as an independent nation. European Union officials hailed the accord, which paves the way for talks to begin between Serbia and the European Union, demonstrating, as one official put it, that both Serbia and Kosovo were finally able to "focus on the future rather than staying entangled in the past."[90] This hopeful response must nevertheless be greeted with a measure of caution. Ashton herself, although commending the prime ministers of Serbia and Kosovo for having "the courage to imagine a better future for their peoples" and expressing the hope that the western Balkans, after being known for the past century "as a cradle of war," would henceforth become known "as a cradle of peace," emphasizes that this future is her hope, but "it is not yet a certainty."[91] As amply suggested in the body of this chapter, before the agreement proves to be the "milestone" in Serbia–Kosovo relations claimed for it, bringing enhanced stability to the Balkan region,[92] a great deal of history will have to be overcome.

2

THE FALL OF MASADA AND MODERN JEWISH MEMORY

"**K**nowledge of the past," wrote the late Lewis A. Coser, "is mainly preserved by the chronicling of events in written sources or by oral tradition. But these events are not all treated in the same manner. Many of them escape notice because potential carriers of the message remain indifferent, while others assume high saliency. How then does one explain that an event that was neglected for almost two thousand years suddenly moved into the forefront of Jewish Israeli consciousness in the twentieth century?"[1] The event Coser refers to is the alleged mass suicide of the Jewish defenders of the mountaintop fortress of Masada in 73 C.E., one of the final acts of the Jewish revolt against Rome that had begun seven years earlier and, with the destruction of Jerusalem and the Second Temple in 70 C.E., resulted in the centuries-long dispersion of the Jews from their homeland. Why was the Masada incident neglected by Jews in the first place? What occasioned the sharp reversal of this neglect in the first half of the twentieth century? And—a question Coser does not address—how is it that, after being front and center in Jewish national consciousness for almost half a century, roughly from the late 1920s to the early 1970s, the heroic image of Masada thereafter began to lose some of its mythic allure? In this chapter, I address each of these questions in turn.

PHASE ONE: THE LONG PERIOD OF
JEWISH NEGLECT OF MASADA

Information about what happened at Masada derives from a single contemporary source, Flavius Josephus's *The Jewish War* (or *The Wars of the Jews*). Two Roman sources refer to the Masada site but pass over completely the events described by Josephus. Similarly, there is no mention in sacred Jewish texts of the alleged encounter between Jewish and Roman warriors at Masada; even the Talmud, in which historical events often come under discussion, makes no allusion to such an episode.[2] Before addressing the question of why Jews remained ignorant of Masada for centuries, let me briefly summarize Josephus's account.[3]

The first thing to be noted about this account—and it is of more than trivial interest—is that aside from a few scattered references to Masada in the body of the work, only a very small portion of *The Jewish War* deals with the events that attracted so much attention among Jews in Palestine and Israel in the twentieth century. The bulk of the work consists of a detailed account of developments leading up to the Jewish revolt and the various phases of the revolt itself, culminating in the Roman siege of Jerusalem, which began in the spring of 70 C.E., and the destruction of the Second Temple in August of that year. It is only at this point—in the final chapter of *The Jewish War*—that Masada becomes the main focus of Josephus's narrative. A rock plateau on the eastern edge of the Judean Desert overlooking the Dead Sea, Masada was initially fortified in the early first century B.C.E. and subsequently much improved by King Herod (r. 37–4 B.C.E.) for use as a refuge.[4] In the early stages of the Jewish revolt, a terrorist group known as the Sicarii (Daggermen), which had been formed in the 50s, captured the fortress, exterminating the Roman soldiers occupying it. The Sicarii, under the leadership first of Menahem and then of Eleazar, son of Jairus, made Masada their base throughout the ensuing conflict.[5] (In the remainder of this chapter, I use the alternate spelling "Elazar ben Yair," which is more common in modern sources.)

After the destruction of Jerusalem, the Roman forces engaged in mopping-up actions against the remaining pockets of Jewish resistance. The last of these pockets was the Sicarii stronghold on Masada, which the new governor of Judea, Flavius Silva, was determined to destroy. Greatly outnumbered and unable to defend against the Roman use of battering

FIGURE 2.1 The way leading up to Masada. (Photographer unknown, early twentieth century. Courtesy of the Library of Congress.)

rams and fire, the Jews faced the certain prospect of capture and enslavement. At this point, according to Josephus, Elazar spoke to his men:

> My loyal followers, long ago we resolved to serve neither the Romans nor anyone else but only God. . . . [N]ow the time has come that bids us prove our determination by our deeds. At such a time we must not disgrace ourselves: hitherto we have never submitted to slavery . . . we must not choose slavery now. . . . For we were the first of all to revolt, and shall be the last to break off the struggle. And I think it is God who has given us this privilege, that we can die nobly and as free men. . . . [I]t is evident that daybreak will end our resistance, but we are free to choose an honourable death with our loved ones. . . . The fire that was being carried into the enemy lines did not turn back of its own accord towards the wall we had built: these things are God's vengeance for the many wrongs that in our madness we dared to do to our own countrymen. For those wrongs let us pay the penalty not to our bitterest enemies, the Romans, but to God—by our own hands.

Elazar thus sought to persuade his people, after setting fire to all their possessions except their store of food, to commit mass suicide. Their wives would in this way "die unabused" and their children "without knowledge of slavery," while the preservation of their food supply intact would "bear witness when we are dead to the fact that we perished, not through want but because . . . we chose death rather than slavery."[6]

The contrast between freedom and slavery articulated by Elazar eerily echoes the one at the heart of the Kosovo covenant, in which again the choice presented was between freedom through courageous death and living in shame as slaves. There is one striking difference, however. Defeat at the hands of the Romans was, in Elazar's eyes, a divine punishment for the "many wrongs" the Sicarii had committed against their fellow Jews. Among these wrongs, doubtless very much on his mind, was a night raid some years earlier during the Passover holiday on the small town of Ein Gedi a few miles north of Masada. In the raid, the Sicarii butchered more than seven hundred Jewish women and children (the men, who might have offered resistance, having scattered before they could seize their weapons), stripped bare the inhabitants' homes, seized the ripest of the crops, and brought everything back to Masada.[7]

Elazar's speech persuaded some of his followers. But "others less heroic," Josephus tells us, "were moved by pity for their wives and families, and certainly too by the prospect of their own end." Fearful lest their families' tears and laments weaken the resolve of their more hardhearted comrades, the Sicarii leader therefore made a further appeal to the entire group, this time in a longer and more dazzling display of oratory in which he placed much emphasis on the immortality of the soul and the freedom that death alone conferred.[8]

After this second speech, all enthusiastically agreed to Elazar's plan: "In the end not a man failed to carry out his terrible resolve, but one and all disposed of their entire families, victims of cruel necessity who with their own hands murdered their wives and children and felt it to be the lightest of evils!" Ten of the men were chosen by lots to be the executioners of the rest, after which, again by lots, one of them was given the task of killing the other nine and then himself. In all, 960 met their end in this manner, only two women and five children escaping the slaughter by concealing themselves in the conduits that brought drinking water to the fortress. When the Roman soldiers arrived on the scene, the women emerged from hiding and provided them with a detailed account of what had transpired.[9]

Let us now return to the question of why Jews neglected Josephus's narrative for centuries after the Masada event. First, there's the matter of language. *The Jewish War* was originally written in Aramaic, the native tongue of its author and of many of his compatriots living in ancient Judea. The Aramaic version was at some point lost and is no longer extant. However, Josephus states in the preface that he later translated his work into Greek to make it more accessible to the diverse inhabitants of the Roman Empire, many of whom either spoke Greek or at least had some proficiency in the language.[10] He also hoped, through the translation, to correct the distortions and inaccuracies in earlier accounts written by people without firsthand knowledge of the war. He himself had been a major participant in the early stages of the revolt, when he was commander of the Jewish forces in Galilee, and had been a spectator at close quarters of the final phases of the conflict (by which time he had long since gone over to the Roman side), in addition to having access to published and unpublished Roman sources.[11] It may also be argued, somewhat tentatively, that although rendering of *The Jewish War* into Greek made it more accessible to educated Hellenized Jews in Josephus's own day and for some time thereafter, it eventually became an impediment to continuing Jewish familiarity with the work as Hellenized Judaism declined and was absorbed (according to some) into early Christianity.

Whatever the case in regard to language, a far more substantial reason for Jews' neglect of *The Jewish War* had to do with Josephus's betrayal of the Jewish side early in the rebellion against Rome, as the author himself openly acknowledged and documented. When the future Roman emperor Vespasian (r. 69–79), after a long and bloody siege, finally triumphed over Josephus in the fortified Galilean town of Jotapata in July 67, the Jewish commander secreted himself in a large cave that already contained forty of his men. When their hiding place was discovered, Vespasian sent one of his tribunes, an old friend of Josephus's, to inform the Jewish leader that if he turned himself in to the Romans, he would be dealt with generously. The others in the cave, who were prepared to take their own lives rather than surrender to the enemy, were enraged when they saw their commander weaken: "Are you so in love with life, Josephus, that you can bear to live as a slave? How quickly you have forgotten yourself! How many you have persuaded to lay down their lives for liberty! False, utterly false, was the reputation you won for courage and shrewdness, if you really expect to be spared by those you have hit so hard, and if, even supposing their offer of pardon is genuine, you stoop to accept it! . . . We will lend you a sword and a hand to wield it. If you die willingly, you will die as commander-in-chief of the Jews; if unwillingly, as a traitor."[12] After attempting without success to persuade his followers not to go through with their plans for mass suicide, Josephus finally yielded to his men's wishes. All of them, including their leader, drew lots and killed each other in turn, prefiguring what was later to take place at Masada. At the end, only Josephus and one other man were left alive.[13] The former easily persuaded the latter to join him in surrendering to the Romans, whereupon, as Yael Zerubavel wraps up what was to follow, "Josephus joined the Roman court and devoted his life to historical writing, leaving behind a most important source on Jewish history in Antiquity, including a detailed account of the Jewish revolt from 66 to 73."[14]

But before all that came to pass, Josephus engaged in a further piece of treachery against the Jews, this time in a much more exposed setting. In the climactic days of the Roman assault on Jerusalem, when the armies of Vespasian's son Titus had all but defeated the city, Titus on more than one occasion deployed Josephus as an intermediary to talk to the Jewish defenders in their own language (Aramaic), using his impressive oratorical skills to persuade them to surrender and thereby save their beloved city from total destruction. These appeals, as Josephus himself attested to on one such occasion, "were received by the defenders generally with howls of derision or execration, sometimes with showers of stones," sealing Josephus's reputation as a traitor to his people.[15] After the war was over, Josephus apparently never revisited his native land, despite being given a large estate there by Vespasian and exemption from the land tax by a later emperor (Domitian, r. 81–96). Fellow Jews were, he claims, jealous of his good fortune. "But," as the Josephus scholar Mary Smallwood suggests, "the conduct which had resulted in that good fortune will surely have rankled still more deeply, and it was not safe to set foot again among people who could not let bygones be bygones."[16]

As earlier noted, the defeat of the Jewish defenders of Masada occupies only a minute part of *The Jewish War*. Certainly, it was of very small consequence as compared to the vastly more significant destruction of Jerusalem. The real question, therefore, is not why the Jews neglected Masada, but why they neglected Josephus's account of the fall of Jerusalem. And the most plausible answer surely is that the author of *The Jewish War* was shunned by his Jewish compatriots for having betrayed their trust and then flaunted that betrayal (in his writing) for all to see. Indeed, Josephus's work might have been permanently lost had it not been for its preservation by elements within the Christian Church, who viewed it as an essential source on early Christianity.[17]

The fact that the surviving version of Josephus's book was written in Greek is, as previously suggested, certainly also a reason for its eventually being forgotten. After the book had been neglected for hundreds of years, some time around the tenth century an Italian Jew named Josippon (or Joseph ben Gorion) produced a Hebrew adaptation of *The Jewish War*, which in different renderings was widely read among Jews and in later times often reprinted and translated into other languages, including Yiddish. Josippon altered Josephus's account of the Masada episode in one important particular: Elazar's men, after dispatching their wives and children, bravely went out and fought the Romans to the death instead of committing suicide. However, even with this partial sanitization of one of the more bothersome aspects of Josephus's narrative, the Masada events as such appear to have had little impact on medieval Jewish readers, the chief reason more than likely being that prior to the dawn of Zionism in the late nineteenth century whatever happened at the mountaintop fortress did not speak meaningfully to contemporary Jewish life and concerns.[18]

PHASE TWO: NATIONAL REBIRTH AND THE NEW AWARENESS OF MASADA

Zionism, with its emphasis on Jews returning to their ancient homeland, reversed this neglect dramatically. The emergence of the Zionist movement in Europe resulted from a number of factors. One such factor, very broad in nature, was the growing strength of nationalism on the continent in the course of the nineteenth century,[19] accompanied by the sense among beleaguered minorities, including the Jews, that they would not be safe until they either relocated to countries that opened their doors to immigrants or built a state of their own. In the closing decades of that century, new fears of anti-Semitism, much stimulated by the outbreak of the Dreyfus Affair in France in 1894, worked to magnify such sentiment in western Europe.[20] The wretched political and economic circumstances of Jewish communities in eastern Europe also gave a major push to Zionism.[21] A wave of pogroms that erupted in Russia in 1881 and further bloodshed against Jews in the Bessarabian provincial capital Kishinev in 1903 heightened public concern about the situation of Russia's Jewish population. One response to this shocking situation was involvement in radical politics, which at the turn of the twentieth century claimed a disproportionate minority of young Jewish recruits.[22] Far more popular, in numerical terms, was the option of leaving Europe altogether. The pogroms resulted in large-scale Jewish immigration to the United States; they also prompted the first serious efforts by Jews (in much smaller numbers) to resettle in Palestine.[23]

As Jews began to migrate to Palestine, the circumstances of their lives changed in profound ways. One of the most important of these ways was the emergence of a new curiosity about the ancient Jewish past, which now seemed far more relevant than during the long centuries of dispersion. An essential prelude to this shift had been the dawn of serious scholarly interest in Jewish history, one expression of which was the first Hebrew translation of Josephus's works in 1862. Zionist interest in the ancient national past not surprisingly also drew attention to the Judean wars of liberation, and when a modern Hebrew translation of *The Jewish War* appeared in Palestine in 1923, it was applauded as a document of towering historical and national significance. The way was now paved for Masada, despite making up only a very small part of Josephus's work, to be reconstituted "as a major turning point in Jewish history, a locus of modern pilgrimage, a famous archeological site, and a contemporary political metaphor."[24]

All of these things did not, of course, take place at the same moment in time. Like many events of the remote past that are unusually susceptible to multiple interpretations (often including outright falsification), especially when they are not well documented historically, Masada was invested with distinctly different meanings by successive generations of Jews living in Palestine.[25] During the first few decades of Jewish emigration there, lasting from the early 1880s until the outbreak of World War I, Masada was still not on the Jewish radar screen. Until the end of the war, Palestine remained a part of the Ottoman Empire. The numbers of eastern European Jews who went there were minuscule compared to the numbers who went elsewhere (mainly to the United States), and immigrants to Palestine were reduced by half during the war years as a result of privations suffered under weakened Turkish rule, fighting between the British and Turkish forces (especially in Gaza toward the war's end), as well as natural disasters against which the settlers had little protection.[26] Palestine became an important destination for Jewish migration only after the end of the war.

The reasons for this focus on Palestine were multiple. First, growing anti-immigration sentiment in the United States resulted in severe restrictions on immigration in 1921 and even severer ones in 1924 with the introduction of national origins quotas. The consequences were striking. In the period from 1885 to 1921, some 85 percent of the more than two million Jews emigrating from eastern Europe were taken in by the United States. However, in the four years from 1921 to 1925, the number of Jews admitted to America plummeted from 119,036 to 10,292, a reduction of 91 percent, and on a much smaller scale the same pattern held elsewhere in the West.[27]

Second, complex changes that took place in Europe, in part as a direct result of World War I and the manner of its official termination, generated an increasingly uninviting environment for Jews still living there. Although nationalism had been growing on the continent throughout the nineteenth century, it finally triumphed with the collapse of the old empires during the war, placing a pronounced emphasis on national purity. Gone were the days, Mark Mazower writes, "when it was possible for ethnic Germans to rise to high positions in Tsarist administrations, and for diplomats representing the Ottoman Empire in international congresses to be Greek. The war of 1914–18 swept this world away." Versailles, he adds tellingly, gave "sixty million people a state of their own, but it turned another twenty-five million into minorities."[28] What to do about Jews, Gypsies, and other minorities was a much-discussed problem during the postwar period, but no good solution was found. Hitler did not rise to power in a vacuum: "indigenous traditions of anti-Semitism" were widespread, "common to the modernizing, state-building national elites of authoritarian *and* democratic countries alike through much of central and eastern Europe."[29]

Within this broad setting, a significantly different dynamic was played out in Russia as a consequence of the February and October revolutions of 1917. With the Kerensky government's annulment of all religion- and nationality-based restrictions placed on Russian citizens, Jews for the first time acquired full civil rights in Russia, and support for the Zionist movement increased dramatically, causing Chaim Weizmann to proclaim that the primary motive force fueling Zionism wasn't, as commonly believed, the longstanding suffering of Russia's Jews, but the yearning of the Jewish people for a home of their own. In a matter of months, however, the Mensheviks' liberal decrees were overturned under the Bolsheviks, who saw Zionism, with its transnational ties and commitment to a Jewish national home outside Russia, as in profound conflict with their own political and ideological objectives.[30] The Communist campaign against Russian Zionists and all expressions of Jewish culture was carried on energetically, with thousands of Jews being incarcerated or exiled. Many more of Russia's Jews suffered terribly from the violence attending the revolution and its aftermath, the number of Jewish casualties in the Ukraine alone estimated at between 60,000 and 130,000.[31]

A third factor encouraging Jewish settlement in Palestine was a change in the latter's administrative and political status owing to the collapse of Ottoman rule during World War I. An agreement had earlier been reached between Britain and France that in the event of a victory by the Entente powers Palestine would come under British protection. A letter dated November 2, 1917, from the British foreign secretary Arthur James Balfour to Baron Walter Rothschild, a leader of the Jewish community, for transmission to the Zionist Federation of Great Britain and Ireland incorporated a formal statement of British government policy: "His Majesty's government view with favour the establishment in Palestine of a national home for the Jewish people, and will use their best endeavours to facilitate the achievement of this object, it being clearly understood that nothing shall be done which may prejudice the civil and religious rights of existing non-Jewish communities in Palestine." Also included in what came to be known as the Balfour Declaration was an explicit statement that the declaration was to be taken as an indication of the British government's "sympathy with Jewish Zionist aspirations."[32]

Owing to all these developments, there was a substantial increase in Jewish migration to Palestine in the years from 1919 to 1923, which, together with an additional wave of immigrants who went to that territory (often now referred to as the British Mandate) in the late 1920s, more than tripled the Jewish settler population, bringing it by 1931 to just shy of 175,000. From the standpoint of longstanding Zionist goals, this development was encouraging, but the good news was tempered in several ways. Many of the new Jewish immigrants who went to Palestine did so not because they were impassioned Zionists, but because they had no other option once the gateway to America was effectively blocked. Large numbers who came from Russia had been traumatized by their experiences during the revolutions and civil war and were in desperate shape emotionally. Immigrants from Russia and later Poland were often destitute, and social services in Palestine that might relieve their plight were extremely limited. Apart from the *halutzim* (vanguard or pioneers)— those committed Zionists who received special training in agriculture prior to leaving their countries of origin and who took the lead in championing cooperative living and working of the land in Palestine—many migrants were ill equipped to survive in their new home's very different physical environment. Moreover, a significant number of the early settlers, although dedicated Hebraists, had little more than a rudimentary command of the language and faced problems communicating, and from the beginning there were tensions between the new migrants and the Arab population long resident in the area. As an indication of how bleak and depressing life was for many Jews in Palestine between 1922 and 1929, for every hundred new Jewish settlers roughly thirty Jews migrated again, in most cases returning to their lands of origin.[33]

It was during this period that the Masada story first attracted the serious attention of Jews living in Palestine, and, significantly, in stark contrast to the interpretation of the story in later decades, when Masada was associated primarily with the image of a small number of intrepid Jewish warriors defending themselves heroically against a far larger and more powerful adversary, the story's meaning in the 1920s pertained above all to survival.[34] Articulating this meaning most powerfully was the long poem *Masada* published in 1927, which, by giving agonized expression to the tension between hope and despair of Palestine's Jews, almost overnight won an enthusiastic readership among the settlers, becoming in Bernard Lewis's judgment "probably the most significant landmark in the restoration of Masada to the Jewish consciousness."[35] The author of the poem, Yitzhak (or Isaac) Lamdan, had been born in 1899 in the Ukraine. After being raised as a boy in a traditional Jewish environment, Lamdan had received a general and Hebrew education. When the fighting accompanying the revolution and civil war engulfed his hometown, he and his brother were separated from their parents.

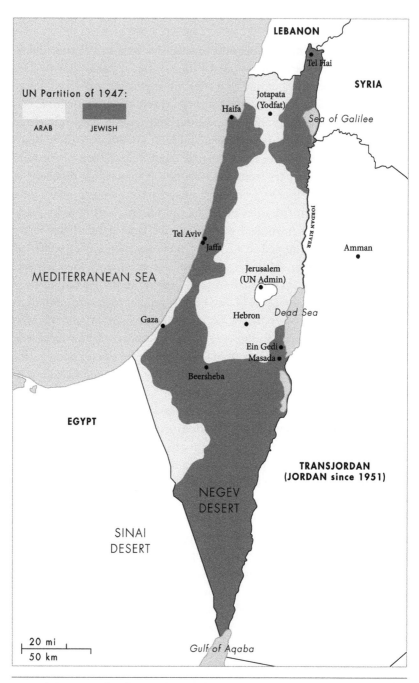

MAP 2 Palestine under the British Mandate, 1922–1948, and the UN partition of 1947. After Israel's victory in the Six-Day War (1967), the territory under its control as a result of the partition increased dramatically.

FIGURE 2.2 Yitzhak Lamdan. (From Leon I. Yudkin, *Isaac Lamdan: A Study in Twentieth-Century Hebrew Poetry* [London: East and West Library; Ithaca, N.Y.: Cornell University Press, 1971]).

The brother was later killed in a pogrom, and Yitzhak, initially won over to the revolutionary cause by the Kerensky government's emancipation of Russian Jewry, joined the Red Army. However, after barely escaping a wave of anti-Jewish violence that swept over the Ukraine,[36] he decided to "ascend" to Palestine, where he arrived in 1920 as part of the post-war wave of Jewish immigration.[37] In Palestine, after spending several years engaged in road construction and agriculture, Lamdan abandoned manual labor to take up writing full-time.[38]

Coursing through the poem *Masada* are its author's deeply conflicted feelings.[39] At one pole is Lamdan's dark, pessimistic view of Jewish history, a history in which Jews have forever been victimized by an unforgiving fate; at the other pole is the slenderest flicker of hope and optimism, in which the individual defiantly mounts a rebellion against fate. In terms of physical and psychological spaces, the poem gravitates back and forth between the impossibility of continued Jewish life in eastern Europe and the daunting difficulties and uncertainties facing Jewish efforts to make a new life in Palestine. The former space is articulated in seemingly autobiographical terms right at the start of the poem, followed by a terse symbolic allusion to the latter space:

> One Autumn night, on a restless couch far from our ravaged home, my
> mother died:
> In her eyes, a last tear glistened as she whispered me a dying blessing.
>> Before I went to campaigns on distant, foreign fields, with my army kit
>> pressing on my shoulder . . .
> On Ukrainian paths, dotted with graves, and swollen with pain,
> My sad-eyed, pure-hearted brother fell dead, to be buried in a heathen
> grave.
> Only father remained fast to the doorpost wallowing in the ashes of
> destruction,
> And over the profaned name of God, he tearfully murmured a prayer.
> Whilst I, still fastening my crumbling soul with the last girders of courage,
> Fled, at midnight to the exile ship, to ascend to Masada. . . .
> The final banner of rebellion has been unfurled there . . .
> Against the hostile Fate of generations, an antagonistic breast is bared
> with a roar:
> "Enough! You or I! Here will the battle decide the final judgement!"[40]

Throughout Lamdan's poem, Masada refers allegorically to Jewish Palestine. But, although it is the Jews' last best hope, the likelihood that it will bring salvation is laughably weak. Early in the poem, anonymous "friends" present the options available to Jews in eastern Europe in the horrific aftermath of the Russian Revolution. Each of the first three options—taking revenge, remaking the world by joining the revolution, and passively waiting for the end—is contrasted with a Masada alternative that is variously described as a fiction, a "ruined fortress" that failed once and will fail again, and an illusion.[41]

In the midst of utter hopelessness, Masada (Palestine)—the fourth option—is offered as the only possible route of escape, the only place where, according to a secret voice, the fugitive from Europe can find atonement. He hearkens to the voice and makes his way there. Although he betrays scant confidence in the voice's trustworthiness—"High, high is the wall of Masada, therefore does the ravine that crouches at its feet go deep . . . And should this voice have cheated me, then would I cast myself from the heights of the wall into the ravine that there be no record of the remnant, and nothing remain!"[42]—the night bonfires at Masada offer a powerful burst of hope.

> These nights, there are no weary in the camp. No one stumbles thirsty
> for rest when the air infuses strength, pouring joy into the limbs.
> A wondrous roar—extra power—goes from the chest to the throat; there
> is a scorching fire in the arms, and a flame of strength in the soles of
> the feet.
> At such a time are night bonfires raised on to the wall, and round them
> the children of Masada go out with flaming dances. . . .
> Bonfires, like eternal avenues, are planted on all of Israel's paths,
> bonfires—the marks of every path that ascends to Masada. . . .
> On nights of terror did bonfires illuminate the dream of Masada from afar;
> by bonfires let us now illuminate its realisation, near at hand. . . .
> Into bonfires did our fathers jump with deathful joy to become an
> enigma; around bonfires now do children dance the dance of
> the solution. . . .
> The chain is still not broken, the chain still continues, from father to
> child, from bonfire to bonfire, the chain still continues. . . .
> Ascend, chain of the dance! Never again shall Masada fall! Does the leg
> stumble? Let us ascend! The son of Yair* shall again appear. He is not
> dead, not dead! . . .
> If the age-old Fate derides: "In vain!" we will pluck out Its inciting
> tongue! And in spite of itself, the derisive negation, defeated, shall nod
> its head: "Indeed, indeed. Amen!"[43]

But the momentary hope, like the bonfires themselves, does not last:

> Ah, as God was absent from accepting the offering of our lives, and the
> sacrifice of youth and love when we raised the bonfires, so does He now
> not listen to our weepy plaints as the bonfires die. . . . Surely Masada weeps
> too, and how should she not? All of us, with thirsty arms, are suspended
> about her neck, and seek motherly pity, protection and deliverance—
> and she knows that she can give nothing, that she can deliver no more!
> She cannot deliver that consumed by the curse of generations; she cannot
> deliver that which Fate has commanded not to deliver.

---

*Elazar ben Yair, the commander of the Jewish defenders of Masada in 73 C.E.

In the depths of despair, the poet, filled with a selective nostalgia, questions yet again why he left Europe. He remembers "scenes of yesterday:
on soft carpets of forgetfulness I rolled as a young foal rolls on grass beds
in the Spring," and asks, "Why did I come to wallow in Masada nights in
the ashes of dying bonfires?" He remembers "the nest of the motherland,
upholstered with ancestral love," where "[g]ay mornings used to greet me
when I rose, and laughing Springs would extend their arms to me," and
asks, "So what was the bad dream that uprooted me, and dragged me
here?" He, of course, knows the answer to this question: he has come to
Masada (Palestine) to atone for the blood of his martyred brothers and
sisters in the land of his birth, who pleaded with him, "Atone, O remnant,
atone for our blood!" But even as he yields to their plea and commits
himself to atonement, he realizes that "there is no atonement, none," and
wonders, "Where can I now take the plea of my martyrs?"[44]

Again and again, as the poem moves toward its finish, Lamdan's
imagery alternates between the sufferings endured in the old country
and the imperviousness of the new land to the needs of those seeking
refuge in it. The counterpoint to the buoyant "Never again shall Masada
fall!" is the cruel reality that, just as in the first century, Masada (i.e.,
Palestine) cannot possibly meet the demands placed on it by twentieth-
century Jews. And there is another equally disheartening parallel to the
earlier Masada: when Lamdan writes that "[n]o one would know if we
were to fall here, as no one would know if we were to triumph," he
alludes to the psychological as well as the physical separation from the
larger Jewish community that the meager numbers answering the call of
Zionism have experienced in making their way to Palestine. But the isolation he describes is no less apt a characterization of the small cluster of
first-century defenders of Masada, toward whom most Jews at the time
were at best indifferent.[45]

In the final part of *Masada*, Lamdan's narrator initially assumes the
part of a supplicant, begging God to be a father and guardian to the weak
and weary, to "soften the hard rocks of Masada at their heads" and "let
them not be struck by the hail of sorrow, or dried up by sudden heat-
waves. . . . To those who from their wallowing ascended to the wall, the
ashes of destruction on their head and sacks of mourning on their loins
to derive comfort in the battle of Masada—bolster their spirit, O God,
bolster their spirit when comfort delays!"[46]

But the mood quickly shifts as the book on the past is closed and the future, dreaded and uncertain, is contemplated:

"This is the frontier; from here onwards there are no more frontiers, and
    behind—to no single exit do all paths lead."
We have finished the books of all the paths; experience, heavy with years,
    reads out in tears and blood, and we follow with a signature:
"Finished!" (Finished, finished and completed, though not "finished and
    completed with praise to God, creator of the world."[47] We have no
    praise for God, creator of the world)—
As from now, a new book of Genesis is opened on the wall.
And as did our fathers on finishing the book of the Law [the Torah] before
    starting it again, let us roar with a new and last roar of the beginning!
Be strong, be strong, and we shall be strengthened![48]

Lamdan's apocalyptic poem, which begins and ends with a roar of defiance against the seemingly intractable course of Jewish history, makes frequent use of military metaphors. But the enemy—fate—is not a human enemy, and the weapons used are not sticks and stones. Scholars have sometimes asked why, if the Jews were looking for heroic material from their past to bolster spirits in the present, they didn't fasten upon a more straightforward (and in the early twentieth century far more widely known) example, such as the revolt of the Maccabees, who against great odds seized portions of Judea from the Seleucid Empire and founded the Hasmonean dynasty in the second century B.C.E. The best answer to this question, as far as Yitzhak Lamdan and other Jews who arrived in Palestine both before and in the immediate aftermath of World War I were concerned, is that the main problem they encountered in their new home was not a military threat (which the British protectorate precluded), but adaptation to a strange and deeply discouraging environment.[49]

In this situation, the metaphor Lamdan felt called upon to probe in his poem was not military conquest, but rather the more ambiguous rebellion against a callous and unforgiving Jewish past. For this metaphor, the Masada of the first century C.E., as it was known to Lamdan (very possibly from Josephus's account), was tailor-made, and his success in portraying the existential struggle facing Jews in Palestine during the 1920s was a major factor in his poem's immense popularity among the settlers, according to Barry Schwartz, Yael Zerubavel, and Bernice Barnett: "The reality of the historical Masada articulated (1) the settler's sense of being in a situation of 'no choice'; (2) their realization that the Zionist cause was a last stand against fate; (3) their sense of isolation from the main body of the Jewish people; (4) their despair and the essential ambivalence of their commitment to one another and to their new homeland; and (5) the very real prospect that the second Masada would fall in the same manner as did the first—by self-destruction." In short, the overriding effect of Lamdan's poem was to invest the settlers' situation with meaning. Their ultimate concern was "not dominance, but survival," which perhaps explains how it was that "in one of the bleakest and least significant events of their history," they saw part of themselves.[50]

Masada was reprinted numerous times, was for years the subject of lively discussion in the literary press, and, prior to its waning popularity in the late 1960s, occupied an important place in the Hebrew school curriculum.[51] It is interesting in this connection to note that, as in the case of Serbian history, at a key historical moment a work of literature took a major part in the shaping of Jewish consciousness.[52] The differences between the two cases, however, are striking. One such difference is that the Kosovo myth as developed in Petar Petrović Njegoš's play *The Mountain Wreath* embodied a significant element of religion and religious belief, whereas the Masada story (especially as Lamdan framed it) was deeply antireligious, appealing primarily to secular-minded settlers, not to highly religious Jews. Another difference: Njegoš's overriding aim in writing *The Mountain Wreath* was not to recall to Serbian minds the fourteenth-century Battle of Kosovo, which they already knew only too well as the major turning point in their history—it was to free Serbia from the yoke of the Ottoman Turks. In contrast, the historical Masada has been described as "a mopping-up operation" that was far less noteworthy historically than the destruction of Jerusalem and the Second Temple. The importance of Lamdan's work was that he almost single-handedly reconstructed Jewish memory of Masada and moved it from the periphery of the periphery to the very center of the consciousness of Palestine's Jews.[53]

Once Masada was embedded in Jewish collective memory, however, the meaning(s) of the mythology surrounding it evolved in response to changing circumstances first in Palestine and later in Israel. Early in his sensitively wrought portrait *The Israelis: Founders and Sons*, Amos

Elon describes the celebrations marking the twentieth anniversary of the founding of the State of Israel, held in Jerusalem in May 1968. He imagines the sense of pride, verging on disbelief, that the aging founders viewing the parade must have felt about what had been accomplished in their lifetime:

> In one short lifetime, a modern welfare state had grown up in what had been a backward, partly barren, thinly populated Ottoman province. In one short lifetime, a nation, spirited and cohesive, had developed out of a horde of frightened refugees, the outcasts of Europe, survivors of concentration camps and primitive, half-literate masses from the shoddy souks of the Near East and North Africa. A common language, painfully resurrected from the dead, had emerged from a babel of tongues. In one short lifetime, big cities, theaters, orchestras, ballet troupes, had sprouted in a profusion rarely found in much larger nations. Zoos, ports, and airfields, industries, superhighways, traffic jams, great universities; all were the realization of their dreams.[54]

In the space of just four decades after the publication of Lamdan's poem, the environment in which it was written and to which it spoke, along with the people inhabiting that environment who had greeted the poem as the perfect reflection of their emotional torment, had been utterly transformed. In addition to the remarkable advances Elon describes, these four decades bore witness to a number of other changes and developments that had an appreciable effect on the fate of the Jewish community and gradually changed the context in which Jews thought about Masada as a symbol.

One such development was the emergence of Arab nationalism and growing friction between Arabs and Jews. The earliest Jewish settlers often seemed naively oblivious to the Arabs as a potential source of conflict, but in the first years of the twentieth century, as Arab nationalism grew in tandem with Jewish nationalism, signs of a budding problem began to appear. After World War I and the establishment of the British Mandate, as Arabs became increasingly fearful of the Jewish threat, sporadic protests, demonstrations, and acts of violence erupted among them. "Living in tiny Palestine," the renowned author J. C. Brenner wrote not long before being killed by rioting Arabs in Jaffa in May 1921, are "no fewer than six or seven hundred thousand Arabs who are, despite all

their degeneracy and savagery, masters of the land, in practice and in feeling, and we have come to insert ourselves and live among them, because
necessity forces us to do so. There is already hatred between us—there
must be and will be."[55] In August 1929, a major disturbance took place in
Hebron, resulting in the deaths of sixty-seven Jews.[56] And the situation
worsened in the 1930s when, in reaction to the massive influx of Jewish
refugees from Europe,[57] a series of Arab attacks on Jews took place, peak-
ing during the rebellions of 1936–1939 (which were supported in part by
the Axis powers).[58]

Another change that became increasingly conspicuous during the 1930s
was the makeup of the Jewish community. During the early decades of the
twentieth century, the Jewish population in Palestine had consisted largely
of immigrants from eastern Europe. But by the 1920s and 1930s, the proportion of native-born Jews steadily grew. The members of this younger
generation differed from their parents in important ways. They had no
direct memories of a prior existence in Europe marked by discrimination,
persecution, impoverishment, and violence. Hebrew was their mother
tongue, not a language they had to struggle to learn. Also, they didn't have
to adapt to a different climate, a different physical environment, different
food, and a different lifestyle. To this generation, Palestine was home.

As conditions for Palestine's Jewish population steadily improved in
the decade or so following the publication of Lamdan's *Masada*, the
nature of the poem's appeal gradually shifted. By the time it became
integrated into the Hebrew school curriculum in the late 1930s and early
1940s, many young Israelis, like some Zionists earlier, read it less for the
gloomy and uncertain feeling conveyed in the poem as a whole than for its
periodic bursts of optimism. In this highly selective reception, the ambi-
guities and fears that were such a large and key part of the poem were
passed over in favor of a reading that accentuated the work's message of
defiance and heroism.[59] The line "Ascend the chain of the dance! Never
again shall Masada fall!" now became for many young people emblematic
of the poem in its entirety.

The full flowering of Masada as a patriotic symbol came in the early
1940s in direct and indirect response to the outbreak of war in Europe. As
reports came in of the methodical destruction of European Jewry by the
Nazis, the defenders of Masada were increasingly acclaimed as a prin-
cipled alternative to the submissiveness of Europe's Jews in the face of
Nazi persecution. The Holocaust confirmed for Jewish youth in Palestine

what their Zionist education had long taught them: that, as Zerubavel puts it, "the future belonged to the national revival in the Land of Israel; Jewish life in Exile could only lead to death and destruction."[60]

Apart from the situation of the Jews in Europe, Palestine's Jewish population faced a more immediate threat in the form of German field marshal Erwin Rommel's Afrika Korps, which was advancing toward Egypt in North Africa. The British had a plan for the evacuation of all British from Palestine if the German army invaded. But Arabs and Jews were of course not included in the plan, which meant that if the British withdrew, the Jews would be confronted with two adversaries, the Germans and the Arabs. The latter (as well as non-Arab Muslims in the Middle East and North Africa) had been bombarded with Arabic-language Nazi anti-Semitic propaganda during the war, which obviously did little to moderate longstanding animosities between Jews and Arabs.[61] Responding to these circumstances, underground armed organizations with an ideology of direct action, such as the Palmach (the elite fighting force of the Haganah, the Jewish paramilitary organization), formulated plans to defend the Jewish community, one of the best known of which was the "Masada Plan," envisioning a last stand against the Germans in northern Palestine.[62]

In this increasingly tense and unsettled environment, youth groups actively fostered the Masada story as an important part of Jewish national identity. The hike through the desert to Masada and then the arduous climb to the top became a rite of passage for thousands of Jewish youth. With the threat of a German invasion looming, Shmaria Guttman, an early promoter of the Masada symbolism, in January 1942 organized a week-long seminar at the top of the fortress for forty-six youth movement guides (among whom was the future Israeli political leader Shimon Peres), which elicited the following impassioned account in the magazine *Bamaale*:

> Before our eyes, the world is on fire. We see nations disintegrate when they confront the diabolic Nazi power. . . . We must strengthen ourselves and stand on guard for our land and freedom with all our might. . . . For this readiness, we must intensify and amplify the mental connection with the chain of Hebraic heroism in the past. Before us we must imagine Masada—fortress of Israel that stood in the battle for the freedom of the people and the land against the legions of Rome. . . . The people

who fight today . . . rely for their power on the heroes of their people in the distant and recent past. When the young Hebraic generation defends its homeland, it will rely on the heroes of its people, the fighters of Masada and the defenders of Tel Chai [Hai].[63]

Zerubavel points out the irony that the narrative of Masada that gathered increasing force among Hebrew youth during the prestatehood years laid special emphasis on how the Masada defenders died "holding their weapons." This emphasis, which became the core of the heroic Masada myth, circumvented the most troublesome part of Josephus's account, according to which the defense of the mountaintop fortress ended in mass suicide. Yet it became pervasive and long-lasting. In the interviews Zerubavel conducted in Israel in the late 1970s, both students and their parents repeatedly referred to the Masada warriors as having fought "to the bitter end," "until the last breath," or "until the last drop of blood."[64]

The hold that the Masada myth acquired among Jews was powerful enough to overcome any possible sense of irony over discrepancies between the myth and the historical account from which the myth derived, at least ostensibly. In point of fact, many people, having never read Josephus, were familiar *only* with the myth. For instance, in interviews that Nachman Ben-Yehuda conducted in the early 1990s with celebrated commanders of the Israel Defense Forces (IDF), the interviewees were asked to look back on the attitudes they had decades earlier. The following responses were typical:

The question is what is more important. There is no perfection. Exactly who these people were [on top of Masada, Sicarii or Zealots]—it is not important! Were they Jewish? That is what is important! Of course, it is possible to find things that would show that not everything was in order. But, overall, there are struggles for this land. And when we look at this struggle, it becomes a potentiating charge that reinforces our struggle today. A heritage and tradition that we can rely on.

It is not important at all if this myth is true or not. As long as it helps to activate the people and its light can be used for educational purposes. . . . We are all selective, as a people and as individuals. We remember what was done to us. Myths are myths. It is good that there are myths. But it is not good for a people to live *only* on myth.

We accepted things as they were. Like "It is good to die for one's country." This was an oral Torah [accepted truth]. I am telling you these
stories so that you can understand how [they] could catch us so easily
in our naïveté and build myths for us. . . . Today [they] are moving in
totally the opposite direction. Trumpeldor was a pimp, Ben-Gurion a
pickpocket. Everyone corrupted [laughing]. But then, [they] accepted
things as they were. . . . This was a naïve and romantic period, and part
of it was this business of Masada.[65]

A major development in Jewish history took place with the establishment of Israel as an independent state on May 14, 1948. The United
Nations (UN) General Assembly had voted on November 29, 1947, on the
proposal to partition Palestine into two states, one Arab and the other
Jewish, with Jerusalem placed under UN administration (see map 2)—a
plan the Jewish leadership in Palestine supported and the Palestinians'
representatives opposed. There were 650,000 Jews and 1,220,000 Arabs
living in Palestine at the time, and almost immediately after the UN vote,
which went in favor of partition,[66] enraged Arabs attacked buses, homes,
and shops throughout the land. After at first being thwarted by the British, the Haganah was finally able to respond with major offensives all over
Palestine. In the end, thousands were killed and hundreds of thousands
(mostly Arabs) were driven from their homes. On May 15, 1948, a day
after the official declaration of Israel's independence, the British Mandate formally ended, and Palestine was invaded by five neighboring Arab
states. The war went through three phases and didn't finally end until
early the following year. Although there were times when the outcome
was uncertain, Israel was ultimately victorious, ending up with somewhat
more territory under its control than had originally been allotted to it
under the UN partition. Separate armistices with four of the invading
Arab countries were signed in 1949.[67]

The Israeli military arm that fought in the 1948 war and in all subsequent conflicts in which the new state became involved was the IDF,
a conscript army formed mainly out of the Haganah and other prestatehood armed groups and officially established on May 26, 1948, by
David Ben-Gurion, the minister of defense and first prime minister of
Israel.[68] The Haganah had for years made much of the Masada story
in its internal training and ideology, which carried over into the IDF
after statehood. Indeed, as in the case of the Kosovo myth in Serbia, the

state in Israel now became seriously engaged in the propagation of the Masada story to justify and muster support for national goals. Masada was, in Bernard Lewis's words, "made the center of something verging on a national cult."[69]

The state's role was manifested in a variety of ways. Over the years, hundreds of thousands of IDF soldiers trekked to and ascended Masada as part of their education—a ritual that had special meaning for members of the armored units, who until the early 1990s regularly climbed to the fortress's top on completion of their basic training to take an oath of allegiance to the State of Israel and the IDF.[70] Extensive excavations of the Masada site in the mid-1960s, under the direction of Yigael Yadin, a professional archaeologist (and former IDF chief of staff), also had substantial government backing. Yadin, whose work was widely publicized both in Israel and abroad, was motivated at least as much by patriotic enthusiasm as by the search for truth about the Jewish past (an inclination that did not go uncriticized).[71] The state also organized important ceremonial events at Masada, a particularly striking example of which was the reburial in 1969 of twenty-seven skeletons excavated at the site (and presumed to belong to the last defenders) in an elaborate military funeral conducted on the top of the Masada cliff.[72] More recently, on VIP visits to Israel, the state has added an official stop at Masada, along with the Yad Vashem memorial to the Jewish victims of the Holocaust in Jerusalem. "The visit to the isolated and remote site that is surrounded by the open vistas of the desert," Zerubavel writes, "provides visitors with a visual representation of contemporary Israel as standing alone, surrounded by Arab countries, left to defend itself or face a destruction similar to that of the ancient Masada people."[73]

The state has vigorously promoted the understanding of Masada as a negative political metaphor, laying stress on "the fragility of Jewish survival and . . . intended to legitimize Israel's current concerns about its own security," and this understanding has become an influential strain in Israeli political culture, leading many contemporary Israelis "to look at their own situation as if they were situated at the top of besieged Masada" and to take a dim view of the value of compromise in negotiations with the Palestinians and Arab countries.[74] This shift toward a more extremist politics has been reinforced by a number of long-term trends in Israeli society, which Peter Beinart summarizes: "an ultra-Orthodox population that is increasing dramatically, a settler movement that is growing more radical and more entrenched in the Israeli bureaucracy and army, and a Russian immigrant community that is particularly prone to anti-Arab racism." An Israel Democracy Institute poll in 2009, according to Beinart, "found that 53 percent of Jewish Israelis (and 77 percent of recent immigrants from the former USSR) support encouraging Arabs to leave the country," and another poll taken in March 2010 "found that 56 percent of Jewish Israeli high school students—and more than 80 percent of religious Jewish high school students—would deny Israeli Arabs the right to be elected to the Knesset."[75]

PHASE THREE: THE FADING OF THE HEROIC MASADA MYTH

At the same time that the state's role as the custodian of national memory has grown in Israel, along with an increasingly widespread perception of Masada as a powerful negative metaphor, the heroic interpretation of the Masada myth, once so prominent nationwide, has weakened—or at least become more complicated—in the minds of many Israelis owing to a number of important new developments.

Although at the beginning of the life of certain ideas there is a brightness and allure about them that captivate people's minds and hearts, sooner or later a process of degradation often sets in: the nobility of the ideas fades, and they lose their purity and freshness. This is, at any rate, what seems to have happened with the heroic Masada narrative in Israel beginning in the late 1960s and early 1970s. The narrative did not disappear. Even today when Israelis visit Masada, the tangible reality of the site, together with the stunning biblical landscape over which it towers, can stir deep feelings of symbolic connectedness with Jewish antiquity and a sense of historical proprietorship over the land to which Jews, starting in the late nineteenth century, had begun to return. This sense of connectedness also took a religious turn in the 1960s with the discovery of an ancient synagogue and two ritual baths (*mikvah*) at the Masada site during archaeological excavations,[76] an event that for Orthodox and ultra-Orthodox Jews not only changed the definition of

Masada to a religiously sanctified ground but also reframed the collective suicide of the Jewish defenders of the fortress as a form of martyrdom (*kiddush ha-Shem*).[77]

Nevertheless, for a number of reasons, the optimistic patriotic narrative that was so much a part of the Masada myth appears to have been drained of much of its energy and idealism at its apogee—the naïveté and romance alluded to by one of Ben-Yehuda's IDF informants. A major factor contributing to this weakening was the increasing commercialization of the Masada site as a result of the excavations. What had once been a profound collective experience for Israeli youth—the long, difficult, and precarious trek that was the heart of the Masada pilgrimage—was now transformed into a showy attraction designed for the benefit of tourists. The once wild and unruly Masada site was changed into a national park run by the state, which now charged admission. To encourage tourism, the state staged performances at Masada such as a sight and sound show to mark the thirtieth anniversary of Israeli statehood and a performance of Mahler's Resurrection Symphony by the National Orchestra of Israel to celebrate the fortieth anniversary. Masada as a tourist site has been a huge success. From some 42,000 visitors in 1965 and 1966, the number of tourists reached a half-million per year during the 1970s and 1980s and increased still further in the mid-1990s. Also significant, the number of visitors from Israel in time became much smaller than the number of foreign visitors: in 1995, out of 740,000 tourists who went to Masada, only 115,000 were Israelis. Foreign tourism was further encouraged with Masada's designation as a UNESCO World Heritage site in 2001.[78]

Another factor contributing to the weakening of Masada as a patriotic national symbol was that as a result of changed circumstances in Israel the symbol suffered a decline in relevance, becoming increasingly less appropriate as a metaphor for the country's societal and national goals. The Six-Day and Yom Kippur wars provided an important impetus to this process of attenuation. Any war involving Israel—in addition to the 1967 and 1973 conflicts, there had of course been the war of 1948, and in 1956 Israel clashed with Egypt over the issue of access to the Suez Canal—was bound, in part because of structural factors, to have a profound impact on Israeli society. For one thing, there is the country's Lilliputian size, both in geographical and demographic terms. (The population in 1970 was a little more than 2.5 million.) "Intensity of experience," Elon writes with specific reference to the Six-Day War, "is inordinately heightened in Israel by the closeness of everything. . . . The war has been mostly a 'limited' one, but in a country as small as Israel even 'limited' calamities easily assume an air of sickening abundance."[79] Also to be taken into account is the proximity of the action in all of the major wars Israel has been involved in: the fighting in every instance has taken place on Israel's or a neighboring Arab country's soil. War has never been far away. Finally, there is the fact that military service is mandatory for all non-Arab Israeli citizens (with minor exceptions) and, when time spent in the reserves is factored in, often lasts for many years. What these three circumstances taken together mean is that, in stark contrast to the situation in the United States in the early twenty-first century, where for many citizens the Iraq and Afghanistan conflicts have occasioned little sense of personal connection,[80] when Israel goes to war, all Israeli families and individuals are deeply affected.

A graphic sense of what the militarization of Israeli society has meant is provided by the case of David Grossman, one of Israel's foremost writers. Born in 1954 in Jerusalem, Grossman entered the army in 1971. In 1973, shortly after the Yom Kippur War, he became acquainted with another conscript, who subsequently became his wife. When Israel invaded Lebanon in 1982, Grossman—then in the army reserves—was called up and spent five weeks on active duty. Both of his sons served in the army in the first decade of the new century. One of them was killed in 2006 in the Second Lebanon War. In the summer of 2010, Grossman's daughter, after graduation from high school, began her three years of military service.[81]

Both the 1967 and 1973 wars, although often contrasted in their emotional impact on Israelis, contributed to a weakening of the Masada symbol, albeit in different ways. One consequence of the crushing victory over the Arab side in 1967 was that, by quadrupling the territory under Israel's control, it brought more than a million often not very friendly Arabs under Israeli rule. This large increase in territory and rule, combined with the defeated Arab countries' refusal to make peace when the war was over, promised long-term security problems for Israel, prompting the chief architect of Israel's triumph, Moshe Dayan, to complain bitterly that "we are doomed to live with [the Arabs] in a state of permanent belligerency."[82] Dayan's prediction was borne out by the Yom Kippur War, which despite Israel's victory was far more traumatic than the Six-Day War. The coordinated attack by Syria and Egypt on Yom Kippur day (October 6) in 1973 came as a complete surprise, raising serious concerns about the state of Israeli intelligence. The Arabs' early battlefield successes caused deep anxiety and fear among Israelis. And although the war lasted only three weeks, Israeli casualties were heavy. The result was that the sense of invincibility and complacency bequeathed by the 1967 war was severely undermined.[83]

Already in the years and months preceding the Yom Kippur War, evidence of the weakening grip of the heroic Masada myth abounded. Some of this evidence came in the form of critical commentary by Israeli and non-Israeli Jewish intellectuals. An Israeli social scientist for whom "Masada was a dynamic symbol" when he was growing up in the 1940s and 1950s observed that "when Masada became a tourist attraction (with restored archaeological finds and a cable car) and a subject of a television series, it became impoverished as a cultural symbol for the 'country' itself . . . a waning glow of a flame that was once vigorous." Another Israeli social scientist saw the Six-Day War as having "eclipsed Masada and made it redundant," Israel's spectacular victory providing the country with the symbolic center it had previously lacked: "the whole of Jerusalem [previously under UN control] and the Western Wall at its center." The Wall synthesized the alternative traditions of Masada and Yavneh,[84] "superceding and encompassing both—the martial and the learned, adaptation and last stand—within its own unbroken continuity growing out of the Land of Israel, something built, and not built on, a signpost for both secular historicity and religious yearnings."[85]

In April 1973, a young Israeli historian, Benjamin Kedar, writing in the Hebrew-language daily *Ha'aretz*, sharply criticized the Masada myth's aptness as a symbol for the State of Israel. He argued (as summarized by Robert Alter) that, on the contrary, "the suicides at Masada were an aberration from Jewish values and a historical dead-end, while it was rather Yavneh that was the key to underground survival and ultimate national rebirth." Masada, according to Kedar (now in his own words), was "less an inspiring model than an obfuscating obsession, a complex that could pervert moral criteria. For if in fact our situation is as desperate as Masada's, the lines of demarcation between forbidden and permitted begin to waver."[86]

The diminished salience of the Masada myth-story over time may also be seen from another perspective: at the height of the story's impact, Israel, in terms of both its size and military strength, played David to the Arab world's Goliath; but after the 1967 war this perception was gradually reversed, as Israel, with the most powerful military in the region, assumed the mantel of Goliath, and the Arab world, despite its overwhelming demographic advantage, became the new David.[87] In June 1973, after describing Israel as "the looming military power in the region," Alter wrote: "Every day Masada seems less appropriate as an image of Israel, encircled though it is by belligerent states that would, if only they could, drive it into the sea."[88]

Alter's conclusion was not really affected by the outcome of the Yom Kippur War. Indeed, in the years following the war, the gap between Israel's military strength and that of the Arab world widened, if anything.[89] In Dayan's 1976 autobiography, he wrote of having to justify to the United States the actions of Israeli pilots who in July 1970 had gotten into a skirmish with Soviet aircraft over Egypt and shot down five of them, an action the Americans feared might drag the Soviet Union into active combat. Israel, Dayan told the Americans, also had no interest in such an outcome. However, he added, "Israel was not Czechoslovakia, and our generation was not the generation of Masada, where the defenders of the last Jewish outpost in the war against the Romans . . . held out to the end and then committed suicide. We would continue to fight and live."[90] Even Yadin, in an interview for *Newsweek* a few months prior to the Yom Kippur War, made essentially the same point, noting that although Israelis still made the pilgrimage to Masada, it wasn't necessarily because they considered the example of the Masada defenders "worth emulation but in order to remind themselves to keep their country strong enough that they [would] never be faced with the Zealots' desperate choice." Writing in 1979, Baila Shargel, after quoting Dayan and Yadin's comments, concluded that "by the middle of the 1970s, Masada had become for many a symbol of what Israel did *not* want to become. . . . Today, virtually no Israeli citizen accepts the Zealot–Sicarii fanatics as role models, and public speakers and popular writers seldom present their story as a paradigm for the virtues of freedom and independence."[91]

Zerubavel, although pursuing a quite different interpretive tack, arrives at a not entirely dissimilar position. Where in an earlier time it was common for Jews to see Masada as the antithesis of the Holocaust, in the 1960s, in part as a result of the testimony of Nazi concentration camp survivors during the Eichmann trial in 1961, many Israelis' view gradually began to shift. This shift was accelerated by the new sense of vulnerability Israelis felt after the Yom Kippur War, which tempered earlier criticism of Holocaust victims for "going like sheep to the slaughter." In the 1970s and 1980s, Lamdan's "Never again shall Masada fall!" increasingly became the symbolic equivalent of "Never again!"—both slogans functioning "as national vows conveying Israelis' determination to avoid recurrence of a deadly situation, alluding to Masada and the Holocaust respectively." Masada, Zerubavel continues, "provides contemporary Israelis with a metaphor for their own situation: a small group of Jews living on top of an isolated cliff, surrounded by the desert and besieged by a powerful enemy, with no one to turn to for help." But, like Dayan and Yadin, she has increasingly come to see it less as a positive symbol to be emulated than as a negative metaphor for a situation to be avoided at all costs.[92]

As Nachman Ben-Yehuda and others have shown, the changing Israeli view of Masada in the 1970s and 1980s was reflected in a waning interest in Masada as a site of symbolic and mythic power. This decline in interest became apparent within the secular youth movements, Masada losing much of its earlier appeal as a destination for youth pilgrimage. It was also reflected in the fact that the IDF's armored corps eventually ceased holding its ceremonies at the fortress, and although the Ministry of Education recommends a trip to Masada for high school students, it is no longer mandatory, and some educators even oppose it on ideological grounds.[93]

In addition to some of the reasons already given for this weakening of the hold of the heroic image of Masada, we mustn't discount some of the broad changes taking place in Israeli society from the 1970s on, changes that have resulted in an increasingly diverse and divided population. As of 1970, almost 50 percent of Israelis were native born; a highly developed economy and modern welfare state had come into existence; and young Israelis, less oriented toward their forbears' collective ideals, were often more focused on materialistic needs and quality-of-life issues. To be sure, given the reality of the security situation facing Israel and the ever-present dangers of living there,[94] military service was still an accepted obligation. But the values of heroism and sacrifice of self for country that were so important to earlier Israelis and that made the secular patriotic Masada myth so alluring had lost much of their appeal,[95] all too often being replaced by the negative image of Masada as a metaphor for a fate Israelis must do all in their power never again to experience.

Nachman Ben-Yehuda begins his book *The Masada Myth* by describing a painful weekend he spent in 1987. He had been reading an article by an American scholar, David Rapoport, discussing terrorist groups in three different cultural traditions. One of the groups Rapoport dealt with was the Sicarii, who had flourished at the time of the revolt against Rome in the first century C.E. and had advocated the use of assassination and terror. Ben-Yehuda describes his reaction at the time:

> One can imagine my amazement, indeed indignation, at Rapoport's statement that this "bunch of assassins" perished on top of Masada. I still vividly remember reading this and skeptically thinking, "Here is another American who wants to tell *me*, the Israeli, what happened on Masada." After all, I "knew" what happened on Masada. I learned it in school, in the army—I climbed to the top of Masada. I *knew* that there was a group of Jewish freedom fighters who fled Jerusalem, after its destruction by the Roman Imperial Army in 70 A.D., to Masada. There, they staged the final fight against that army. When the Romans were about to conquer the fortress, all these heroic Jewish freedom fighters chose to commit collective suicide rather than surrender to Rome and become slaves or die in some strange and painful ways (e.g., in the arena). But to think that these Jewish freedom fighters were in fact a group of detested assassins?

Curious to find out how Rapoport could possibly have made such an egregious error, Ben-Yehuda checked the article's references and discovered that the author's main source was Flavius Josephus's *The Jewish War*. He spent the weekend "frantically reading" the relevant sections of both the Hebrew and English renderings of Josephus's work and by

Saturday night discovered to his chagrin "that Rapoport was right and I was wrong." Ben-Yehuda, moreover, was not alone in his mortification. Toward the end of his book, he notes that when he told people about the nature of his work on Masada and the ways in which Josephus's account diverged from what they had been taught and led to believe, their responses ranged from "mild disbelief to (much more frequently) anger and open hostility."[96]

I empathize with Ben-Yehuda's pain and that of the other Israelis with whom he discussed his work, well remembering how shocked I was, after growing up believing a simple, idealized vision of Lincoln as "the great emancipator," to learn in college that, despite his personal concerns about slavery, Lincoln's priority from start to finish was not to free the slaves, but to save the union.[97] But from my standpoint as a historian, Ben-Yehuda's response to his discovery struck me as methodologically misguided. His book is for the most part devoted to an eminently useful discussion of the consistency with which Jews in Palestine/Israel have believed in the "truth" of the mythic account of Masada, in spite of its significant departures from Josephus's historical account. So far so good. Where I part company with him is in regard to his view that "the credibility and reliability" of Josephus's work are "a side issue" because it is "the only true account we have."[98] From my perspective, it may indeed be the only account we have, but that doesn't make it "true." As more than one scholar has contended, there is a strong likelihood that the story recounted by Josephus contains major distortions and fabrications.[99] Apparently, therefore, what we have in the twentieth century is not a mythic account and a true account, but rather a layered set of myths— one mythic account built on (and diverging from) another, the latter in turn being built on and diverging from whatever it was that actually happened at the Masada fortress in 73 C.E.

The word *myth*, in everyday parlance, often implies something "fabricated" or "not true." My own use of the term, although not excluding this connotation, is broader and more nuanced and is focused on a somewhat different set of concerns.[100] Not the least of these concerns is the very issue of what, indeed, "truth" is in a historical sense. Once assertions about the past enter deeply into people's minds and hearts, once they become the stuff of popular memory, it is arguable that they acquire a truth of their own, even if this truth does not at all coincide with what in fact happened at some point in past time. At the very least, such assertions are true statements about what people *believe* and therefore must occupy a central place in any history of human consciousness.

Beyond this, insofar as what people believe (regardless of whether it is true or false in the ordinary sense) exerts a powerful influence not only on how they feel and think, but also not infrequently on their behavior, such beliefs become agents that generate and condition historical action of the most undeniably "real" sort. "The past is a malleable substance," one writer has observed, "which we work into expressive shapes that in turn shape us."[101] During the twentieth century, the myth of the American frontier more than once influenced Washington's foreign policy and through books and films shaped popular beliefs concerning violence, masculinity, race, material progress, and a host of other matters.[102] In more recent American history, the Tea Party movement's insistence upon the current relevance of a frozen-in-time reading of the Founding Fathers—"with their white wigs, wearing their three-cornered hats, in their Christian nation, revolting against taxes, and defending their right to bear arms"—has exerted a powerful impact on the political environment in which the Obama presidency has been forced to operate.[103] Myths gain their potency from their ability to persuade. It doesn't matter whether the Opium War (1839–1842) in fact ushered in the beginning of the "modern" era in Chinese history. If most Chinese are convinced that it did, as appears to be the case, and if this conviction is deeply enough held, it becomes, on some level, "true"—an efficacious working myth.[104]

Something very much along these lines happened in regard to the Masada myth in twentieth-century Palestine/Israel and to the myths and legends surrounding the Battle of Kosovo in modern Serbian history. In both Palestine/Israel and Serbia, what was vitally important was to have a compelling *story*, an operative "truth" that related not so much to what actually happened in the past as to what people believed—or wanted to believe—happened. Such stories, as we have seen in the case of the Masada narrative, may be modified, sometimes in significant ways, to enable them to address people's shifting worries and concerns. And if historical conditions change sufficiently, as eventually happened in Israel, the grip of a story on popular memory may weaken considerably. But however committed professional historians may be to identifying and demolishing the myths of the past, for most human beings stories with substantial mythic content have an emotional power and appeal that strenuously resist the results of serious scholarly inquiry. Although historians of George Washington have long since laid to rest the cherry tree myth, Mason Weems's life of the first American president, "which created the myth, still remains in print as the most popular biography of the man ever written."[105] If at some point in time such stories lose traction within a community, it tends to be because they no longer resonate meaningfully with new historical circumstances, not because the members of the community suddenly discover (as did Ben-Yehuda) that the stories are little more than myths with scant grounding in historical truth.

3

CHIANG KAI-SHEK, CHINESE NATIONALIST POLICY, AND THE STORY OF KING GOUJIAN

Stories and their protagonists, whether historical or fictional or (as is most often the case) somewhere in between, have taken a vital part throughout Chinese history as didactic metaphors, prototypes to be followed or avoided in the historical present. An important example in the twentieth century—although it has been largely invisible to Western observers—is the close affiliation that existed between the Guomindang (Nationalist Party) political leader Chiang Kai-shek and Goujian, king of the ancient state of Yue, one of the more or less autonomous political units into which China was divided prior to its unification under the Qin dynasty in 221 B.C.E. Chiang identified strongly with Goujian, and his government's actions and policies in the run-up to the Sino-Japanese War of 1937–1945 were, in important respects, modeled on those of the Yue king. After the Guomindang's defeat by the Communists in the civil war of 1945–1949, moreover, writers in Taiwan, with official encouragement, regularly highlighted the parallels between the circumstances of Yue and those faced by the Nationalists, even going so far as to portray Goujian, at least implicitly, as a stand-in for Chiang. The link between the Nationalists and the Goujian story, in brief, not only was part of Chiang Kai-shek's personal makeup but also prevailed in the thinking of the Nationalist government and the Chinese public at large both before and after 1949.[1]

THE GOUJIAN STORY IN ANTIQUITY

But before getting to this intriguing connection between ancient narrative and recent history, we need a brief introduction to the Goujian story itself, as it was known in antiquity. The earliest sources relating to the story are *Zuo zhuan* (The Zuo tradition) and *Guo yu* (Discourses of the states), both of which were probably compiled during the late fourth century B.C.E. (though based on earlier materials both oral and written) and provide a bare-bones account of political and military events concerning the Yue king.[2] Although these early works clearly have some degree of fictional content, they "most certainly include a good deal of accurate historical information" as well.[3] At the very least, there is a strong likelihood that their depictions of such basic essentials as the year in which an important war was fought, the identities of the rulers involved, the reasons for the war, and its outcome are a reasonably faithful reflection of what in fact took place.

Although the main thematic structure of the Goujian story (above all, the interplay between humiliation and revenge that lies at its core) has persisted with little change from the story's first emergence in ancient times right up to the present day, the story itself, like most ancient Chinese historical narratives, evolved over time, some elements being reworked, others dropped, and still others added.[4] A favorite diversion of Chinese opera fans that was not part of the original story, for example, is the alleged romance between Fan Li, Goujian's prime minister, and the ravishing beauty Xi Shi (whose very historicity some Chinese scholars have questioned).[5] The text of the story, in other words, in contrast with the relatively stable texts of a Chekhov play or a Jane Austen novel, has been a soft or pliable one. In fact, to even speak of a "text" in the case of the Goujian saga is probably misleading. Oral transmission was still strong in China during the period when accounts of Goujian's career first emerged. And in subsequent times, much as in the trail of stories inspired by so many other historical figures globally (Joan of Arc comes to mind), the narrative was recycled almost continuously in accordance with the requirements of different audiences, historical moments, and authorial predilections.[6] The importance of the recounting of Goujian's life and career for Chinese during the past century and more, it is clear, has resided less in its embodiment of historical truth (although many Chinese may see it as such) than in its many-faceted allure as a story. It is significant, in this connection, that the version of the story that directly or indirectly served as a principal source for many of the renderings that circulated in the twentieth century was a work that has been described as China's first historical novel: *Wu Yue chunqiu* (The annals of Wu and Yue), originally compiled by the Eastern Han author Zhao Ye from 58 to 75 C.E.[7] The following summary of the Goujian narrative is based mainly on this work.

The setting for the Goujian story is the rivalry beginning in the latter phase of the Spring and Autumn period (722–481 B.C.E.) of the Zhou dynasty between the neighboring states of Wu (roughly coinciding with the modern province of Jiangsu) and Yue (modern Zhejiang), two newly ascendant powers on the southeastern periphery of the contemporary Chinese world. In 496 B.C.E. the king of Wu, Helu (or Helü) took advantage of the opportunity created by Yue's preoccupation with funeral observances for its recently deceased king to mount an attack. The new Yue ruler, Goujian, at the time only in his early twenties, counterattacked and, employing exceptionally brutal tactics, defeated the forces of Wu. (Goujian is said to have sent three waves of convicted criminals toward the Wu front lines, where with a great shout they proceeded to cut their own throats; while the Wu forces stood stupefied, the Yue army launched a surprise attack from another direction.) Helu was mortally wounded in the fighting, but before dying he summoned his son and successor, Fuchai (or Fucha), and asked him never to forget that Goujian had killed his father. Accordingly, after assuming the kingship, Fuchai devoted himself energetically to planning his vengeance against Yue. Goujian saw what was happening and, overconfident from his earlier triumph, asked his trusted minister Fan Li what he thought about a preemptive strike against Wu. Fan Li, observing that Yue was not nearly as strong as Wu, urged the young king to be patient. Goujian, however, convinced that he knew best, went ahead and attacked Wu anyway. The year was 494 B.C.E. It did not take long for the Wu army, led by King Fuchai, to quickly rout Yue's troops, obliging Goujian and a remnant force of five thousand men to retreat to Mount Kuaiji (southeast of modern Shaoxing city in Zhejiang province), where they were surrounded by the Wu forces.

This point was critical in the sequence of events. Goujian, facing certain defeat, was fully prepared, we are told, to fight to the finish. But his high officials remonstrated with him, arguing the case for a less suicidal course. In the interest of saving Yue from extinction, they contended,

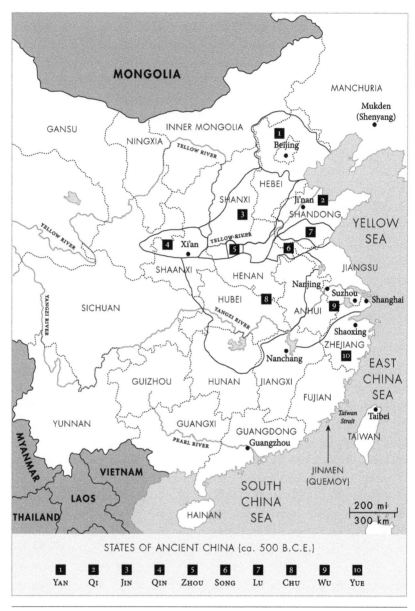

MAP 3 Eastern and central China, c. 1900–1950. The locations of ancient states are also indicated.

Goujian should do everything possible to bring about a peaceful resolution of the conflict, mollifying Fuchai with humble words and lavish gifts and even evince his willingness to go with his wife to Wu as slaves of the Wu king. Swallowing his pride, Goujian, not without misgiving, acquiesced in this strategy. It was also decided that Fuchai's grand steward, Bo Pi (or Bo Xi), well known for his greed and lust, should be secretly bribed with beautiful women and precious gifts in order to gain internal support for Yue at the Wu court.

Goujian and his wife's servitude in Wu began in the fifth year of his reign (492 B.C.E.). His top minister, Fan Li, accompanied them, while another of his high officials, Wen Zhong, remained at home to look after the governance of Yue during the king's absence. During the ceremonial farewell that took place prior to Goujian's crossing of the Zhe River (the modern Qiantang River) into Wu, his official counselors, in an effort to console and encourage him, pointed to the historical precedents of King Tang of the Shang dynasty, King Wen of the Zhou, and other sage rulers of antiquity who had experienced great setbacks and painful humiliations in their day but had ultimately managed to turn defeat into accomplishment and calamity into good fortune so that their merit was passed down through the ages. Goujian was urged not to berate himself or view his predicament as the result of personal failings; rather, he should endure humiliation for the sake of Yue's survival.

On Goujian's arrival in Wu, Fuchai's prime minister, Wu Zixu, a clearsighted and tough-minded official with long experience, urged the Wu king to kill Goujian forthwith and obliterate the state of Yue. Fuchai responded that he had heard that if one put to death someone who had surrendered, misfortune would be visited on one's family for three generations. His reason for not killing Goujian was not that he felt any affection for him, but rather that it would be an offense against Heaven. In the end, Fuchai, with Bo Pi's encouragement, allowed Goujian to live. During the next three years, the Yue king served as Fuchai's carriage driver and took care of the horses. He, his wife, and Fan Li resided in a humble stone cottage near the palace, where they led the lives of poor working people, experiencing one humiliation after another without betraying the least sign of anger or resentment.

The greatest of these humiliations came in the third year, when Fuchai fell ill. Goujian consulted with Fan Li, who through divination determined that the king's illness was not in fact serious. Fan Li then suggested a plan to Goujian that he said was sure to succeed. Goujian should request permission to inquire after the condition of Fuchai's illness. If permitted to see the king, he should then ask leave to taste Fuchai's stool and examine his facial color. After so doing, he should kneel to the ground and offer his congratulations to the king of Wu, informing him that he would soon get well and would not die. When this prognosis proved correct, Goujian need have no further worries. The following day Goujian asked Bo Pi to arrange an audience with Fuchai so that he could ask about his health. As it happened, at the very moment that Goujian arrived at the palace, the Wu king had just moved his bowels, and Bo Pi was carrying the stool out in a bucket when he encountered Goujian at the entranceway. Goujian greeted Bo Pi and asked if he might taste Fuchai's stool in order to make a prognosis concerning his illness. He then proceeded to stick his finger into the container and taste the stool, after which he went inside and announced to the Wu king: "The captive servant Goujian offers his congratulations to the great king. The king's illness will begin to improve on *jisi*. On *renshen* of the third month he will be completely well."* Fuchai naturally wanted to know how Goujian knew all this. Goujian explained that he had formerly studied with a man skilled in making prognoses on the basis of the smell and taste of fecal matter.

When Fuchai did indeed recover, he was of course overjoyed. Stirred by Goujian's loyalty and honesty, the Wu king ordered a banquet to be held with Goujian seated in the place of honor. On the following day, Wu Zixu, appalled by Fuchai's conduct, went to the palace to admonish him. He warned the king about people who were outwardly friendly but harbored harmful designs in their hearts. He then went into a lengthy account of the real motives behind Goujian's behavior. Goujian "has started out by drinking the great king's urine, but he will end up eating the great king's heart; he has started out by tasting the great king's stool, but he will end up devouring the great king's liver." The very existence of the state of Wu hung in the balance. Having heard enough, Fuchai

---

*One of the basic systems for marking time in China, used from earliest times on into the twentieth century, involved the combining of two sets of counters (one consisting of ten stems, the other of twelve branches) to form sixty unique combinations. The system was used most commonly for identifying days and years. When the sixty-day or sixty-year cycle was completed, it was repeated ad infinitum. In the text, *jisi* and *renshen* represent specific days.

FIGURE 3.1 Goujian tastes Fuchai's stool. (From Wu Hanbi, *Wu jiejie jiang lishi gushi* [Elder sister Wu's history tales][Taibei: Zhonghua Ribao, 1978].)

advised his prime minister to forget the entire matter and not to mention it again. He then went ahead with his plan to pardon Goujian, escorting him personally through the Serpent Gate on the south side of the capital and asking him, on his return to Yue, to always bear in mind his goodwill in forgiving him. Goujian performed a *ketou** and vowed before Heaven that he and his high officials would forever remain loyal to the Wu king

---

*Also *koutou*, a ubiquitous Chinese ritual denoting respect for a superior and involving knocking the head on the ground while in a kneeling position; the origin of the English word *kowtow*.

and never turn against him. He performed another *ketou*. Fuchai raised him up and helped him into his carriage. With Fan Li holding the whip, they drove off.

After his return to Yue, Goujian, with the help of Fan Li, Wen Zhong, and other official advisers, adopted a wide range of policies geared toward the ultimate goal of taking revenge against Wu and becoming the dominant figure in the China of his day. In keeping with this aim, he built up the population and economy of Yue and rehabilitated its military. He also made it his business to do everything possible to weaken the state of Wu through various stratagems designed to exploit Fuchai's vulnerabilities—above all, his fondness for beautiful women and lavish display. A different man from the headstrong, self-indulgent youth of only a few years earlier, Goujian governed in a respectful and circumspect manner, practicing strict economy and avoiding extravagance. Knowing that avenging himself against Wu was something that required elaborate preparation and could not be accomplished overnight, he worked incessantly, never resting his mind or body. When overcome with sleepiness, he would use the sharp smell of knotweed (*Polygonum*) to keep his eyes from closing. In the winter, when it was freezing, he would often carry ice and snow in his arms, and in the heat of summer he would hold a hot brazier in his hands. Although the proverb *woxin changdan*, "sleeping on brushwood and tasting gall," that has long been closely associated with the Goujian story apparently wasn't used until the Song period (960–1279), already in ancient times the Han historian Sima Qian had written in *Shiji* (Records of the historian) that Goujian hung a gall-bladder in his room, which he licked every time he went in and out in order to guard against complacency and as a reminder of the bitter experiences he had undergone.

When Goujian first returned home from Wu, Fuchai restored to Yue a piece of territory one hundred *li** in circumference. Later, when it came to the Wu king's attention that Goujian, since returning to Yue, had shown himself completely content with his circumstances, he decided to confer more land on him, augmenting Yue's territory to eight hundred *li* in circumference. To repay the king of Wu for this kindness, Goujian sent him one hundred thousand bolts of hemp cloth (*gebu*), nine wooden

---

*A unit of length equal to about one-third of a mile.

FIGURE 3.2 Graphic depiction of "sleeping on brushwood and tasting gall." (From Zhao Longzhi, *Goujian* [Taibei: Huaguo, 1953]).

containers of honey, seven multicolored square-shaped vessels, five pairs of fox pelts, and ten boats constructed of bamboo. Fuchai, who had always regarded the remote and insignificant state of Yue as possessing little if anything of value, was struck by this tangible expression of Goujian's loyalty and consideration.

Wu Zixu, after learning of these developments, went home, lay down on his bed, and expressed to his attendants his forebodings concerning the future consequences of the enlargement of Yue's territory. But Fuchai, upon receiving the hemp cloth tribute from Yue, carried out his promise to enlarge Yue's land. The officials and populace of Yue were extremely pleased with the way things were going. All understood the Yue king's strategy for handling Fuchai and fully supported him in his efforts.

Goujian made it clear to everyone high and low that they were not to talk openly of Yue's long-term plans. He led his people in replenishing the granaries and armories and in opening up new lands and plowing the soil so that the populace might be enriched and the state strengthened. He also regularly asked his top officials for advice on matters pertaining to governance. On one such occasion, Wen Zhong argued that the key to good governance was for the ruler to concern himself above all with the people's well-being (*aimin*). In response to this counsel, Goujian relaxed the severity of Yue's laws and punishments and reduced taxes and levies, with the result that the living conditions of the populace improved and all were willing to "buckle on their armor" and go to war to advance Yue's interests.

In the first month of the ninth year of his reign (488 B.C.E.), the king of Yue summoned his top ministers into his presence. He reminded them of Yue's past defeat at the hands of Wu, the abandonment of the Yue ancestral shrine, and his own captivity—humiliations that were known among all the states. His thoughts were constantly fixed on seeking revenge against Wu, just as a lame person thinks constantly of being able to stand up and walk again. But he did not know what strategy was best and appealed to his ministers for guidance. The general consensus was that Fuchai was an arrogant man, consumed by self-love. The conflict between Bo Pi and Wu Zixu was a fatal flaw that, in combination with Fuchai's weaknesses as a ruler, would eventually bring about Wu's fall. But, for the time being, Wu remained militarily powerful. Yue, therefore, should build up its strength in secret while continuing outwardly to demonstrate its loyalty to Wu and wait patiently for the time when Wu, having exhausted itself in fighting against its rivals, the large northern states Qi and Jin, was vulnerable and could be safely attacked.

Goujian now consulted with Wen Zhong and, noting that this minister had saved him from difficult situations in the past, asked him to recommend a plan for taking revenge against Wu. Wen Zhong replied that if Goujian wished to destroy Wu, the first thing to do was to determine Fuchai's desires and indulge them; only after so doing would it be possible to acquire Wu's land and wealth. He suggested nine concrete stratagems that he hoped the Yue king would adopt. If Goujian kept them secret, and if he used his intelligence to gain complete mastery over them, the whole world was his for the asking. What difficulty, then, should he have in bringing the lone state of Wu to its knees? Goujian was delighted with Wen Zhong's advice and immediately set about implementing his recommendations. Wen Zhong observed that Fuchai was obsessed with constructing palaces and towers and had his workmen engage in such construction nonstop. Goujian should therefore make a selection of the finest wood and present it to Fuchai. Goujian had his woodworkers scour the hills for such wood, and once it was located, he instructed the workmen to cut, shape, polish, and decorate it. He then sent Wen Zhong to Wu to present the timber to Fuchai, who was, of course, overjoyed.

Fuchai's prime minister, Wu Zixu, however, was not pleased at all and entreated the king of Wu not to accept the wood. Formerly, he said, when Jie, the last ruler of the Xia dynasty, had constructed the Ling Tower, and Zhou, the last ruler of the Shang, had erected the Lu Tower, these actions had caused yin and yang to be out of joint, winter and summer to come at the wrong times, and the grain not to ripen in the fields, resulting in calamities that brought privation to the people and misfortune to the state. In the end, these two rulers occasioned their own destruction. If Fuchai accepted the presentation from Yue, it would surely spell the end of the state of Wu.

Fuchai predictably paid no heed to Wu Zixu's remonstrance. He accepted the timber from Yue and incorporated it into the Gusu Tower, which took five years to complete. The tower was so high that from the top one could see two hundred *li* in every direction. The workers recruited to construct it underwent enormous hardship and suffering. The common people were in a state of utter exhaustion, unable to earn a livelihood; the nobility were overcome with anguish. "Excellent," exclaimed Goujian, elated by how well Wen Zhong's stratagem had worked.

In the twelfth year of his reign (485 B.C.E.), Goujian told Wen Zhong that he had heard that Fuchai had a weakness for beautiful women and that, when indulging this passion, he completely disregarded the administering of his realm. The Yue king wondered whether by exploiting this failing it might not be possible to undermine Wu's defenses. Wen Zhong responded in the affirmative and, adding that Yue could count on the eloquence of the grand steward Bo Pi to weaken Fuchai even further, urged Goujian to select two beautiful women for presentation to the king of Wu. Accepting this advice, Goujian dispatched someone skilled at reading faces to scour the land. At Ningluo Mountain, this person discovered two beautiful maidens, Xi Shi and Zheng Dan, and brought them back to the capital, where they were fitted with silk clothing and taught how to move gracefully and convey feeling in their facial expressions. They practiced these things for three years, at which point they had become proficient enough to be presented to the king of Wu.

Goujian ordered Fan Li to escort the two beauties to Wu, where Fuchai received them with delight, seeing the gift as yet another sign of Goujian's loyalty. Wu Zixu remonstrated with Fuchai, warning him of the trouble that would ensue if he accepted Goujian's gift. The Wu prime minister described Goujian as a man who, day and night, thought of nothing other than his desire to destroy the state of Wu, a man who paid heed to good advice and surrounded himself with men of virtue and ability. Goujian had already assembled a force of tens of thousands of men who were prepared to die for Yue. If a man of such determination were allowed to remain alive, he would surely become the instrument of Wu's destruction. Men of virtue and ability were a state's treasure, beautiful women the source of a state's ruin. Fuchai should take warning from the fact that beautiful women had brought about the downfall of the Xia, Shang, and Western Zhou dynasties. Fuchai, however, as usual ignoring Wu Zixu's cautionary advice, accepted the gift of Xi Shi and Zheng Dan, an action that, when reported back to Goujian, delighted the Yue ruler.

In the thirteenth year of Goujian's reign (484 B.C.E.), the Yue king told Wen Zhong how pleased he was with the efficacy of the tactics thus far used to weaken Wu and asked what stratagem he should avail himself of next. Wen Zhong advised him to inform Fuchai that Yue had suffered a severe crop failure and wished to purchase grain from Wu. Goujian dispatched Wen Zhong to Wu with this message. Fuchai was strongly inclined, in light of the constancy of Goujian's allegiance to him, to grant Yue's request and, overruling Wu Zixu's objections, announced that he was prepared to lend Yue ten thousand *dan* of grain, to be paid back when Yue experienced a bumper harvest. On Wen Zhong's return to Yue, Goujian gave the grain to his officials to distribute among the people. The following year, after the grain had ripened, the Yue king issued orders for the finest seeds to be selected and boiled. A quantity of grain equal to ten thousand *dan* was then transported to Wu. Fuchai was most pleased and gave instructions for the seeds to be planted. The farmers of Wu sowed the Yue seed, but because it had been sterilized, it produced no crop, resulting in a severe famine.

Goujian, observing that Wu was in straitened circumstances, thought that this might be a propitious time to attack his nemesis. Wen Zhong, however, advised against any immediate action. Although it was true, he said, that Wu had begun to feel the pinch of poverty, it still had loyal ministers at court, and Heaven had yet to give a clear signal concerning its fate. It was best, therefore, to wait for a more opportune moment.

Goujian then spoke with his prime minister. Fan Li had assembled boats and chariots for combat, the king noted, but they were defenseless against swords, spears, and bows and arrows. Was it possible, he wondered, that Fan Li in his military planning had omitted something important? Fan Li replied that all the great rulers of ancient times had excelled at warfare, but in such specific matters as the arrangement of battle formations, the commanding of troops, and the beating of drums to signal advance and retreat, the difference between success and failure hinged entirely on the military skills of the troops themselves. Fan Li knew of a maiden from the forests of southern Yue whose swordsmanship everyone praised, and he urged the Yue ruler to send for her. Goujian thereupon dispatched emissaries to invite the maiden to come to the capital to demonstrate her skill in the use of the sword and halberd.

When the maiden arrived at court, Goujian asked her about her sword-handling skills. She told him that she had grown up in a wild, sparsely inhabited area where there was no opportunity for formal study, but that her secret passion had always been swordplay. Nobody had instructed her. Her mastery had come all of a sudden out of nowhere. Goujian asked her for a detailed account of her technique. The maiden said that her technique was subtle yet quite simple, but that the meaning was veiled and profound. She then supplied a more elaborate explanation, concluding that, after attaining proficiency in her technique, one person could subdue a hundred persons in combat. Goujian was so delighted to hear all of this that he instantly gave the girl the name "Yue Nü" (Maiden of Yue). He then issued orders for the commanding officers and best soldiers in his army to take instruction in sword-handling skills from her and, after achieving mastery, to transmit those skills to the rank and file. Everyone at the time acclaimed the Maiden's swordsmanship.

Fan Li next recommended an outstanding archer from the southern state of Chu whose name was Chen Yin. When Chen Yin arrived at court, the king plied him with one question after another. Goujian was elated with Chen Yin's responses and asked him if he would teach everything he

FIGURE 3.3 The Maiden of Yue teaching swordsmanship to a Yue soldier. (From Xiao Jun, *Wu Yue chunqiu shihua* [A story from the annals of Wu and Yue], 2 vols. [Harbin, China: Heilongjiang Renmin, 1980].)

knew to the warriors of Yue. Chen Yin replied that the secret to archery was hard work. If a person practiced diligently, he would be successful. Goujian thereupon sent Chen Yin to the capital's northern outskirts to give instruction to the Yue army, and at the end of three months the entire army had mastered the techniques.

In the fifteenth year of his reign (482 B.C.E.), Goujian told Wen Zhong that he had persuaded the people of Yue to fully support an attack on Wu and asked him whether Heaven had yet provided a sign authorizing such action. Wen Zhong said that the source of Wu's strength all along had been the presence of Wu Zixu at court. Now, as a result of Wu Zixu's blunt and forthright remonstrations, Fuchai had ordered him to commit suicide. This was a sign from Heaven indicating that the time was ripe for

Yue to attack Wu. Wen Zhong expressed the hope, therefore, that the king would devote himself wholeheartedly to preparing the people for war.

Soon thereafter, Fuchai departed from Wu and journeyed north to Huangchi (in modern Henan province) to attend an important meeting with other state rulers, where a new overlord (ba)* was to be chosen. He took his best troops with him, leaving the crown prince behind with a force of only old and weak soldiers to defend Wu. Seeing his opportunity, Goujian, after getting the go-ahead from Fan Li, dispatched a force totaling almost fifty thousand troops and engaged the Wu defenders in battle. The crown prince was captured and immediately put to death. The Yue forces then entered the Wu capital and set fire to Fuchai's beloved Gusu Tower. Messengers were sent north to report this news to Fuchai. But Fuchai, fearing that he would never be chosen overlord if the other kings got wind of what had happened, kept everything quiet until the meeting was over. At that point, he sent emissaries to Yue to sue for peace, which Goujian, wisely recognizing that he was not yet strong enough to annihilate Wu, welcomed.

Six years now passed, and by the seventh month of the twenty-first year of his reign (476 B.C.E.) Goujian had once again readied the Yue military for a punitive expedition against Wu. But before acting, he sent an emissary to the Zhou court to announce his intention to punish an unprincipled state so that the rulers of the other states would not begrudge him his revenge. Then he issued a formal command to the people of Yue: those who reported for action within five days were his subjects in good standing, but those who took more than five days to report were not his subjects and would be punished with death. Goujian took seriously the need to instill fear in the Yue army. In the course of reviewing his forces prior to leaving the capital, he had three criminals publicly beheaded and then announced to the troops that this treatment would be meted out to those who disobeyed his orders. The following day, in the countryside, he had three more criminals put to death and repeated the same announcement.

For all his severity, Goujian worried that if his warriors were motivated only by fear of punishment and not by heartfelt conviction, it

---

*The ba, sometimes translated as "hegemon," was the top holder of real power in the declining Zhou dynasty.

would be hard to mold them into an effective fighting force. He felt that he had still not succeeded in instilling in them a true willingness to risk their lives for something larger than themselves. Just as he was mulling over this problem, he spied a frog by the roadside, beating its belly in anger and filled with the spirit of one about to do battle. Goujian stood up in his carriage and saluted the frog. When one of his soldiers asked him why he was showing respect for a miserable little creature, he said that he had long hoped for an expression of anger on the part of his men but had not yet found any who were in full concurrence with his mission. The frog he had just seen was an ignorant animal, but when it encountered an enemy, it became infuriated, and so he had shown it a sign of respect. Upon hearing of this incident, all of the warriors committed themselves to a spirit of sacrifice and resolved to lay down their lives for their king.

The fighting against Wu lasted for three years, the forces of Yue winning one engagement after another and eventually forcing Fuchai to go into hiding on the top of Mount Gusu (located southwest of Suzhou in modern Jiangsu). The Wu ruler then sent an emissary to make peace with Goujian, recalling that he, Fuchai, had given offense to Goujian at Mount Kuaiji years earlier and that he would not now dare to flout the Yue king's command. Taking pity on Fuchai, Goujian sent an envoy to Mount Gusu to tell the Wu king that he was willing to arrange for Fuchai and his wife to go to Yongdong (Zhoushan Island in modern Zhejiang) to live and would allot them three hundred families to wait upon them for the rest of their days. Fuchai rejected Goujian's offer, saying that the calamity that Heaven had unleashed on Wu had taken place while he was on the throne. His altars to the earth and grain gods and his ancestral temple had been destroyed, and Wu's land and people already incorporated into the state of Yue. He was an old man and unable to become Goujian's servant. He then took a sword and killed himself.

The final destruction of Wu took place in 473 B.C.E. In the vast majority of twentieth-century renderings of the Goujian story (at least up to the 1980s), this is where the narrative ends. In the ancient texts, however, a darker Goujian emerges after the obliteration of Wu—a part of the story that if included in accounts prior to the last years of the twentieth century would have run the political risk of being interpreted as a veiled criticism of the despotic rule of the author's own time in either the People's Republic of China (PRC) or the Republic of China (ROC) on Taiwan. Shortly after the destruction of Wu, Goujian took a number of steps to reinforce Yue's position as a rising power among the states of the day. Fan Li, knowing his master well and sensing that the Yue king's unbridled ambition and envious nature would now make life extremely dangerous for anyone in his entourage who had accumulated great merit, decided that it was time to leave Yue and seek his fortunes elsewhere. He tried to convince Wen Zhong to do the same. Wen Zhong, however, was not persuaded, to his later regret. Before long, he became the target of rumors at the Yue court raising questions about his loyalty. Goujian thereupon presented him with the royal sword, with which the devoted official committed suicide.[8]

Among the key themes in the Goujian story is humiliation, sometimes externally inflicted (Wu's defeat of Yue), but also at times self-imposed, insofar as Goujian, in order to strengthen the Wu king's trust in him, willingly submitted to a range of humiliating behaviors. A second major theme is the quest for revenge, which characterizes not only Goujian's motivations, but also (in the ancient account) Fuchai and Wu Zixu's. A third important theme in the story, clearly related to the first two, is forbearance. The central idea here, nicely encapsulated in the Chinese proverb *renru fuzhong*—literally, "to endure humiliation in order to carry out an important task"—is that there is a higher order of courage according to which an exceptional individual will abase him or herself, acquiescing in the most degrading forms of humiliation or indignity if by this behavior the possibility of attaining some greater end (in this case revenge) will be enhanced. A fourth theme, which takes up a significant bit of the narrative, is the systematic rebuilding of the state of Yue economically and militarily after Goujian's return from Wu and the establishment of a positive relationship between the king and his people through enlightened and compassionate policies. A final theme, the consummation of the other four, is a small state's ability, through patience, hard work, shrewd planning, and thorough preparation, to triumph against heavy odds over a much larger one, avenging thereby the humiliation earlier inflicted on it by its larger rival.

Each of these central themes in the Goujian story found a welcome reception from Chiang Kai-shek himself and from the Nationalist government over which he presided in both the mainland and Taiwan phases of Nationalist rule, although there were different emphases during the two periods.

REPUBLICAN CHINA: 1920S AND 1930S

The Qing dynasty was finally overturned and a new order brought into being in China in 1911–1912. In the years after 1912, however, the country lurched from one crisis to another—the sabotaging of the young republic by its president Yuan Shikai; Japan's issuance in 1915 of the Twenty-One Demands; the rejection of China's claims at the Versailles Peace Conference; the years of warlordism from 1916 to 1928; the impact of the world Depression; the first civil war between the Communists and the Nationalists (Guomindang) in the early 1930s; and, finally, the Sino-Japanese War and the second civil war, the two lasting from 1937 to 1949. Although positive developments also occurred during the republican period, it was, for vast numbers of Chinese, a wretched time in which to be alive.

During these years of anguish and frequently frustrated hope, one persistent theme was nationalism, a familiar expression of which was the appropriation, reshaping, and wide dissemination of stories of heroic figures from the past with a view to shoring up sagging Chinese spirits in the present. In these circumstances, there was a strong, almost instinctive tendency to match specific stories to specific situations. In the wake of mounting Japanese aggression in the 1920s and 1930s, interest in Zheng Chenggong, who had liberated Taiwan (since 1895 a Japanese colony) from foreign (Dutch) control in 1662, was naturally revived;[9] and equally predictable, the Ming dynasty general Qi Jiguang (1528–1588), famous for having led the fight against Japanese pirates off the Zhejiang and Fujian coasts in the 1550s and 1560s, was now reconstituted as a Chinese nationalist hero.[10] Other figures from the Chinese past who were celebrated in the republican era for their heroic resistance to external invasion include the Southern Song scholar-official Wen Tianxiang (1236–1283), whom the Mongols executed for refusing to capitulate to them; Shi Kefa (1601–1645), a Ming loyalist who died at the hands of the Manchus;[11]

and the Song patriotic hero Yue Fei (1103–1142), who was praised for his patriotism in Guomindang propaganda and whose stirring words, "Give us back our rivers and mountains," were scrawled on walls all over occupied China during the Sino-Japanese War.[12]

The Goujian story, although also adapted in important ways to the anti-Japanese nationalism of the first half of the twentieth century, is not part of the previous grouping. Why? One reason, surely, is that unlike these other patriotic heroes, Goujian lived at a time prior to the establishment of China as a recognized political entity. True, we think of the Zhou as a Chinese dynasty, and when leaders such as Goujian acquired the status of overlord, they regularly acknowledged the ritual paramountcy of the Zhou in a symbolic Chinese world. But China's political unification still lay far in the future in Goujian's day. We would never identify the Yue king as a "Zhou loyalist," and we certainly would not conceptualize the periodic conflicts between Yue and Wu as conflicts between a "Chinese" and a "non-Chinese" state.

It has been observed in regard to China that "whenever invasion threatened this otherwise civilian-oriented society, military heroes were resuscitated."[13] This connection applies to most of the patriotic heroes apotheosized in the republican years, including Goujian. But once again there is a crucial difference between Goujian and the others: Goujian alone was a king. Where, for the others, the quality of loyalty to ruler and dynasty was of overriding importance and lay at the very core of the original heroic image, it was a nonissue for Goujian (although, of course, it was very much an issue in the Goujian story writ large). This distinction had a crucial bearing on how the story functioned in political China. Chiang Kai-shek (1887–1975) could admire Yue Fei greatly,[14] but, as we shall see shortly, it was with Goujian that he *identified* during the 1920s and 1930s.

One further reason for distinguishing Goujian from the other patriotic heroes canonized during the republican years is the prominence of the theme of *guochi* (national humiliation) in his story. Although during the Spring and Autumn period of the Zhou dynasty, *guochi* referred to the humiliation not of a nation, but of a ruling house,[15] by the late nineteenth century the former meaning had already gone far toward displacing the latter. As national humiliation became increasingly central to Chinese political discourse, other heroic figures—an early example was Zheng Chenggong[16]—were also linked to this theme, but none anywhere near as consistently or steadfastly as Goujian. As a consequence, during the years from the establishment of the republic in 1912 to the outbreak of the Pacific War in the late 1930s, as China experienced one humiliating setback after another (mostly at the hands of an increasingly assertive Japan), the example of Goujian was called upon again and again as a morale booster and guide to proper thinking.

A landmark event in this process was the Japanese government's secret presentation to China of the Twenty-One Demands on January 18, 1915. The demands were originally divided into five groups, the fifth of which would have required the virtual transfer of Chinese sovereignty to Japan if assented to. As a result of intense Chinese opposition and international pressure, Japan eventually withdrew the fifth group. On May 7, however, Tokyo presented the remaining demands in the form of an ultimatum, and on May 9 the Yuan Shikai government acceded to them.[17]

Beginning in the 1920s, the Goujian story became a regular and prime feature of Nationalist rhetoric and propaganda. In 1996, the Guangzhou municipal government invested 36 million yuan (more than US$4 million) in the restoration of the complex of buildings that had housed the Whampoa Military Academy on an island in the Pearl River just west of Guangzhou's commercial port.[18] The original academy, which was destroyed by Japanese bombing in 1938, had been founded in 1924 with Chiang Kai-shek as commandant, its purpose to train a new generation of Chinese military officers who would be indoctrinated in the tenets of Guomindang ideology, loyal to the party and its leaders, and fundamentally different from the warlord model then widely prevalent in China. Significantly, the front entrance of the original (and restored) academy shows on either side the ROC and Guomindang flags and at the top center, draped across the archway, a large light-colored banner on which is written in bold black characters the Goujian story proverb *woxin changdan*.[19]

Allusions to the Goujian story were a standard part of the official ritual repertoire of the Guomindang after its attainment of national power in 1927, especially in connection with the growing tensions between China and Japan. For example, in 1928 at the Guomindang-sponsored observance of National Humiliation Day on May 9—the date on which the Yuan Shikai government accepted the Twenty-One Demands of Japan in 1915—a party official referred in a speech in Nanjing (the Nationalist capital) to *woxin changdan* as part of what Chinese must do to prevail against the Japanese.[20] This was just days after the Ji'nan Incident of May 3, in which Chinese soldiers taking part in the Northern Expedition for the reunification of the country engaged in a bloody clash with Japanese troops in Ji'nan, Shandong, resulting in several thousand Chinese deaths (including that of a diplomatic official, Cai Gongshi).[21] A year later, on May 9, 1929, a newspaper notice placed by the Propaganda Department of the Executive Committee of the Shanghai Branch of the Guomindang called on citizens "to sleep on brushwood and taste gall" and to vow to wipe clean China's national humiliation.[22] At Guomindang Central Committee and National Government observances of the May 9 anniversary in the same year, Chinese were enjoined to adhere to the spirit of *woxin changdan* if they wanted to expunge the national humiliation and make the country strong.[23] Two years later, an announcement of the May 9 anniversary meeting, to be held under the auspices of the Shanghai Branch of the Guomindang, stated that the focus of the meeting would be on how Chinese, holding fast to the spirit of *woxin changdan*, must erase the humiliations of the Twenty-One Demands and the more recent Ji'nan Incident.[24]

In the aftermath of the Mukden Incident of September 18, 1931, which sparked the Japanese takeover of Manchuria, the Commercial Press in Shanghai issued a volume entitled *Guochi tu* (National humiliation illustrated), which, like so many other books published subsequent to the Guomindang's assumption of national power, clearly reflected the ruling party's point of view. The book contains ten large, full-color foldouts of charts, maps, and other pictorial material pertaining to China's victimization at the hands of imperialism. One of the foldouts, titled "A Chart of the Different Kinds of National Humiliation," shows a list of the wrongs China had suffered as a result of the unequal treaties, superimposed over the proverb *woxin changdan*, "to sleep on brushwood and taste gall," drawn in large block characters.[25] On either side of the foldout is depicted a sword passing through a crown of thorns—a symbol, interestingly, derived from Christian iconography, where it represents the mocking humiliation of Christ by the Roman soldiers who placed the crown on Jesus's head. From each crown of thorns is suspended a gallbladder dripping bile into the open mouth of a Goujianesque figure clad only in shorts—it was common in illustrations from this period for a man's bare upper body to signify a state of oppression and victimization—and lying against a pile of brushwood. As in the other shorthand allusions to the Goujian story that we have previously encountered, it is taken for granted that Chinese readers will know that *woxin changdan*

FIGURE 3.4 Illustrated chart of the different kinds of national humiliation. (From *Guochi tu* [National humiliation illustrated] [Shanghai: Shangwu, 1931 or 1932].)

refers to the story of Goujian and the burden of suffering and shame (including the mockery) he endured and will interpret the contents of the image accordingly.[26]

Although it cannot perhaps be demonstrated in a categorical way, it is certainly plausible to argue that the Guomindang's strong identification with the example of Goujian during these years reflected the profound sense of connection that Chiang Kai-shek himself felt with the Yue king. Howard Gardner, the distinguished student of educational theory and human intelligence, has argued that stories are important for all leaders and that leaders achieve their effectiveness through the stories they communicate and embody.[27] This was certainly true of Chiang. His sense of connection with the Goujian story doubtless had something to do with the fact that he hailed from the same geographical area—the modern province of Zhejiang—in which the ancient state of Yue had been situated. But I wouldn't put undue emphasis on this geographical connection.[28] Far more important, in my judgment, were the personal qualities exhibited by the Yue king—the forbearance in the face of repeated humiliations, the willingness to absorb temporary setbacks for the sake of achieving ultimate victory—and the appeal to Chiang of the larger strategy adopted by Goujian over time in his dealings with the state of Wu.[29]

These aspects of the Goujian story so attracted Chiang that in the spring of 1934, two years after his appointment as chairman of the Nationalist government's Military Affairs Commission, his Field Headquarters (in the city of Nanchang, Jiangxi), which had a lead role in the military's political indoctrination, ordered the compilation of biographies of Goujian and his two top ministers, Fan Li and Wen Zhong. The Goujian biography was put out in two versions, one in literary Chinese, the other in more colloquial style for popular consumption.[30] It devotes particular attention to military matters: the engaging of people of unusual skill to instruct the Yue army (such as the expert swordswoman known as the Maiden of Yue and the master archer Chen Yin), Goujian's training of his soldiers (including the harshness of his disciplinary regime), and so on. The stool-tasting episode is omitted; Yue's use of beautiful women (Xi Shi and Zheng Dan) to divert Fuchai from affairs of state is alluded to only in passing; and although the account briefly notes that after the destruction of Wu, Goujian was appointed overlord of North China, there is no hint of postconquest tension between the Yue king and his ministers. In a manner reminiscent of Laurence Olivier's cleaning up of the character of Henry V in his film production of Shakespeare's play (see chapter 5), this rendering of the story—what was included and what was omitted or deemphasized—conformed to the contemporary needs of the Nationalist military, which at the time the order was given for the story's compilation was engaged in the final "extermination" campaign against the Communist forces in Jiangxi province; it also conformed to the puritanism and military discipline that were conspicuous features of the New Life Movement, which Chiang launched in 1934 in an effort to refashion China into a modernized, secular Confucian society.[31]

In an article on Chiang Kai-shek's Japan strategy in the years leading up to the outbreak of war between China and its neighbor, based mainly on Chiang's unpublished diaries, the well-known historian Yang Tianshi has written that the rare "power of restraint" Chiang exhibited at the time "can only be related to the influence of Goujian."[32] During this period, Chiang insisted that, given China's comparative weakness militarily, before engaging Japan, it must first achieve domestic political unity and second await the emergence of a more favorable international environment. After the outbreak of the Mukden Incident and the ensuing Japanese takeover of Manchuria, Chinese societal pressure to resist Japan mounted, and Chiang's stance became increasingly difficult to maintain. He faced particularly vocal opposition from students, intellectuals, and writers. When, for example, a play titled *Xi Shi* was staged in Nanjing in the mid-1930s, winning high praise from the Nationalist authorities, the left-leaning playwright Tian Han, who was in Nanjing at the time, wrote a blistering critique in which he castigated the government's policy of nonresistance and its Goujian-like advocacy of "forbearance" (*woxin changdan*). Tian had only recently been released from a Guomindang jail. His review, in which he disparaged Goujian's credentials as a popular leader and contended that any plan for saving China would have to rest on the masses and not on some ravishingly beautiful woman, was a thinly concealed attack on Chiang Kai-shek and his famously good-looking wife (Soong Mayling).[33]

In this difficult and decidedly unfriendly environment, Chiang often bolstered his spirits by recalling the attitude and conduct of Goujian, who also, faced with a far more powerful adversary, had to postpone indefinitely the gratification of his consuming desire for revenge. Two days after the Mukden Incident, Chiang wrote in his diary: "Goujian slept on brushwood and tasted gall, expanding the population and wealth of his state and instructing and guiding its people, as a result of which Yue became overlord; today it is my time to do the same."[34] A week later, deeply burdened by the loss of Manchuria, Chiang elaborated on these themes, expressing the wish that all Chinese would unite under the leadership of the Nationalist Party, that they would "increase in numbers and economic strength and be properly indoctrinated [*shengju jiaoxun*], observe strict order and submit to discipline, in the hope that within ten years, we will wipe away the supreme humiliation of the present and bring to fruition the great cause of the national revolution."[35] Both the phrase *shengju jiaoxun* and the reference to "ten years" were derived directly from the Goujian story.

When the headstrong young Goujian, shortly after succeeding to the Yue throne, attacked Wu against his ministers' advice and suffered a humiliating defeat, Fan Li scolded him, making the key point (as interpreted by commentators) that "if the opportune moment has not arrived, you cannot force things; if conditions are not ripe, you cannot force a successful conclusion." Chiang, doubtless thinking of his own stance vis-à-vis Japan, liked this interpretation and copied it into his diary.[36] He also had great admiration for Goujian's capacity to withstand the most horrific abuses and indignities: "During Goujian's captivity, not only did he lie on brushwood and taste gall, he also drank urine and tasted excrement. Compared with me today, his ability to put up with hardship and tolerate humiliation was many times greater!"[37] It is interesting to note in this context that Chiang, who several years after his marriage to Soong Mayling in September 1927 had converted to Christianity, was also deeply drawn to the figure of Jesus, whom he refers to often in his diary. On May 4, 1934, he wrote, "Believers in Jesus must control themselves, endure insults, and be patient in suffering. Every day [they] must bear the cross along with Jesus." In March 1937, several months after the Xi'an Incident, in which Chiang on a visit to Xi'an in northwest China was taken prisoner by two of his own top generals and forced to agree to an anti-Japanese united front with the Communists, the Nationalist leader compared his ordeal at Xi'an with the trials and humiliations of Jesus.[38] According to Yang Tianshi, Chiang also absorbed into his thinking Laozi's dictum that it was necessary to yield in order to gain and the ancient Daoist notions of "retreating in order to advance" and "overcoming hardness with softness." Repeatedly in his diary and other writings of the 1930s, he alluded to such ideas in order to remind himself that China, in its response to Japan, "must exercise the greatest patience," "accept the unacceptable and endure the unendurable."[39]

These ideas also formed an important part of Chiang's more public pronouncements. At the time of the Ji'nan Incident of May 3, 1928, when (according to him) "the Nationalist Government and the Revolutionary Army were thoroughly humiliated by Japan and severely criticized by the people," he issued the following directive to the officers and men of the army: "In order to avenge our country's humiliation, you must free China from imperialist oppression and must attain the objectives of independence and liberty. Today you can only endure insults and prepare yourselves for vengeance. It will take ten years to train the population in the firm belief of our forefathers that the lost territories can and must be recovered and the national humiliation avenged."[40] This is a loose rendering of the original Chinese text of Chiang's speech, which used such phrases as *woxin changdan, shi nian shengju,* and *shi nian jiaoxun*—all directly taken from the story of Goujian.[41]

In less formal remarks to subordinates in Zhejiang on February 5, 1934, Chiang was more explicit in his adulation of Goujian: "We must emulate King Goujian of Yue, everyone must become a King Goujian of Yue. . . . In all our actions, all our methods, we must follow his example. . . . With such a model as Zhejiang's King Goujian of Yue, if we are unable to save the nation, truly we will be unable to face our ancestors."[42]

Up until the middle of the 1930s, Chiang Kai-shek pursued mainly a policy of accommodation and concession toward Japan. Although this policy began to stiffen perceptibly in the fall of 1936, owing in part to further Japanese encroachment in the North and in part to the Nationalists' suppression of anti-Nanjing rebels in the southern provinces of Guangdong and Guangxi and an upturn in the Chinese economy (two developments that gave Chiang renewed confidence),[43] criticism of the government's policy from within the Guomindang as well as from outside it had for years been unrelenting. This was especially so in areas, such as the far South and the Northwest, where Nanjing's capacity to exert control over the press was weakest.[44] In 1935, Zou Lu, a veteran Guomindang member and chancellor of Zhongshan (Sun Yat-sen) University in Guangzhou (Canton), penned a searing critique in which he noted that ever since the Mukden Incident of September 1931, Nanjing had steadily surrendered China's territory and rights to the Japanese, to the point where everyone likened the authorities to the Song dynasty traitor Qin Gui, a man reviled through the ages for his involvement in the killing of the patriotic hero Yue Fei in 1142. Nanjing, according to Zou, disputed this characterization, describing itself as a Goujian that tolerated temporary humiliations for the sake of long-term goals (*renru fuzhong*). He did not buy this analogy at all, however, claiming that Nanjing had not done a fraction of the things Goujian had done to strengthen the country and that in any case China's current adversary Japan was hardly to be equated with the weak and bumbling Fuchai. Even the depiction of the government as a Qin Gui was, in his view, inappropriate because Qin Gui, by pursuing a policy of peace toward Jin, had at least managed to get some of China's territories returned, whereas the Nanjing authorities had accomplished nothing in this regard.[45]

Some of the themes in Zou Lu's critique were developed in 1936 in an article entitled "Wo wei Goujian, ren fei Fuchai" (We are Goujian, but the other side isn't Fuchai), which appeared in the newly established Xi'an paper *Xibei xiangdao* (Northwest guide) and was written by one Lin Guanghan. The gist of the article was that "Goujianzhuyi" (Goujian-ism), whatever its strengths (and Lin acknowledged them to be considerable), was wholly inadequate as a response to China's current crisis. The main precondition for Goujian's success had been Fuchai's ineptitude and muddleheadedness, but Japan, bluntly put, was no Fuchai. The only policy for dealing with the Japanese, therefore, was immediate resistance. Responses to Lin's piece in subsequent issues of *Northwest Guide* were enthusiastically supportive of his stance.[46]

One thing that Chiang Kai-shek's unabashed exaltation of Goujian and the criticism of this exaltation as misguided clearly suggest is that on all sides of the political divide in the mid-1930s there was a general recognition that the example of Goujian—what Lin Guanghan called "Goujianism"—was the guiding spirit underlying Nanjing's Japan policy. More broadly, both the adulation and the denigration it provoked supply fascinating instances of the psychologist Jerome Bruner's contention that we "cling to narrative models of reality and use them to shape our everyday experiences." Stories become "templates for experience." What is astonishing about such stories, Bruner adds, "is that they are so particular, so local, so unique—yet have such reach. They are metaphors writ large" or "root metaphors of the human condition."[47] When the Goujian story is understood as a root metaphor in Bruner's sense, it assumes a far more imposing historical presence than we would ever guess from the standard narrative accounts of twentieth-century Chinese history. In Chiang's remarks to his subordinates in Zhejiang and in the criticisms—Gardner would characterize them as "oppositional 'counter-stories'"[48]—by Zou Lu, Lin Guanghan, and others, the figures Goujian, Fuchai, and Qin Gui were deployed as symbolic touchstones for talking about and assessing contemporary historical situations.

Contrary to what one might expect from the strident criticisms of Chiang Kai-shek's Japan policy, the Nationalist leader, even before the fall of 1936, was by no means completely unreceptive to a strategy of resistance. Indeed, in the years after the Mukden Incident, Chiang, even while being forced repeatedly to give ground to Japan, simultaneously intensified his planning for war. In two respects, these preparations echoed strategies that Goujian himself had pursued more than two millennia earlier. First, Chiang, operating from a position of relative military weakness, engaged in a succession of diplomatic efforts designed to bring about an international environment favorable to the Chinese cause (an alliance, for example, with the Soviet Union against Japan), much as Goujian, in his plans for avenging himself against Wu, had paid close attention to Yue's—and Wu's—relations with the large northern states Qi and Jin.[49] Second, just as Goujian took care to conceal Yue's military ambitions from Wu, Chiang's hot pursuit of the Communists during the Long March in 1934–1935 was intended in part to divert Japanese attention from the secret preparations simultaneously in progress to create a rear base in the Southwest for eventual Chinese resistance against Japan.[50] Thus, Yang Tianshi concludes, "at the same time that Chiang Kai-shek made one concession to Japan after another, he also went ahead with preparations for military resistance, drawing inspiration from the spirit of self-imposed hardship and restraint in the face of provocation shown by Goujian."[51]

CHIANG KAI-SHEK'S TAIWAN

For the Communists, successive victories in the Sino-Japanese War and the civil war of 1945–1949 created a fundamentally new historical situation in which the major humiliation of foreign imperialism had become a thing of the past. But for Chiang Kai-shek's Nationalists, after their retreat to the island province of Taiwan, the most salient change arguably was that the area under direct government control had been dramatically reduced. The Guomindang, from its perspective, still faced the task of eliminating both foreign imperialism (now in the guise of the Soviet Union) and its mainland Chinese accomplices.[52] There remained, in other words, a major humiliation to be eradicated, requiring the same qualities of forbearance, hard work, belt tightening, and tireless effort—or *woxin changdan*—that had been staples of the Goujian story as it had been articulated in earlier decades. In these circumstances, the story was predictably from the outset widely disseminated among all sectors of the population on Taiwan.

In late 1949 and the first half of 1950, Chiang Kai-shek's embattled government was readying itself for an amphibious Communist invasion that appeared imminent and that American observers assumed, given the deplorable state of the Nationalist military, would be successful. Then in June 1950 the Korean War broke out, and the East Asian world changed overnight. Communist forces, which had been assembling in southeastern China in preparation for the final act of the civil war, were redeployed to the northern part of the country, and the United States, determining that Taiwan was now an important part of its defense perimeter in East Asia, moved its Seventh Fleet into the Taiwan Strait. "For the Nationalist Chinese," Nancy Tucker writes, "the struggle in Korea had come as if by magic at the last possible moment before disaster engulfed them."[53]

Significantly, although Chiang Kai-shek regularly referred in his speeches of 1950 (as he had in earlier years) to the precedent of Goujian's coming back after sustaining a serious defeat, his tone was noticeably more optimistic after the outbreak of the Korean War than before it.[54] Provided with the breathing space it had previously been denied, the Chiang government during the 1950s moved in a number of broad directions that were to distinguish the Taiwan scene for the next three decades. After an examination of past errors evocative of the pained self-scrutiny Goujian engaged in following his humiliating defeat at Mount Kuaiji,[55] the Nationalists reorganized and rebuilt their armed forces, fashioning a military that by the end of the 1950s was six hundred thousand strong and bore "little resemblance to the disorganized, demoralized units" fleeing the mainland in 1949. Education was promoted vigorously, with some 93 percent of primary-school-age children enrolled in school as of the late 1950s.[56] A number of important economic and social developments also took place during this decade, laying the groundwork for the vigorous economic growth that Taiwan experienced in the 1960s and 1970s.[57]

The foundational policy that drove these developments for several decades after 1950 was the goal of retaking the Chinese mainland. The manifestations of this goal, succinctly embodied in such slogans as *fangong fuguo* (launch a counterattack and recover the nation) and *fangong dalu* (launch a counterattack against the mainland), were encountered everywhere: on billboards in public venues, in magazines and books, in school primers, in political speeches, on radio and television, and in newspapers. Typical were Chiang Kai-shek's remarks in 1963 in his annual October 10 (Double Ten) message, celebrating the anniversary of the outbreak of the Revolution of 1911: "On our shoulders lies the heavy responsibility of delivering our compatriots, recovering the mainland, and destroying the Chinese Communist regime, that scourge of mankind. . . . To us recovery of the mainland is a sacred mission."[58]

The supreme Nationalist goal of counterattack and recovery, reversing the stinging humiliation of defeat in 1949, resonated in a powerful way with the story of Goujian. It is no surprise, therefore, that in one form or another the story was widely encountered not only in educational materials in Taiwan, but also in juvenile literature, opera, spoken drama, fiction, film, radio, and television. The narrative was often tailored, either implicitly or explicitly, to the specific circumstances in which the Nationalists found themselves. Indeed, although doing so was hardly necessary, given the story's central theme, many renderings actually incorporated the phrase *fuguo* (recovery of the nation) in their titles, thereby underscoring the intimate association between the Goujian story and Nationalist government policy.[59]

One thing Westerners sometimes have difficulty understanding is the great importance Chinese governments have routinely attached to literature as both an index and molder of correct political thinking. Although common enough in earlier periods as well, this practice was especially rife in the twentieth century. The Communists had used theater with great effectiveness as a political weapon in their conflict with the Nationalists,[60] and, belatedly recognizing this connection, the Nationalists themselves, after their arrival on Taiwan, began to pay serious attention to the propaganda value of the arts. Nancy Guy, in her illuminating study of the relationship between opera and politics in the ROC, argues that "Peking opera was closely associated with—and, in fact, was employed to advance—the Nationalists' dominant ideology of mainland recovery."[61] Symbolic of this close association was the Ministry of Defense's deep involvement in the promotion and control of opera on the island. It certainly surprised no one in Taiwan when Chiang Kai-shek in 1955 issued an appeal for "literature for the sake of war" (*zhandou wenyi*).[62]

This appeal was clearly answered in the treatment of Goujian in dramatic works that appeared in Taiwan in the first decades after 1949. It will be recalled that Goujian was presented in ancient times as a man consumed by ambition and envy after his conquest of Wu, who would not tolerate anything that stood in the way of his quest for more territory and power and who in time found ways to rid himself of those in his official entourage whose heroic achievements threatened to overshadow his own. What is interesting is that in the three theatrical works I have examined— Chen Wenquan's play *Goujian yu Xi Shi* (Goujian and Xi Shi, 1959), Tan Zhijun's play *Goujian fuguo* (Goujian recovers his country, 1950s or early 1960s), and Zhang Daxia's opera *Goujian fuguo* (1982)—these unattractive facets of Goujian's character are completely passed over (calling to mind again the changes Olivier made in his film adaptation of *Henry V*, to be discussed in chapter 5).[63] After committing his one big mistake shortly following his accession to the kingship—a mistake that caused enormous suffering among the people of Yue and that he profoundly regretted—Goujian in each of these three works becomes an archetypically model ruler. He listens to his official advisers' counsel. He makes use of talent wherever it turns up. He lives an ascetic life and doesn't fritter away scarce resources. Never wavering in his commitment to avenge the earlier humiliations that the king of Wu inflicted both on him personally and on Yue, he works tirelessly over many years to enlarge the population of the state, rebuild its economic life, and strengthen its military. He adopts enlightened social policies. And he consistently demonstrates humaneness and compassion in his day-to-day dealings with the Yue people.

If we ask why the authors of these works chose to portray Goujian in this way, I don't think we have to search far for answers. For one thing, the central theme in all of them is the recovery of full control over the territory of Yue and the avenging of the humiliations the state had suffered as a result of its earlier defeat. These goals were achieved with the final victory over Wu and the suicide of Goujian's main antagonist Fuchai. At the end of Chen Wenquan and Tan Zhijun's plays, when the Yue king, still in the Wu capital, addresses his soldiers and officials and tells them, in almost identical phrasing in the two plays, that he hopes they will continue untiringly to work together in the building of their "new country" (*xin guojia*), there is a natural sense of ending.[64] This is the moment both plays have been pointing toward from the beginning. We are not told what happens next, and from a dramatic point of view we don't really care.

For another thing, given the almost perfect fit between the Goujian story, as developed in these works, and the supreme Nationalist goal after 1950 of returning to and reestablishing its rule over the Chinese mainland, it is safe to assume that readers or viewers of these productions would instinctively identify Goujian, the leader of Yue's *fuguo* mission, with Chiang Kai-shek, until his death in 1975 the dominant political figure associated with the policy of *fuguo* (mainland recovery) in Taiwan. Moreover, much as Alexander Nevsky's flawless character as a leader in Eisenstein's film inevitably suggested to Soviet moviegoers in the late 1930s and early 1940s "a thinly veiled representation of Stalin" (see chapter 5), it is not hard to imagine teachers in Chinese classrooms drawing similar parallels between Chiang Kai-shek and Goujian for their students. Indeed, when we take into account that an authoritarian political system and police state environment prevailed in post-1949 Taiwan—the emergency decree of martial law, enacted in 1949, was not lifted until 1987, not long before the death of Chiang's son and successor Chiang Ching-kuo—we might infer, given the likely identification with Chiang, that to portray Goujian as anything other than an exemplary ruler would be at best in poor taste and at worst a delicate and possibly risky business.

I do not, however, want to suggest that the favorable portrayal of Goujian was an entirely manipulative action, cynically carried out by individuals who didn't sincerely believe in the messages they transmitted. After all, for most Chinese who fled to Taiwan in 1949, the hope of returning to their homes and being reunited with family members on the mainland was a genuine one, and if this hope could be kept alive and bolstered by stories from the Chinese past that touted the likelihood of success against overwhelming odds, provided one had the proper attitude and spirit, this was all to the good. It did not matter what one might think of Chiang Kai-shek personally. The fact was that one could not read a narrative like the Goujian story in the circumstances then prevailing in Taiwan without associating Chiang with the story's protagonist; it was desirable if not incumbent, therefore, that Goujian, like Chiang himself,[65] be depicted in an adulatory way.

The idealization of Goujian as a ruler applied not only to the world of theater, but also to that of popular education. This is amply documented in Huang Dashou's efforts to publicize and promote the story of the Yue king starting in the 1950s. Born in 1920 in Jiangxi province and educated at Sichuan University, Huang became one of Taiwan's best-known and most prolific writers on historical subjects.[66] He did his first rendering of the Goujian story in 1950, not long after arriving in Taiwan following the Nationalist defeat. It was entitled "Goujian mie Wu" (Goujian destroys Wu) and was published in a monthly magazine for young people. The same

FIGURE 3.5 Portrayal of Chiang Kai-shek on the cover of Huang Dashou, *Zhongxing shihua* (Historical accounts of national resurgence) (Taibei: Shijie, 1955).

piece (slightly revised), along with other stories dealing with the theme of national revival, formed the basis for a series of radio broadcasts Huang made in 1952. Readers and listeners urged him to put the stories into book form, which resulted several years later in a little volume entitled *Zhongxing shihua* (Historical accounts of national resurgence).[67]

The match-up between the contents of *Historical Accounts of National Resurgence* and the contemporary political situation in Taiwan in the early 1950s was made immediately clear by the drawing on the book's cover, which shows a self-assured Chiang Kai-shek, his feet planted squarely on a raised base in the shape of Taiwan, with a drawn sword in his right hand and, in his elevated left hand, a lantern with the characters "fight [or oppose] communism" (*fangong*) emblazoned on the side. This connection is reinforced on the title page, at the foot of which appear the slogans: "We need to launch a counterattack against the mainland! The mainland needs us to launch a counterattack against it!"

It was the historical episodes recounted in the book, however, that established the real link with the contemporary circumstances of Taiwan. In each of the chapters of *Historical Accounts of National Resurgence*, Huang reconstructed in lively, informal prose encounters from China's past in which, by a combination of hard work, preparation, unflagging determination, and astute leadership, a weaker adversary was able to prevail over a far stronger one. Following the lead chapter, which deals with the Goujian narrative, a story from the Warring States period (403–221 B.C.E.) recounts how, after the state of Yan had attacked the state of Qi and seized some seventy of its cities, the people of Jimo (in modern Shandong province), one of only two Qi cities remaining uncaptured, chose as their new commander Tian Dan, who, using a brilliantly unconventional stratagem, led the Qi army in a surprise night attack against the encircling Yan force, putting it to rout and recovering the captured cities. Among the other stories included in the book are the saga of Liu Xiu's restoration of the Han dynasty (in 25 C.E.), bringing an end to the ruinous civil disturbances that had erupted in the last years of the usurper Wang Mang's rule and establishing the prototype for later dynastic revivals; an account of the celebrated battle of Red Cliff (Chi Bi) on the Yangzi River (208 C.E.), at which Sun Quan and Liu Bei's southern naval forces decisively defeated the northern general Cao Cao's far larger and more powerful army, forcing Cao Cao to abandon his goal of extending his dominion over the entire country; the story of Guo Ziyi's (697–781) reestablishment of peace and order to the Tang after the dire threats posed by the An Lushan rebellion and other disturbances of the mid-eighth century; and, finally, an account of Sun Yat-sen's revolution—also, of course, the triumph of a small group of dedicated individuals over a vastly larger and wealthier adversary (the Qing dynasty).

Two former high officials under the Nationalists, Huang Jilu and Cheng Tianfang, wrote prefaces to *Historical Accounts*, underscoring the parallels between the stories contained in it and Taiwan's current situation. Cheng praised the book as "the best extracurricular reading material for the youth of Free China,"[68] and author Huang Dashou, in his own introductory statement, was equally explicit: "All these events were of epoch-making significance in Chinese history," he wrote, "and in each case the first phase of the event's trajectory may be said to bear a close correspondence to our present situation, in which we are using Taiwan as a base for rejuvenation and for preparing our counteroffensive against the mainland. After reading these seven historical accounts, how can we not feel confident? As long as we are prepared to endure hardships and stick it out to the finish, how can we not be victorious in our struggle against the Communists and Russians? How can our recovery of the mainland [*guangfu dalu*] not be crowned with success?"[69]

Taiwan in the years of Chiang Kai-shek's rule was saturated with stories like those included in Huang Dashou's book. I will mention just one other example, which was incorporated in a mass campaign launched by Chiang in the mid-1960s. The campaign was built around a four-character piece of calligraphy the Nationalist leader had presented to the local elite of Jinmen (Quemoy), a small ROC-held offshore island within sight of the Chinese mainland, in 1952. The phrase Chiang wrote, *wuwang zai Ju*, or "Never forget our time in Ju," alluded to an episode in ancient Chinese history in which a ruler who had lost most of his territory found refuge in the region of Ju and eventually turned the tables on his enemy and recovered his kingdom. The meaning of the phrase in the early 1950s was clear: Ju was Taiwan, the kingdom that the ruler recovered was the Chinese mainland. Although the Ju Guang (Glory of Ju) campaign soon faded in importance in society at large, it had a lasting impact on the Nationalist military. "Glory of Ju" was the name given to the army's weekly compulsory political education. Starting in 1976, all Jinmen militia units were required to take part in Glory of Ju training, the goal of which was "to heighten the patriotism of the citizenry and strengthen their anti-Communist consciousness." "Glory of Ju," Michael Szonyi notes in his instructive account of this episode, is still remembered in today's Taiwan in village and street names and in the brand names of a variety of products.[70]

Although there is no need to summarize Huang Dashou's recounting of the Goujian story, it is worth noting that his treatment of the Yue ruler is in some respects even more highly idealized than that found in the theatrical versions of the story discussed earlier. This sanitization of Goujian, especially noteworthy in light of the clearly implied effort in the book as a whole to link the heroes of the stories recounted in it to an embattled Chiang Kai-shek, is coupled with a portrayal of the Yue king as a model ruler. In addition to dressing and eating simply, Goujian labors in the fields alongside his people, setting an example of hard work that the farmers of Yue emulate. He listens respectfully to anyone, even the lowliest individual, who proffers advice. And local leaders follow the example set by him in the administration of their own areas.

Huang Dashou's telling of the Goujian story, like the theatrical treatments dealt with earlier and in keeping with the title he gave it, concludes with Yue's conquest of Wu and ignores entirely the less attractive behavior of the postconquest Goujian found in ancient renderings of the story. Another aspect of the conclusion that is of interest is the final paragraph, which symbolically is suggestive of the consummation of Chiang Kai-shek's dream of reestablishing Nationalist rule over the Chinese mainland: "On the next day, as the sun rose to the east, the Yue king and his ministers met in the Wu palace atop Mount Gusu to go over plans for the future administration of Greater Yue. Goujian, having taken the place of Fuchai, was the new ruler of Wu; the flag of Yue fluttered in the air above the Wu palace, reflecting in the golden splendor of the eastern sky the immeasurable glory of the moment."[71]

Because the Goujian story resonated so closely with the situation the Nationalist government found itself in after 1949 and the staple policy of *fangong fuguo* that it adopted in response, it comes as no surprise to learn that the state actively supported the story's dissemination in a variety of ways. This was plainly evident in the case of Huang Dashou's popularization efforts. Huang's accounts of the story appeared in books that, as often as not, contained prefaces by top-ranking former Nationalist officials.[72] His broadcasts of the story were aired over radio and television stations that were owned in part (and of course controlled) by the Guomindang party-state.[73] And his use of the story in the late 1950s as a morale builder for former members of the Nationalist military took place under the auspices of the Vocational Assistance Commission for Retired Servicemen, which at the time was headed by Chiang Kai-shek's son Chiang Ching-kuo.[74]

The government's imprimatur was even more explicit in the case of a comic book titled *Woxin changdan* (Sleeping on brushwood and tasting gall), compiled and illustrated by one Lan Hong.[75] Lan Hong's work was published in 1976 with the support and authorization of the powerful National Editorial and Translation Office—the producer, among other things, of the textbooks used in the national school system and therefore in a key position to determine what reading material the youth of Taiwan should be exposed to—and was awarded the office's first prize in the category of comic books for that year.[76] The book's main thrust is that with belief in one's cause, a willingness to endure repeated humiliation, and hard work over a span of many years, it is possible to

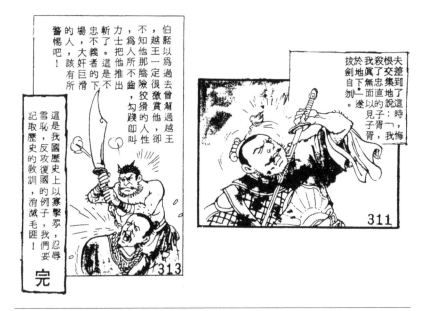

FIGURE 3.6 Propagation of Nationalist government policy via a comic book. At the very end of Lan Hong's comic, the author explicitly links the Goujian story with Taiwan's current situation (in a boxed message). Also shown are images of Fuchai's suicide and Bo Pi's execution. (From Lan Hong, *Woxin changdan* [Sleeping on brushwood and tasting gall] [Taibei: Dongguang, 1976].)

achieve final victory, even when the odds are heavily stacked in favor of the other side.

In addition to foregrounding these familiar themes of the Goujian story, Lan Hong's work suggests clear parallels between the story and Taiwan's contemporary circumstances. It does this in part by the use of code phrases known to all in post-1949 Taiwan. Thus, when Goujian learns to his delight that Fuchai, succumbing to Yue's strategy, has fallen passionately in love with the Yue beauty Xi Shi, he steps up the drilling of the Yue army so that it will be battle ready to "launch a counterattack and recover the country" (*fangong fuguo*) at the right time. And when shortly thereafter he hears that Fuchai has taken his best troops north to the Huangchi conference (where Fuchai is to meet with the other state rulers of the day to choose a new overlord), he announces to his top advisers that "the time has come to counterattack and avenge the wrong done us" (*fangong xuechi*).[77] The tie-in between the Goujian story and Taiwan's situation in the 1970s is established with even greater explicitness at the comic's end, where, after giving an account of Yue's conquest of Wu, Lan Hong inserts a boxed message articulating for his youthful readership the following moral: "This is an example from our country's history of the few attacking the many, of enduring humiliation and wiping out disgrace, of launching a counterattack and recovering the nation [*fangong fuguo*]. We must bear in mind the lessons of history and obliterate the Mao bandits!"[78]

After Chiang Kai-shek's death in 1975, real power in Taiwan passed to his son Chiang Ching-kuo. Like his father, the younger Chiang was resolutely opposed to communism and "steadfastly refused to yield the Nationalist claim to jurisdiction over all of China."[79] Nevertheless, during and after his years in power, as a result in part of external events (such as the end of the Mao era on the mainland in 1976 and the emergence of a new leadership in Beijing dedicated more to economic modernization than to political and social revolution) and in part of his own initiatives (for example, the legalization of opposition political parties in the ROC in 1986 and the granting of permission in 1987 for residents of Taiwan to visit relatives on the Chinese mainland), vitally important changes took place in the political, economic, and cultural relationship between Taiwan and the mainland. These changes developed still further under Chiang's successor, the Taiwan-born Lee Teng-hui (Li Denghui), whose administration in the early 1990s formally proclaimed that the ROC no longer considered itself the lawful government of the whole of China.

In this rapidly evolving environment, the features that had characterized Taiwan's stance toward the Chinese mainland in the early decades after 1949 and that, from the perspective of the island's mainlander refugee population and Nationalist party-state, had made the story of Goujian so compelling faded one by one from the scene. It is interesting to note what happened as a consequence. Broadly paralleling what took place in Israel in the 1970s and thereafter as changing historical realities weakened the hold of the heroic Masada myth on Jewish minds (see chapter 2), with the abandonment of the foundational policy of launching a counteroffensive and retaking the mainland, the central theme of the Goujian story—the theme of a small state triumphing improbably over a much larger one through patience, hard work, shrewd planning, and thorough preparation and avenging thereby the humiliation inflicted on it earlier by its larger rival—was drained of relevance. As a result, beginning in the 1980s, a major change became apparent in both the number and nature of Taiwan publications dealing with the story. In contrast to the abundance of material on the Goujian narrative published in the period from the early 1950s to the early 1980s, I have been able to identify only five books with a primary focus on either Goujian or the *woxin changdan* theme for the two decades from the mid-1980s to the first years of the present century.[80]

The tenor of these five works, moreover, differs strikingly from that of writings on the Goujian story in the 1950s, 1960s, and 1970s. For one thing, there is the remarkable fact that at least three of the five did not originate in the ROC at all but were reprints of writings by PRC authors, a circumstance that alone spoke dramatically to the vast changes that by the 1990s had taken place in the relationship between Taiwan and the Chinese mainland. For another, in four of the writings (and possibly a fifth, which I have been unable to examine) the repellent side of the post-conquest Goujian is prominently displayed, something that happened only rarely during the Chiang Kai-shek years.[81]

This last development is of critical importance. While Chiang Kai-shek was alive and a highly authoritarian system remained in force in the ROC, it was natural to link Goujian, the top person in the state of Yue, with Chiang, the leading power holder in the Nationalist party-state.[82] This linkage, moreover, for reasons discussed earlier, was almost invariably a positive one. However, once the political controls put in place by Chiang Kai-shek began to loosen—first under his son and then even more under Lee Teng-hui—the inclusion of the negative aspect of the king's character in renderings of the Goujian story ceased to carry the political risk that obtained during earlier decades and became a regular feature of ROC publications.

Significantly, something very similar also happened on the Chinese mainland. From the 1920s until the end of the 1970s, in the many versions of the Goujian narrative that I have seen, the protagonist's unattractive features that emerged after his triumph over Wu were either avoided entirely or explicitly subordinated to Goujian's extraordinary achievements in rejuvenating Yue. As an instance of the latter, a commentator in 1934 (when Chiang Kai-shek was the most powerful political figure in China), after noting Goujian's harsher side (including his responsibility for the forced suicide of Wen Zhong), asked his readers to bear in mind "how the king erased the humiliation Yue had experienced, how he built up the strength of the state, and how in one leap he went from being the ruler of a vanquished state to the chief of all the lords. If we conceive of the matter in this vein, despite the shivers Goujian sends down our spines, we will immediately be filled with admiration for this extraordinary man . . . [and] treat Goujian as our teacher."[83]

The almost total suppression of the bad Goujian on the mainland was especially true of the years of Mao Zedong's supremacy (1949–1976), when exposure of the brutal, ruthless side of the Yue king might too easily have been read as indirect criticism of Mao himself. After the end of the Mao era, however, this pattern underwent a decisive shift. The shift occurred in two phases. In the early 1980s, in works by two politically intrepid writers, Xiao Jun and Bai Hua, the Yue ruler's callously ambitious, hard-hearted side, largely absent from renderings of the story in the first eight decades of the twentieth century, was reinstated, with the clear intent of censuring Maoist tyranny (something that at the time was still too risky to do in more open ways).[84] Then, with the progressive relaxation of state control over society and depoliticization of everyday life in the PRC that marked the 1990s and 2000s, a succession of major fictional and multipart television adaptations of the Goujian saga appeared, all of which without exception incorporated the Yue king's brutal side.[85] By this point in time, unlike the early 1980s, there was no apparent fear that inclusion of this component of the story would be misconstrued as politically motivated. In the rapidly developing Chinese economy of the turn of the twenty-first century, the promotion of the Goujian narrative (not to mention hundreds of other stories from China's cultural heritage) was driven above all by commercial gain. Entertainment had now taken precedence over political guidance, and the more frightening features of Goujian's character could be given full play simply because they made for a better story.

The attention given the Goujian story in the politically unremarkable circumstances prevailing in the 1990s and 2000s was atypical, the result of two unprecedented changes in the Chinese environment that fed off one another synergistically: the emergence starting in the early 1980s of a mass television audience and the rapid growth of domestic tourism.[86] Prior to the last years of the twentieth century, it was much more common for the story's impact to be greatest in times of unresolved crisis, when one outcome (victory or survival) was vastly to be preferred over another (defeat or extinction). The right story, in such circumstances, evoked a picture of the world that incorporated either the proper spirit to be embraced or the desired resolution of the crisis or both. The Goujian story embodied both, inasmuch as Goujian, through his evocation of the *woxin changdan* spirit, was able to breathe new life into his state and triumph over his adversaries. This basically optimistic narrative was made to order for the perils facing Chiang Kai-shek in the two crisis periods dealt with in this chapter—the run-up to the Sino-Japanese War and the Guomindang's defeat in the civil war and retreat to Taiwan. More broadly, the functioning of the Goujian story in these circumstances revealed much about the interior of the Chinese world in time of stress, how those inhabiting it felt—and how they talked and wrote—about the predicaments facing them, individually and collectively. Such stories and the root metaphors they incorporated formed an undercurrent of meaning—often unrecognized by non-Chinese—that flowed beneath the surface of conventional renderings of Chinese history in the twentieth century.

4

THE ENIGMA OF THE APPEAL OF JOAN OF ARC IN WARTIME FRANCE

Unlike the story of Masada or the mythic themes surrounding the Battle of Kosovo, the saga of King Goujian concerned, first and foremost, the achievements, character, and motivational drive of a lone individual. This is also true of the story of Joan of Arc. Although no two historical figures could have been more unlike, both Joan of Arc and Goujian had the capacity, through their stories, to appeal not only to nations, but also to other individuals, including such national leaders as Chiang Kai-shek in Goujian's case and Charles de Gaulle and Philippe Pétain in the case of Joan of Arc. Another similarity between the Goujian and Joan of Arc narratives is that both are immensely complex, speaking to a great diversity of historical themes and situations, as compared to, say, the siege of Masada, which ultimately is a simple story about a people threatened with defeat—and very possibly annihilation—at the hands of a more powerful adversary.

Related to their thematic complexity, there is also a third way in which the Goujian and Joan of Arc stories are similar: over the centuries each was refashioned again and again, often in heavily fictionalized form, in response to the demands of different historical environments, different audiences, and different authorial agendas. Thus, although the aspect of the Goujian story that I have dwelt on in this book has been its inspirational power in relation to large-scale political–military challenges (Japanese aggression against China in the 1930s and the Communist threat to the Guomindang on Taiwan after 1949), as the sphere of private interests and concerns widened appreciably in the People's Republic of China,

Goujian was frequently called on during the 1990s and 2000s to serve as a source of personal motivation for individuals struggling to make it in a vastly changed Chinese world. Young job hunters, to take but one example, were told that they shouldn't insist on getting the perfect position right away. Putting up with adversity in the short term, two writers counseled them, wasn't really such a bad thing. "As a twenty-first-century 'Goujian,' you will be more self-confident and have a greater competitive edge" when you try out for your next job."[1] Similarly, the story of Joan of Arc spoke (or could be made to speak), depending on historical context, to republicans in the political center, socialists on the political left, royalists and reactionaries on the right, the spirit of the French nation, Anglophobia, resistance against foreign invasion, an absolute faith in God, the appeal of modesty and innocence, piety and saintliness, courage in battle and in the face of death, rebellion against authority, subversion of social convention, female empowerment, and more.

There are also, of course, substantial differences between the stories of Goujian and Joan of Arc, one of the most striking of which is the latter's much wider geographical and cultural appeal. At the turn of the twentieth century in China, Joan of Arc was widely hailed as a patriotic hero—she was often likened to the homegrown female warrior Hua Mulan[2]—and in her flouting of conventional gender norms was also held up as a model by a growing number of Chinese feminists,[3] whereas very few people in the Euro-American world had ever heard of King Goujian. It isn't that the Goujian and other ancient Chinese stories didn't travel at all, but their reach, at least until quite recently, was generally confined to the East Asian cultural sphere. Educated people in Korea, Japan, and Vietnam, who in centuries past were trained in Chinese writing and steeped in the cultural traditions of China, knew the stories well, much as European elites were versed in the classical learning of Greece and Rome. But, with few exceptions, that was where the spread of Goujian's story ended, whereas the story of Joan of Arc inspired biographies, novels, plays, poems, operas, films, paintings, sculpture, children's books, and such aspects of popular culture as advertising, television, video and computer games, comics and animation *globally*,[4] including creative works by such prominent non-French cultural figures as William Shakespeare, Robert Southey, and the Irish-born George Bernard Shaw in England; Bertolt Brecht and Friedrich Schiller in Germany; Carl Dreyer in Denmark; the *manga* master Yoshikazu Yasuhiko in Japan;

Mark Twain, Cecil B. DeMille, and Maxwell Anderson in the United States; Giuseppe Verdi in Italy; P. I. Tchaikovsky in Russia; and the film director Gleb Panfilov in the Soviet Union.[5]

Equally of interest, just as French retellings of the Joan of Arc story over the centuries were as often as not deliberately designed to reflect contemporary issues or the author's personal concerns or both, the same was true of non-French renderings. John Flower makes this point again and again in his wide-ranging study of Joan of Arc's global appeal. Shakespeare's portrayal of Joan in *Henry VI, Part I* (1592) as a "damned sorceress," "fell banning hag," "virgin strumpet," "ugly witch," and "foul accursed minister of hell" mirrored the anti-French and xenophobic political mood of late-sixteenth-century England. In DeMille's film *Joan the Woman* (1916), the white-hooded people at the heroine's trial and death were a clear allusion to the iconic garb of the white nationalist Ku Klux Klan, which had been revived in America the previous year and was part of a rising tide of nativism sweeping the country. More broadly, against the backdrop of an America deeply divided over whether to enter World War I (the picture was distributed in the winter of 1916–1917, only a few months before full-scale American mobilization began), the film, which incorporates a double plot involving Joan of Arc's relationship with a young soldier who is a knight in the latter stages of the Hundred Years War and then reappears as a British officer in World War I, was "prophetic in recasting history in the service of a call to arms" and became part of "public discourse enlisting support for an embattled France symbolized by Joan of Arc." The published version of Shaw's *Saint Joan* (1924) was introduced by a lengthy preface in which the playwright clearly expounded his main political, social, and moral concerns, including praise of Joan for her refusal to accept a woman's lot and her "quite unconcealed contempt for official opinion, judgement, and authority." And Brecht's play *Die Heilige Johanna der Schlachthöfe* (Saint Joan of the stockyards, 1932), imbued with the author's recently acquired Marxist views, departs sharply from the original Joan story, taking the action away from France entirely and replacing rebellion against an authoritarian church with the struggle of oppressed workers in the Chicago stockyards against an exploiting class of capitalist owners and bankers; the heroine of the play is Joan Dark, the youthful leader of the local Salvation Army, who after an initial failed effort to remedy the workers' problems with charitable reformism espouses the militant Marxist message that

FIGURE 4.1 The U.S. government's use of Joan of Arc in the latter stages of World War I to encourage American women to support the war effort. (Poster created by Haskell Coffin. Courtesy of the Library of Congress.)

the only hope for laboring people is through struggle against those who would keep them in chains: "Only force helps where force rules, and only men [as opposed to God] help where men are."[6]

Why Joan of Arc has attracted such astonishing interest worldwide is an intriguing question, especially given the brevity of her career and the fact that at the time of her death in 1431 her cause was losing. Part of the answer, certainly, is supplied by the extraordinary story of a seventeen-year-old girl of humble social origin who did not hesitate to tell her king what he must do and commanded French soldiers in battle. It also has to do with her seemingly incongruous personal qualities: she was intelligent but also headstrong, alternately vain and pious, brashly self-confident though at times verging on arrogance, worldly in spite of her inability to read or write, tough-minded but easily moved to tears, steadfast and loyal yet impatient and quick to anger when she did not get her way.[7] Joan's magnetism results in part, of course, from the horrifying way in which she died and the striking importance—at least in popular memory—of the part she took in her country's history, but also in part, as Mary Gordon suggests, from the sense that "[w]e need her as the heroine of our better selves."[8]

JOAN OF ARC: THE STORY

Although the exact date of Joan of Arc's birth is unlikely ever to be known, it was probably in the winter of 1412,[9] the year before Henry V ascended the throne of England. France at the time had for some seventy years been involved in a series of intermittent military conflicts with England that came to be known as the Hundred Years War. During the reign of King Henry V, a brilliant military strategist, the war had gone strongly in England's favor, and in 1420 France and England concluded the Treaty of Troyes, by the terms of which Catherine, the daughter of French king Charles VI and queen Isabeau (or Isabel, Isabella), was given in marriage to Henry V and the dauphin Charles was disinherited, clearing the way for the king of England to reign also as king of France. Two years later, on the deaths of both Henry V and Charles VI, the duke of Bedford was appointed regent for France because Henry VI, the child of Henry V and Catherine, was only a year old at the time, and the dauphin withdrew, destitute and disconsolate, to his castles in the Loire Valley. France's fortunes were at a low ebb, creating opportunities that a young maid from the village of Domremy on the north bank of the Meuse River in easternmost France was to seize.

The farming family Joan of Arc was born into was reasonably well off, owning in addition to a house nearly fifty acres of land. Joan's father exercised some leadership functions in Domremy, including responsibility for the village's defense. As was common enough during the Hundred Years War, life in the village was not always peaceful. France had devolved into a state of near civil war following the death of Charles VI, and villagers throughout the country were regularly subjected to the threats and depredations of brigands and soldiers, some of them marauding groups of English and Burgundians (generally allied to the English).[10] Apart from this political instability, Joan's childhood appears not to have been unusual. She helped with the plowing at times and took her turn watching the sheep and other animals. Also, along with the other girls and women of the village, she engaged in sewing and spinning. She was also not atypical in her religious training, although some of her age peers poked fun at her at times for being too devout and others judged her to be more serious than most girls her age. The differences between Joan and the others became more striking around the time she turned thirteen, though "none of those who knew her in Domremy mentioned any of the events that she claimed changed her life in the summer of 1425."[11]

An additional contextual factor that helped prepare the ground for the mission Joan was to claim for herself was a spate of prophecies that erupted in Europe in the late medieval period, which called attention to, among other things, the notion of a virgin who would bear arms. According to a popular story derived from a work of the twelfth century, the wizard Merlin had prophesied that a maid would come out of a wooded area near Domremy who could work miracles and save France. An unusual number of late medieval prophecies came from women who, responding to the weakened power and prestige of the Roman Catholic Church (owing in part to the turbulence of the time and in part to the Great Schism within the papacy in the late fourteenth and early fifteenth centuries), felt called upon to issue warnings about the dire consequences of the crisis for society.

Joan first heard her voices in 1425. She appears to have told no one in the village about this experience at the time, describing it only later in answer to questions put to her at her trial in 1431:

> When I was thirteen, I had a voice from God to help me to govern myself. The first time, I was terrified. The voice came to me about noon: it was summer, and I was in my father's garden. I had not fasted the day before. I heard the voice on my right hand, towards the church. There was a great light all about. . . .
>
> I saw it many times before I knew it was Saint Michael. Afterwards he taught me and showed me such things that I knew it was he.
>
> He was not alone, but duly attended by heavenly angels. I saw them with the eyes of my body as well as I see you. And when they left me,

I wept, and wished that they might have taken me with them. And I kissed the ground where they had stood, to do them reverence.

Above all Saint Michael told me that I must be a good child, and that God would help me. He taught me to behave rightly and to go often to church. He said that I would have to go into France.*

He told me that Saint Catherine and Saint Margaret would come to me, and that I must follow their counsel; that they were appointed to guide and counsel me in what I had to do, and that I must believe what they would tell me, for it was our Lord's command.

He told me the pitiful state of the Kingdom of France and he told me that I must go to succour the King of France.

Saint Catherine and Saint Margaret had rich crowns on their heads. They spoke well and fairly, and their voices are beautiful—sweet and soft.

The name by which they often named me was *Jehanne the Maid, child of God.*

It appears that at the same time that she first heard her voices, Joan swore to remain a virgin "for as long as it should please God." For the next three years, two or three times a week, the voices would instruct her to go into France to defeat the English and lead the dauphin Charles to his coronation at Rheims. The voices also informed her that Robert de Baudricourt, the overlord of the inhabitants of Domremy who lived in the town of Vaucouleurs just north of the village, would supply her with a company of soldiers and that she would lift the siege of Orléans.[12]

Little is known of the period from 1425 to 1428, the year when Joan first left home. In May 1428, she sought a meeting with Baudricourt to inform him of God's instruction that he send her with an escort to the dauphin Charles in Chinon. This first effort failed, Baudricourt sending Joan back to her family for a good thrashing. Later in the same year,

---

*Although from the perspective of modern France Joan was already in France, Domremy being situated near the eastern border abutting the Holy Roman Empire, France was deeply divided politically during the period of the Hundred Years War, some areas being ruled by the French throne (the central and southern parts of the country), others (mainly in the northern part of the country and the southwestern coast) under English control, and still others in the hands of the English-allied Burgundians (eastern central France, just south of Domremy, and the far Northeast). See map 4.

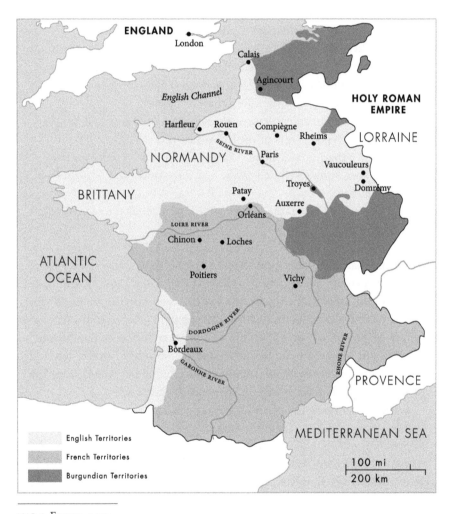

MAP 4 France, 1429.

however, she contrived to visit Vaucouleurs again, much to the vexation of her parents (who had tried unsuccessfully to marry her off), and this time, stubborn and self-assured, she managed to win the support of Baudricourt, who outfitted her with boy's clothing, a sword, and a horse. With a retinue of six men, Joan left for Chinon in February 1429.

The ride to Chinon, which was in west central France in the heart of the Loire Valley, took eleven days. Because their route took them through Burgundian territory, they traveled mostly at night to avoid encounters with unfriendly soldiers. On reaching Charles's castle, Joan was asked the nature of her business. Although at times in her brief career she described her mission broadly as being to drive the English from France, in this instance she appears to have announced that she had two objectives: to raise the English siege of Orléans, which had begun some months earlier, and to escort the dauphin to Rheims to be anointed and crowned. Because Joan, although only a simple country lass, claimed to be acting on orders from God, she was interrogated by members of the clergy in Poitiers (where the French Parlement, loyal to Charles, was in exile). She was also subjected to other tests, including physical inspection by a group of women led by Charles's mother-in-law to confirm her virginity. When one of her clerical examiners asked her for some sign demonstrating the truth of her claims to have been sent by God, she answered: "Take me to Orléans and I will show you signs proving why I was sent."[13] After completing their examination of Joan, the clergymen gave their support to her stated mission and recommended that she be given a complement of soldiers to go to Orléans.

Joan returned to Chinon, where in late March she was presented to the full court of Charles, who, having had his doubts about his unusual supplicant removed in Poitiers, now announced his formal backing of her mission. The dauphin's court thereupon unleashed a barrage of promotional material shaping and reshaping the image of Joan for public consumption. For example, the following prophecy written by a member of Charles's court circulated in Latin, German, and French: "The virgin, her maidenly limbs clothed in male attire, at God's prompting, hurries to raise up the fallen lily-bearer and king, [and] to destroy the abominable enemies, especially those who are now at Orléans, outside the city, and beset it with a siege. And if men have a mind to commit themselves to war, and to follow her arms, which the kindly [Maid] now prepares, she believes that the deceitful English will also succumb to death, when the

French overthrow them with maidenly war; and then there will be an end to fighting."[14]

At the same time, the Maid of Lorraine (a title now more and more frequently used for Joan) appears to have been put through an intensive training course in the arts of warfare so that when she led her soldiers into battle, she would look the part of the legend that was being constructed around her. Clearly, she was an apt student. Jean, duke of Alençon, a member of Charles's court who became in time Joan's favorite companion and would fight at her side in many of the battles in which they took part, recalled years later that in "war she was very talented, as much in wielding a sword as in assembling the army. . . . All were full of admiration that she could comport herself so skillfully and prudently in military activities, as if she had been a war captain for twenty or thirty years, and above all in the preparation of artillery, in which she excelled."[15]

Before departing for Orléans, Joan had to be fitted with a suit of armor and mail. She also required a new sword to validate her standing as a warrior. Charles wanted to present her with one, but she said she wanted the sword behind the altar in the church of St. Catherine of Fierbois outside Chinon, which she claimed to know about from her voices. When an armorer was sent to fetch it, he found it covered with rust, but the rust fell off easily on being rubbed by the priests, revealing a sword with five crosses on the blade and the names "Jesus" and "Maria" inscribed on its edge. This was Joan's special sword, which certified her as a warrior of God. The names "Jesus" and "Maria" were also embroidered on the banner that was made for her, which she claimed to be even more attached to than her sword.

In late April 1429, on the way to Orléans with a small contingent of soldiers, Joan sent the English a provocative letter she had dictated more than a month earlier in Poitiers. In the letter, she offered peace if the English ended their siege of Orléans and evacuated the other places they had occupied in France, but she promised "great harm" at the hands of God, working through her, if they did not. The French in Orléans had initially held off the English attackers, but after a disastrous battle that took place in mid-February 1429 the tide had turned against the French. It was at this point that Joan of Arc and her soldiers entered the picture. Their journey to Orléans had many of the trappings of a religious crusade, with much hymn singing along the way. En route, Joan learned from her soldiers that they had been instructed to approach the city from the south of the

Loire. Upon arriving at the river and discovering that the wind was blowing strongly against them, preventing them from crossing, Joan, fearing that she was being tricked, angrily challenged the Bastard of Orléans (and future count of Dunois), who was in charge of the city's defense, telling him that she would depend on the counsels of God, at which point the wind abruptly changed direction, enabling her to cross the river. Whether this was a miracle (as was widely claimed) or not, the Bastard, who had expected Joan to just sit on her horse and do what she was told, was rendered speechless. He and the other military men in the city now had to reckon with her in all their decisions, in the course of which Joan began to win her men's devotion and trust.

After nightfall, Joan's entry into the city with two hundred soldiers was accomplished safely. Her ride through the streets with her standard carried before her and the Bastard at her side, followed by nobles, officers, and regular soldiers, was a magical moment for the inhabitants of Orléans, who, believing Joan to be the prophesied instrument of their deliverance, rushed from their homes "carrying a great number of torches, and showing such joy that it was [as] if they had seen God descend among them."[16]

In the ensuing days, a number of battles were fought against the English, who called Joan a whore and hurled other insults at her. On a number of occasions, when French military leaders wanted to rest their men and regroup, Joan was determined to continue on the offensive, and in each instance the English were routed. Joan's stature as a leader was enhanced as a result, and when the English fortress at Les Tourelles south of the river fell to the French in heavy fighting on May 7, she and her soldiers crossed the bridge spanning the Loire and entered the city, where they were greeted joyously by an adoring populace. Joan had suffered an arrow wound to the area between her neck and shoulder in the battle, but her refusal to break off from the fighting weakened the resolve of the English, who had become terrified of the seemingly invincible seventeen-year-old girl warrior whom they branded a witch.[17] On the following day, May 8, the English abandoned the siege of Orléans. The French victory, although it did not end the Hundred Years War, fulfilled one of Joan of Arc's promises to Charles. As such, it did much to raise French morale and marked an important turning point in the war.

A few days after the raising of the siege, Joan and the other French captains went to Charles's castle at Loches (not far east of Chinon) and entreated him to provide them with additional men so that they could press the fight forward. Charles made the duke of Alençon head of the French army, and for a time in the latter half of May Joan stayed with the duke and his family. Joan, who by now identified personally and sartorially as a knight (thereby implicitly rejecting the commoner status to which she had been born) and had begun to see herself as the savior of France, was no longer content with the fulfillment of her original goal of liberating Orléans from the English. While waiting for the war to resume, she honed up on her military skills and spoke with some brashness of the French soon celebrating in Paris. Part of her strengthened confidence presumably came from the easy relationship she had developed with her soldiers, whose company she clearly enjoyed and who, in turn, had become increasingly in awe of her.

In the week from June 10 to June 18, the French side won several key battles against fortified towns south and north of Orléans, thereby largely clearing the Loire Valley of English. On a number of occasions during this period, Joan, confident of God's backing, overruled the less daring Alençon—decisions that were made out in the open so that the soldiers, if they harbored any lingering doubt, now knew that Joan was basically in command of the French forces. Joan took a more direct part in the fighting than previously and was wounded slightly at one point when a stone struck her helmet, causing her to fall to the ground from the ladder on which she had been standing holding her standard aloft. She jumped up quickly, telling the soldiers that God had condemned the English and that they should therefore press the attack. The besieged town promptly fell to the French after this incident.

Following the lopsided French victory at Patay just northwest of Orléans, Joan said to Alençon: "Have the trumpets sounded and get on your horse. It is time to go to the noble king Charles to lead him to his coronation at Rheims" ("the second part," in Marina Warner's words, "of her God-given mission").[18] Persuading Charles to go to Rheims to be formally crowned king turned out to be rather complicated because of the clashing political interests of court factions, but Joan finally prevailed. The route taken to Rheims passed through territory in which many of the towns and cities were lightly garrisoned by the English. Auxerre offered no resistance, but the sizable city of Troyes, more strongly defended, was unwilling to submit. Charles and the other French leaders were divided as to whether they should simply bypass Troyes or besiege the city.

FIGURE 4.2 Joan of Arc, demonstrating her moral zeal, drives prostitutes from her soldiers' encampment. (From Martial d'Auvergne, *Vigiles de Charles VII* [ca. 1470], reprinted in Joseph Édouard Choussy, *Vie de Jeanne Darc* [Moulins, France: Imprimerie Bourbonnaise, 1900].)

Joan predictably favored the latter course and told Charles to order his men to prepare for an assault. Troyes fell within two days, and Charles entered the city in splendor, Joan riding by his side with her standard raised high. "Thanks to Joan the Maid," writes Larissa Taylor, "momentum was now on the French side. Throughout Europe and beyond, people spoke of her deeds with wonder and awe."[19]

On the evening of July 16, Charles, Joan of Arc, and a French army by now possibly twelve thousand strong reached Rheims, where they were warmly greeted by the leading citizenry of the city and high church officials. Rheims was the place where French kings were formally crowned, something Joan knew well and that her voices, from the very beginning, had instructed her to bring about. It was in Rheims that Clovis, the first French king, had been anointed with holy oil following his conversion to Christianity in the late fifth century. Rheims was also the capital of the empire of Charlemagne. In a situation in which the French Crown was being seriously contested, it was of utmost importance, therefore,

FIGURE 4.3 Joan of Arc in full armor astride her horse. Engraving by Léonard Gaultier (1612). (From Jean Hordal, *The History of the Most Noble Heroine Joan of Arc, Virgin of Lorraine, Maid of Orléans* [in Latin], illustrations by Léonard Gaultier [Ponti-Mussi, France: Apud M. Bernardum, 1612], reprinted in Joseph Édouard Choussy, *Vie de Jeanne Darc* [Moulins, France: Imprimerie Bourbonnaise, 1900].)

for reasons of both religious and political legitimacy, that the coronation ceremony in the cathedral at Rheims be executed quickly and properly.

Although preparations for the coronation were rushed, and last-minute substitutes had to be found for certain props that were unavailable, the ceremony took place as planned on July 17, 1429, and was by all accounts a most impressive event. It was presided over by the archbishop of Rheims. Joan stood by Charles throughout, holding her standard high. When the ceremony ended, she knelt down before him, clasped his knees, and, weeping with joy, said: "Gentle king, now the will of God has been accomplished, who wished that I should raise the siege of Orléans and bring you to this city of Rheims to receive your solemn consecration, showing that you are the true king, that you are he to whom the kingdom of France should belong."[20]

This was a critical moment in the career of the Maid from Domremy. The tangible goals that Joan's voices had instructed her to fulfill—the raising of the English siege of Orléans and the coronation of Charles VII in Rheims—had been achieved. These goals, moreover, were anything but secret in nature, having been presented to Charles in Chinon in early 1429, approved by examining clerics in Poitiers, formally supported by the king himself in late March, and publicized in the court's propaganda thereafter. The question after the crowning of Charles was, What next? Although Joan claimed in the months ahead to be in periodic touch with her voices, it is not clear that she was ever again given a set of explicit instructions from them with concrete goals comparable to the ones she claimed to have received as a girl in Domremy. And even if she had, it quickly became apparent following the coronation that the plans she now had in mind diverged sharply from those of her king. Charles, ever the more cautious of the two, wanted an end to the fighting—at least for the time being. Joan, emboldened by her past successes, wanted to continue the war against the English until they had been driven from France altogether.

What happened in the course of the ensuing months made it perfectly plain that Rheims, for Joan, represented the high point of her career, or, as one of her biographers, Vita Sackville-West, puts it, "her feet" were hence-forth "set on the sharply sloping path which fetched up at the stake."[21] Up to that point in time, against all odds, Joan had gone from triumph to triumph, confirming for many—and certainly to herself—the authen-ticity of her voices. After Rheims, however, the sacred script she had been following appears to have come to an end, and now, the magic having run dry, she stumbled badly. In September 1429, her attempted assault on Paris (together with the duke of Alençon) ended in disaster—her first great defeat—despite her having promised her soldiers that they would take the city without fail and (according to one account) enrich themselves in the process. (Significantly, at her trial, when she was asked whether she had followed the counsel of her voices in launching the attack on Paris, she acknowledged that she hadn't.[22]) Then, in late May of the following year, the final blow came with Joan's capture by an Anglo-Burgundian force laying siege to the northern French city of Com-piègne. A French nobleman, commenting at the time on this shattering outcome, wrote: "She had too much confidence in her own powers and opinions. . . . She . . . did everything according to her own pleasure. . . . God allowed Joan the Maid to be taken because of her pride and the rich clothing she wore. She had not done what God had commanded but followed her own designs."[23] Although despite such judgments Joan continued to believe that she was France's last best hope, her career as a warrior was over.[24]

The Burgundians, after initially resisting English demands that their prize prisoner be turned over to them, finally relented, selling her to them for twelve thousand pounds. In late November 1430, it was decided that Joan should be tried in Rouen, the capital of English-held Normandy. In January 1431, the English proclaimed that she was to be charged with "crimes of divine treason." The trial began on February 21, 1431, and was concluded in late May. Although Joan defended herself brilliantly, the whole ecclesiastical book was thrown at her (including the charge that her insistence on wearing male dress was an offense against the divine order of things),[25] and threats of torture, trickery, and other knavish devices were used at the trial, the English having made it plain from the outset that anything short of a guilty verdict was unacceptable to them. And, so, on the morning of May 30, Joan emerged from her prison cell wearing a long, loose-fitting dress with a cap on her head inscribed with the words "Relapsed, Heretic, Idolator, Schismatic." Hands and feet in chains, she was taken through the streets of Rouen to the Old Market on a cart pulled by four horses and guarded by more than a hundred English soldiers to thwart any possibility of escape.

Seven to eight hundred people thronged the marketplace for the spectacle. When the preacher who delivered the sermon at one point maligned Charles VII, Joan interrupted, exclaiming, "What you say is not true, because I want you to know that there is no better Catholic than the king!" Pierre Cauchon, the bishop who had presided over the trial proceedings, then summarized the errors and crimes committed by Joan, denounced her as a "rotten member" of the church, excommunicated her, and handed her over to the secular power. Joan was promptly grabbed by English soldiers, passed on to the executioner, and led to the platform that had been made ready for her burning. A board placed in front of it declared: "Jehanne who called herself la Pucelle, liar, pernicious, deceiver of the people, sorceress, superstitious blasphemer of God, presumptuous disbeliever in the faith of Jesus Christ, boastful,

FIGURE 4.4 Joan of Arc at the stake in Rouen. Fresco by Jules Eugène Lenepveu (1886–1890) in the Panthéon, Paris. (From Joseph Édouard Choussy, *Vie de Jeanne Darc* [Moulins, France: Imprimerie Bourbonnaise, 1900].)

idolatrous, cruel, dissolute, invoker of devils, apostate, schismatic and heretic."[26] After being bound to a wooden post on the scaffold, Joan spoke heartrendingly at some length, appealing to "the Father, Son and Holy Spirit, the blessed Virgin Mary, and all the saints of paradise," asking all present to pray for her, and pardoning her judges and the executioner. She asked for a cross, which an English soldier standing close by quickly fashioned out of two twigs and gave to her. She kissed it and, calling out "to God Our Redeemer who had suffered on the cross for our salvation," pressed the cross against her chest. She then requested that the crucifix in the nearby church of Saint-Sauveur be brought to her. A local Dominican priest who had sympathized with Joan throughout the trial, retrieved the crucifix and held it up in her line of vision so that she could look at it uninterruptedly until her death. The faggots were then lit and burst into flames around her. She warned two sympathizers who had joined her on the scaffold to get down quickly. Before expiring, she repeatedly called on Jesus. She appears to have succumbed from smoke inhalation before being completely overwhelmed by the flames.[27]

THE AFTERLIFE OF JOAN OF ARC

Although a church court tried and burned Joan of Arc, the entire process was orchestrated by the English. Taylor argues convincingly, moreover, that the main factor guiding English behavior wasn't the belief held by Bishop Cauchon, the theologians of the English-backed University of Paris, and the duke of Bedford that Joan was a witch or a heretic, but rather that "she had shamed the English on the field of battle and they feared she would do so again." Bedford, in particular, felt this way, having been badly humiliated by the lowly girl from Domremy, and in the weeks following her death he dispatched letters in the name of Henry VI to the most important leaders in Christendom to remove all doubt that, as Taylor frames it, "the witch was dead!"[28]

Bedford hoped that with Joan out of the way there would be a resurgence of English power in France. But this was not how things turned out. He himself died soon, in 1435. Two years later King Charles regained Paris, and in 1453 the English were driven from the rest of France, with the exception of Calais, bringing an end to the Hundred Years War. If there was any question as to the political motives behind the trial and condemnation of Joan of Arc, within three years of the expulsion of the English official nullification proceedings (also not free of political motivation) were commenced in Paris with the pope's support. Focusing on Joan's character and conduct and those of her judges, and relying on the testimony of numerous persons (including villagers from Domremy) who had known her, the proceedings resulted in her complete vindication, which was publicly announced on July 7, 1456, the judges determining that her actions were more to be commended than condemned and that her trial "had been conducted in a vicious, deceitful manner, fraudulently and with ill intent." The judgment exonerating Joan was repeated the following day in the Old Market in Rouen, where she had died in the fire twenty-five years earlier.[29]

In the years following the nullification, the excitement generated by Joan of Arc's career died down, and Joan herself was forgotten by many. For several centuries following her death, her exploits were alluded to from time to time in chronicles and other writings. But it really wasn't until the late eighteenth century that her life and the legends surrounding it became rooted in French popular culture and memory. This trend, with a growing emphasis on Joan as a nationalist symbol, deepened in the course of the nineteenth century, initially in response to the interest Napoleon showed in her as an emblem of French national unity[30] and then in the 1840s owing to the influential writings of Jules Michelet and his student Jules Quicherat.[31] Not long after midcentury, Joan's religious side was also popularized, the bishop of Orléans initiating in 1869 a course of action that led eventually to her being declared a saint on May 16, 1920. As became increasingly clear in the twentieth century, the appeal of Joan of Arc not only straddled the domains of politics and religion but was also deeply ambiguous—an ambiguity nowhere more conspicuously manifested than in the impassioned embrace of her image by representatives of both the Left and the Right in French political life.

THE RIDDLE OF JOAN OF ARC'S POPULARITY DURING WORLD WAR II

In spite of the extensive historical documentation on Joan of Arc found in the trial and nullification transcripts, many of the most elementary questions about her as a person and historical figure remain unanswered. This gap is due in part to the central role Joan's voices played in her life and career, coupled with the circumstance that, as the French philosopher and theologian Jean Guitton has put it, historians will never be able to answer the question "[W]ere her voices true?"[32] It is also due in part to the fact that the greatest concentration of evidence that exists concerning Joan of Arc is tied to her trial and nullification proceedings, two heavily politicized events that inevitably generated documentation with a generous measure of partiality and unreliability. These black holes are part of what has made so many different readings of Joan possible; and it is the multiplicity of readings, in turn, that has enabled individuals representing different sides of deep-rooted French historical and political divides to press her into the service of their core ideas, much as, when civil war broke out in the United States sixty-two years after George Washington's death, the first American president "was embraced by both sides as the personification of their cause: union in the North, liberty in the South."[33] Posthumous images of Joan of Arc often imagined her in female clothing despite the historical Joan's unwavering attachment to male garb as a key part of her identity.[34] Views have likewise been imputed to her that are unlikely ever to have been a component of her actual intellectual and psychological, much less her political, makeup—hence, the baffling circumstance that during the German occupation of France in World War II, Joan, like Washington in America at the time of the Civil War, was venerated by what appears to have been a great preponderance of the French populace regardless of where they stood politically.

FIGURE 4.5 Nineteenth-century engraving of Joan of Arc in women's attire. Based on a frequently reproduced bronze statue by Princess Marie of Orléans (1813–1839), which stands in front of the Hôtel Groslot in Orléans. (From Harriet Parr [Holme Lee], *The Life and Death of Jeanne d'Arc, Called the Maid,* 2 vols. [London: Smith, Elder, 1866], vol. 1.)

The immediate reason for this broad veneration might seem to be that in at least one vital respect—Joan of Arc as a symbol of French national integrity—the alignment between popular image and historical reality was never closer than in time of war. Marina Warner thus observes that in the aftermath of France's humiliating defeat by Prussia and the loss of Alsace-Lorraine to Germany in the Franco-Prussian War of 1870–1871, the stock of national integrity as a symbol shot up, and "all colours wanted Joan for themselves."[35] But, on closer inspection, the eager identification with (and exploitation of) Joan of Arc by both Vichy collaborationists and supporters of resistance during World War II proves to have been a great deal more complicated.[36]

The German dominion over France began following Germany's decisive victory over the French in May–June 1940 and lasted until the second half of 1944. Under the armistice between the two countries that went into effect on June 25, 1940, a large area comprising the North of France and the West Coast was occupied by the German army. In this part of the country (known as the *zone occupé*), the French government, which had been moved to the resort town of Vichy in central France and was headed by Marshal Philippe Pétain (a World War I hero who had been the last prime minister of the Third Republic), was subordinate to the Germans. Most of the rest of France (designated the *zone libre*) was ruled by Vichy. However, with the Allied invasion of North Africa in November 1942, the Germans and their Italian allies immediately established control over the southern part of the country as well, a situation that lasted until after the Allied landings in 1944.

VICHY COLLABORATION

Nothing in the original narrative of Joan of Arc touched on republicanism or fascism or even nationalism. Yet centuries after Joan's time proponents of each of these modern ideologies found themes in the Joan story—either as it first unfolded or as it was later interpreted—that spoke to their most cherished political beliefs. Thus, Timothy Wilson-Smith writes: "As French armies were brushed aside in May 1940, many on the French Right assumed that it alone stood for Joan's vision of France. The collapse of the forces of the atheistic republic before the onslaught of Panzers and Stuka bombers proved that if France recovered, that recovery would be thanks to an ageing marshal, Joan's true representative."[37]

The identification of Pétain with Joan of Arc was achieved in ways large and small. The author of a book on the psychology of Pétainism wrote later that "not a book appeared on Jeanne d'Arc, Henri IV, Louis XIV or Bonaparte in which the preface failed to point out the astonishing similarities between the hero of the work and the glorious Marshal."[38] At the annual celebration of Joan's feast day in German-occupied Orléans in May 1941, the priest delivering the panegyric noted that Marshal Pétain himself had made a surprise visit to the city the day before: "The French flag fluttered over Orléans. The streets and squares reverberated with cries of 'Long live France! Long live the Marshal! Long live Joan of Arc!' The national anthem saluted twenty times the glorious old man whom none will deny carries in his heart the suffering of the fatherland as he incarnates in his person the living will of the country." Officially organized propaganda was equally blatant in its appropriation of the image of Joan in support of Pétain and the policies of Vichy. Pétain's personal propaganda machine (the Bureau de documentation du Chef de l'Etat), for example, published a leaflet with the words "Follow me! Maintain your faith in eternal France" on the front cover and a picture of dueling knights with the insignia "Jeanne / Du Guesclin / Bayard" on the back.* Inside the leaflet there is a picture of Pétain accompanied by an appeal to the young people of France to fashion themselves into a youth that is strong, sound of body and spirit, and prepared for the tasks that will elevate their French souls. "It is on youth and by youth that I wish to rebuild our Country in the New Europe. For this grand enterprise I call upon all young people."[39]

Such uses of Joan of Arc were fairly general and bland in nature. On other occasions, building on tendencies associated with the antirepublican Right in the decades prior to 1940 (most conspicuously the views and activities of the royalist movement and the periodical *Action française* under the ideological leadership of Charles Maurras),[40] Vichy supporters appropriated Joan in more toxic ways. A common theme in Pétainist writings was that in her own day Joan of Arc had been prevented from

---

*Bertrand du Guesclin (1320?–1380) was a French military hero who, as constable of France (1370–1380), was victorious in a number of important battles against the English in the Hundred Years War; Pierre Terrail, Seigneur de Bayard (1473–1524), was another military hero known for his fearlessness and chivalry.

achieving immediate success against the English by cowards, self-seekers, and intriguers who hemmed her in on all sides. Because of these people, she needed to work especially hard to gain a loyal following to carry out her mission. The message Pétainists gleaned from this example was that it was necessary to group tightly around their leader and not be diverted by the fanciful ideas of ethnic or ideological outsiders. If there was any doubt as to what this meant, the zealous Vichy supporter Pierre Pascal filled in the blanks in a May 7, 1942, article—the day of Joan of Arc's feast day—that was framed as an appeal to the "Sainte de la Patrie" (a common designation for Joan). In the piece, Pascal condemned all traitors, from the Jews to the politicians of the Third Republic.[41] What France needed was an officer of justice who would act in the marshal's behalf and would be "empowered to apply the law, punish, and supervise the torture of those who willingly undo, destroy, and reduce to ashes the very work of Saint Joan, that is, France and its wondrous unity, the France of former days that was Christian and European, right-thinking and properly guided." Pascal here placed Marshal Pétain on a level with Joan of Arc. Similar themes were articulated in another article, also dated May 7, in the collaborationist periodical *L'Appel*, which stated: "If Joan had in truth only one wish: to drive out treason by the crowning of her king, the Marshal has only one wish: to drive out treason by the empowering of justice."[42]

As suggested earlier, the formation of a new French youth was a central project under Vichy, and for those in charge of education Joan seemed the perfect exemplar.[43] Here again the effort to link her with Pétain was pervasive. René Jeanneret wrote in the preface to his popular school text *Le Miracle de Jeanne* (1942): "If little boys, and even some big ones, have enjoyed reading of Joan's bravery, might not little girls, who have more of a taste for heroism than some think, . . . enjoy it as well? Inspired by this sublime example they will all discover, as they serve their country, that love and that faith which Marshal Pétain highlights as the two wings that bore Joan to the height of her destiny."[44] Apart from love and faith, teachers in Vichy schools were also expected to instill in their young charges the qualities of duty and sacrifice embodied in the person of Pétain by comparing him with Joan and by singing the national youth hymn "Maréchal, nous voilà!" (Marshal, here we are!). Although Joan of Arc is not referred to explicitly in the hymn's lyrics, in the refrain Pétain, like Joan, is described as "the savior of France."[45]

The image of Joan as the savior of France and more particularly as the girl warrior who had "snatched a military victory from the jaws of defeat" resonated closely with the situation Pétain saw himself and France as inhabiting following the military disaster of 1940. Despite this debacle, the day could still be saved, the marshal believed, if France could undergo moral renewal. A local newspaper from the Massif Central captured this sentiment in the following way: "This victory, which the battlefields refused us, we will win over ourselves. Joan of Arc reminds us how much we must sacrifice and suffer because, today like then, our country has slipped along the paths of divisiveness and selfishness. Enthusiasm and faith remain the necessary virtues from which will emerge our moral and social rebirth. French youth will hear sacred voices. If it were not to, the nation's last chance at salvation would be lost forever."[46]

In place of "Liberté, Égalité, Fraternité" (Liberty, Equality, Fraternity), the universalist watchword of the Revolution of 1789, the core values of Vichy were embodied in the more parochial slogan "Travail, Famille, Patrie" (Work, Family, Country). This slogan did not come out of the blue. Indeed, it represented a distillation of themes that had attracted growing attention in France—and other areas of Europe—during the period following World War I. The terms of the slogan to which the story of Joan of Arc was deemed most pertinent were the last two: *family* and *country*. With respect to family, the image projected by Joan appears at first sight problematic. To be sure, her willingness to sacrifice herself, the role of the supernatural in her life story, her saintly and pristine qualities—so different from Marianne, the competing French female symbol, closely identified with the republic and often portrayed bare-breasted—her robust moral and physical health, and her total devotion to God and France were qualities that fit in well with Vichy values. But there was another Joan—the one who was unmarried and virginal, famed for her military exploits, and insistently androcentric in her clothing preferences. What did this Joan have to do with an emphasis on family that, in the years after the Great War, increasingly pointed to pronatalism as national policy not only in France, but also in Germany, Britain, and other European countries worried about population decline? A fascist publicist described "maternity" as "the patriotism of women," and while World War I was still in progress, the French authorities, in their desperation to encourage births, had circulated postcards exhorting soldiers on leave to "work for repopulation" and asking young women to "work for France."[47] Where—how—does Joan of Arc fit into this picture?

The propagandists of Vichy manifestly had their hands full. One way in which they dealt with the problem was by demilitarizing Joan. The notion of young women bearing arms and engaging in combat clearly did not jibe with the highly traditional notions of womanhood Vichy espoused. So Joan was fashioned into a different sort of warrior. One Vichy writer suggested that her aggressiveness was born of the desire to defend her simple "feminine" world—the "comfort of the home." Slightly more convincing was the stratagem of picking and choosing the aspects of the Joan legend to be emphasized or deemphasized. Thus, Jeanneret noted in his school text that Joan never killed or even tried to kill and that she had made clear her preference for her standard over her sword: "Typical French girl, she loved beautiful clothes, silk and furs; as a warrior she liked pretty armour, but still she preferred her banner to her sword, and could outsew any woman in Rouen." In line with this image, during the Vichy period Joan was often portrayed unarmed.[48]

There were also various efforts to deandrogynize Joan's manner of dressing. Jeanneret asserted that "out of a sort of warrior coquettishness," she wore a sleeveless dalmatic (a skirtlike article of clothing worn by Catholic bishops and English monarchs) above her armor. An issue of a Vichy magazine for youth leaders that dealt with Joan of Arc Day celebrations suggested, following the historical record, that those young people appearing as the girl Joan wear skirts and those emulating Joan at the stake be clad in dresses; in defiance of the historical record, however, its advice to any girl impersonating the warrior Joan was that she dress "in a skirt."[49]

Then there was the problem of what kind of female Joan was. "The Pétainist heroine," one scholar has written, "is either a virgin like Joan of Arc or rabbit-like, such as Mrs Roger Jacquier, who at 21 years of age gave birth to her 7th child without ever bearing twins, and whose model fertility was lauded by the entire French press in January 1942."[50] Although Joan was easily accommodated to the first ideal, it took some doing to align her with the second. Vichy propagandists maternalized her, circulating numerous posters depicting her associated with the Virgin Mary and the cult of motherhood.[51] Ever resourceful, Jeanneret presented her as a kind of godmother (*marraine* in French): in her home town of Domremy, he claimed, "Jeanne loved to be surrounded by children." Vichy used her illiteracy to disparage intellectuals, above all female ones. Sweeping came before learning, a dictum that prompted Eric Jennings to suggest in his marvelous study of the gendering of la Pucelle that Vichy deployed Joan "to promote ignorance, docility and ultimately subjugation for girls." Pierre Jalabert in his strongly collaborationist (and racist) *Vive la France!* portrayed Joan as "feeble and gentle . . . meek and frail" before she began to hear her voices, and Jeanneret depicted her as "a girl suddenly, crying and whining" when she was struck by an arrow in the fighting at Les Tourelles, until her voices restored her courage. In so describing her, both writers thus strongly suggested that Joan's valor was in essence derivative, that she—along with perhaps, Jennings argues convincingly, women in general—was incapable of being brave on her own. Joan's very mission, in Jeanneret's view, represented a great sacrifice, for what she really wanted more than anything was to lead a simple "normal" existence: "Joan cannot read. . . . But she sews, cooks, washes, sweeps, makes the beds and prepares the soup, for men like to have the soup ready when they return from the fields." Even when campaigning, she "inspires respect . . . because she thinks of everything. And the soldiers like her because she cares for them, primarily by cooking . . . Her [mother] would be so proud of her tending to household chores while on military campaign." The true miracle of Jeanneret's *Le Miracle de Jeanne*, Jennings writes, is that he transformed into "a model housewife" the person "who had once been considered France's foremost female fighter." More broadly, Jennings concludes, "[t]he Joan image, perceived today as representing female heroism, stood under Pétain as a protean model for ultra-traditional gender roles," her representation "employed by Vichy schoolbooks to promote uniformity, subservience and resignation for French girls."[52]

If in respect to *famille* Vichy's Joan of Arc had to be made into something she was not, in the process threatening to undermine the attributes that had always been central to her story, the problem in regard to *patrie* was one less of inconsistency than of ambiguity. Was Joan's claim on the hearts of the French people based on a literal reading of her story— of the Joan who was determined to drive the English from France—or was the ousting of the English to be taken as a metaphor for defense of the *patrie* against *any* external invader? In the first instance, Joan's actual historical experience made her the perfect prototype for Vichy's purposes. Just as in her own life she had experienced unprovoked attacks by the English, on May 9, 1942, the very time of her annual celebration and only days after the start of the (largely) British campaign to capture the French colony of Madagascar, Vichy's colonial ministry cabled its Madagascar governor: "At the moment when mainland France and the faithful Empire celebrate with fervour our national Saint, our thoughts go out to our tormented colony and its heroic defenders. Against this same invader this French island is demonstrating the same courage. It is the most fitting homage which can be made to Joan of Arc: sacrifice to the nation and confidence in its destiny."[53] The parallelism was drawn in even greater detail in regard to France's domestic foes. Because Joan in her day had been attacked not only by the English but also by Frenchmen in the pay of the English, the media under Vichy painted Charles de Gaulle, the head of the French government in exile in England, as a modern-day Bishop Cauchon—"a French traitor sent by London to discredit and persecute 'True France.' "[54] In other ways as well, Joan of Arc was tied in with anti-British propaganda. In 1943, the regime issued a poster showing her rising from the ruins of the city of Rouen, which had been bombed by the British. The text read: "The killers always come back to the scenes of their crimes."[55] In a later phase of the war, Vichy (on May 13, 1944) published a series of posters and stickers containing the following message: "So that France may live, like Joan of Arc we must kick the English out of Europe." When, not long after this, D-Day took place, Pétain spoke of it as an invasion (rather than a liberation) of the country, the Free French who participated in it being cast in the role of modern Burgundians.[56]

In the instance where the story of Joan of Arc was read metaphorically to embrace the defense of France against external invaders of whatever stamp, the Germans now taking the place of the English, Vichy's literal reading of the story made Joan in effect into a collaborator with the enemy, a twentieth-century Burgundian. Here again, therefore, as in the gendering and domestication of her, although for different reasons, Vichy risked the subversion of what was truly distinctive about the life of Joan of Arc—an ironic outcome that any number of French people living under Vichy could hardly fail to have detected.[57]

RESISTANCE

If the problem for French collaborators during World War II was how to reconfigure Joan of Arc into a convincing exemplar of the values and policies of Pétainism, the problem for those sympathetic to or actively engaged in the Resistance movement was both simpler and more complicated. It was simpler in that Joan did not have to be made into an anti-Joan, someone completely other than what she really was. It was more complicated in part because the Resistance within France had limited resources available for the effective exploitation of the Joan image and in part because, like all resistance movements, it had to operate in secrecy. As a result, a great deal of the resistance sentiment expressed within the country (as opposed to the operations of the Free French under General de Gaulle in London) was either concealed or coded or "whispered."[58] In this grouping also were rumors, always a major form of communication in wartime, which as the war progressed took an increasingly important part in politicizing the French population, enabling the majority who did not participate actively in the Resistance to adopt it "verbally by positioning themselves as the 'us,' the 'patriots,' against the 'they,' 'them,' 'the collabos,' the enemy."[59]

W. D. Halls notes in his study of French youth under Vichy that in 1941 the nuns of the Pensionnat Notre Dame de Sion in Paris enlivened the celebration of Joan of Arc's feast day by teaching their pupils a sacred song containing lines that could only give offense to the Germans:

> Joan of Arc, Maid of France
> Pray for us, you see our suffering
> Pray for us, be our deliverance
> O model of valour.

In the following year, when they did it again, the Germans learned about it, and the bishop punished the nuns. Although the nuns, in partial self-defense, claimed that they had omitted more insolent lines such as "Let us chase the barbarian / Over the Rhine," the Vichy minister of education was nevertheless placed in the uncomfortable position of having to placate the Germans on their behalf. Halls describes another incident that took place on Joan of Arc's saint's day in 1942. On this occasion, the chaplain of the lycée at Vichy, Father Soras, preaching in Lyons before Georges Lamirand, the official in charge of the government's youth programs, asked his young audience to remember that the prevailing circumstances of the country weren't all that different from those of Joan's day. At that time also, three-quarters of France had been occupied, but Joan had delivered her country from the enemy—words that, Halls observes, could readily have been interpreted as a "call to arms."[60]

Timothy Wilson-Smith has taken note of more muted whisperings of rebelliousness against Vichy. Laying a wreath at the foot of a statue of

Joan of Arc was often seen as an act of patriotic defiance. Some took the annual commemorations of the Maid in Chinon, which habitually cited her battles against the English, as metaphoric signals of anti-German feeling. For others, the national celebration of Joan of Arc Day in early May offered an occasion to pull down a swastika flag. And in the final phase of the war, as more and more of France was liberated, Wilson-Smith writes, "former supporters of Vichy took refuge in silence; and the only acceptable idea of Joan became the idea of her held by de Gaulle."[61]

General de Gaulle liked to think of himself as France incarnate. In a recent biography, Jonathan Fenby states that the general's "identification with France was so intense that, in his mind, the 'historic' de Gaulle and the country he saw himself 'carrying on [his] shoulders' became one." During his presidency of the French Fifth Republic after the war (1959–1969), Fenby continues, de Gaulle "spoke of a murmur rising around him to urge the country on, for all the world like the supernatural voices that drove Joan of Arc."[62] De Gaulle's posture made him an easy target for Anglo-American ridicule. Winston Churchill, although recognizing what was special about de Gaulle, resented his arrogance and was famous for the wisecrack, "The Cross of Lorraine was the heaviest cross I have ever had to bear." But the British leader also wrote the following: "It was said in mockery that he thought himself the living representative of Joan of Arc. . . . This did not seem to me as absurd as it looked." Averill Harriman, the American ambassador to the Soviet Union during the latter half of the war, commended de Gaulle's courage but found his egoism insufferable; in a conversation with Andrei Vyshinsky in November 1943, he described the French leader as "extremely vain and imagines himself a sort of Joan of Arc, and that makes work with him difficult."[63]

Franklin Delano Roosevelt and de Gaulle first met at the Casablanca Conference in January 1943, and the meeting did not go well. The American president took the position, it appears, that he could not recognize the National Committee that had been formed in London in 1941 and under the aegis of which de Gaulle claimed to represent the true France because de Gaulle "had not been elected." De Gaulle's retort to Roosevelt was that Joan of Arc, who had saved France in the fifteenth century, had not been elected either. The Anglo-American joking and mockery at de Gaulle's expense fed on itself over time. Roosevelt, it was claimed, at one point asked Churchill whether de Gaulle really saw himself as Joan of Arc. Churchill was alleged to have answered: "Yes, Mr. President, he thinks he is Joan of Arc, but unfortunately my bishops won't let me burn him." When asked later whether he had really said this, Churchill replied: "No, but it's so witty, I'm sorry I didn't."[64]

One reason—although surely not the only one—why disparagement of de Gaulle was so hard to resist was the visible distance between the Frenchman's ambitious claims and the reality of his position, especially in the early phases of the war. In the summer and fall of 1940, as de Gaulle himself acknowledged, he was far from representing the spirit of the French people, the overwhelming majority of whom considered the armistice with Germany "a painful but necessary act of statesmanship." Reeling under the impact of the one-sided German victory and convinced that Britain's capitulation was only weeks away, "virtually the entire nation rallied around the 'Victor of Verdun' and accepted without question" the correctness of Pétain's decision to ally France with her conqueror.[65] In these circumstances, the situation of the Free French could not have looked bleaker. They represented a small minority even among those French who were in England on the day of the surrender, and most of the latter had asked to be repatriated to France. Few French of standing joined forces with de Gaulle in the early days. But in the ensuing months, things began gradually to change. By August 1940, an agreement had been thrashed out between de Gaulle and Churchill that gave formal status to the Free French and included Britain's commitment to seek the "integral restoration of the independence and greatness of France." By late 1940, a Free French state had been ushered into existence, "with de Gaulle as its unquestioned leader."[66]

De Gaulle's strong identification with Joan of Arc was made manifest in various ways. According to family lore, he was descended from a knight who had fought at Agincourt and was one of the six men-at-arms who accompanied Joan to Chinon in February 1429. In his office in London, de Gaulle received visitors seated beneath portraits of Joan of Arc and Napoleon.[67] Early on in the war, following Admiral Thierry d'Argenlieu's suggestion, the Free French adopted as their emblem the Cross of Lorraine, France's answer to the German swastika and a symbol intimately linked to Joan.[68] De Gaulle alluded to this symbol again and again in his wartime speeches. He also regularly drew parallels between the conditions of France during the war and those pertaining in Joan's time, either holding up Joan's behavior as an example to be emulated by Frenchmen in his own day or using it to castigate the contrasting actions of the Vichy regime. As an instance of the latter, in a message "to all true Frenchmen" broadcast from London on July 2, 1940, he reeled off a number of past French heroes, headed by Joan of Arc, and asked rhetorically whether any one of them would "ever have agreed to surrender French weapons to the enemies of France in order that they might be turned against her Allies?"[69] The following year, in a speech delivered from Brazzaville on the eve of Joan's feast day, de Gaulle drew a detailed comparison between Joan of Arc's France and his own. It is worth reproducing at length:

A country three-quarters conquered. Most of the men in public positions collaborating with the enemy. Paris, Bordeaux, Orleans, Rheims transformed into foreign garrisons. A representative of the invader dictating law in the capital. Treason on all sides. A chronic state of famine. An ignoble régime of terror and delation organized in town and country. The soldiers hiding their arms, the leaders their vexation, the French people their fury. Such was the outward aspect of France five hundred and twelve years ago, when Joan of Arc came forward to fulfil her mission. Such is the outward aspect of France to-day.

I say "the outward aspect of France," for in 1429, notwithstanding oppression, shame, and sorrow, the people were not resigned. I say "the outward aspect of France," for in 1941 the nation is silently fretting the chains of servitude. In olden days, it was because of the same secret faith and hope that from Joan of Arc's sword sprang the great movement that drove the foe from France. To-morrow, the weapons of those who are fighting for our country will drive the enemy from our land, because the same faith and hope still live in the hearts of the French.

Joan of Arc, true, pure, and saintly daughter of France, to-morrow, the National Festival of May 11th—*your* feast-day—will see the whole French nation united in the will to liberation. To-morrow, May 11th, from three to four o'clock in the afternoon, the whole French nation will throng the public thoroughfares of our towns and villages. In silence, millions of glances mutually exchanged will kindle in every heart the flame of national resistance.

Joan of Arc, to-morrow, May 11th, under your aegis, all true Frenchmen will recognize one another.[70]

Because Joan of Arc was a heroine to Pétain as well as to de Gaulle, her feast day could be—and was—celebrated with enthusiasm in Vichy France as well. The question was, What did the "silence" de Gaulle referred to really signify among the participants of such celebrations? Although its meaning can never be known with assurance, on May 19, 1941, in another speech from Brazzaville, the general took the occasion to give his own reading of it: "The French people, sustained by hope, are rising against the invader and his accomplices, as is proved by the colossal national demonstration which, in answer to our call, took place in all our towns and villages on May 11th, the feast-day of Joan of Arc."[71] Some months later de Gaulle claimed to see further signs that his compatriots were awakening to their true situation: "Countless and bloody proofs show that, little by little, the same spirit of national unity that upheld Joan of Arc in her mission, gave birth to the warlike effort of the French Revolution and supported Poincaré* and Clemenceau, is reviving among the people because of their determination to resist the enemy."[72] De Gaulle also made persistent efforts to buck up the spirit of the French, to warn them against compromising with the enemy, and to assure them of final victory. "What would have become of the country," he asked in June 1942, "had Joan of Arc, Danton, or Clemenceau been willing to come to terms? . . . We speak openly to the millions of French men and women who, we know, await but our vanguard's coming to bring out their Crosses of Lorraine and show themselves once more for what they are— children of a great nation capable of sudden and triumphant recovery."[73]

A year later, in June 1943, the tide of the war having turned sharply in the Allies' favor, de Gaulle sent a radio message from Algiers lauding the vital instinct of the French that over the centuries had so often pulled the country back from the abyss:

> It is this instinct that aroused Joan of Arc and led the French to build a centralized state around the King when it appeared that feudal anarchy would bring us under foreign domination. It is this instinct that, at the time of the Revolution, caused the nation to stand up against its enemies and their accomplices and dictated to it, for its salvation, the great principles of the rights of man and of democracy. It is this instinct that, today, prompts all Frenchmen concerned about the future and the greatness of the Country to desire and take steps for the establishment of the Fourth Republic: a republic of national renewal.[74]

---

*Raymond Poincaré (1860–1934) was several times prime minister of France and served as president from 1913 to 1920; he was known for his strongly anti-German policies.

John Flower notes that in contrast to the periodic references to Joan of Arc in de Gaulle's wartime messages, at the time of France's liberation she virtually disappears from his speeches, although he could not have been unaware of the political capital to be made from exploitation of her image. Flower attributes this elision, somewhat enigmatically, to the general's "careful self-image building."[75] Without denying for a moment that de Gaulle cared about his self-image, particularly now that he was no longer operating from abroad and was much concerned with establishing his political authority in northern France in the aftermath of the Allied landings, my own view is that there is a more compelling factor behind the shift away from Joan. For de Gaulle, after all, Joan of Arc was first and foremost a symbol of uncompromising *resistance* to foreign occupation of France. Her story was therefore made to order for the wartime crisis burdening the country and for the organization and activities of the French Resistance that the general did his best to shape from London.[76] But it spoke much less clearly to the Allied victory and not at all to the Gaullist political authority that emerged almost instantly in its wake.[77] There are two reasons for this disconnect. One is the fact that by the time France was finally "liberated" in the fifteenth century, Joan had long since passed from the scene. The other was that in Joan of Arc's France the question of who was to exercise political authority in the country did not have to wait for the ousting of the English to be dealt with; it had already been settled long before with the crowning of Charles VII in Rheims.

Another conveyor of resistance sentiment during the war was the French theater (which I interpret broadly to include oratorios). The repertoire of theaters during the German occupation remained largely unchanged with two key exceptions: plays by Jewish playwrights were banned, and there was "a sudden resurgence of interest in the dramatic potential of Joan of Arc."[78] In light of the prominence of Joan of Arc as a positive model under Vichy, there was nothing surprising about the second exception. Indeed, there were numerous performances of plays about Joan, at least during the first years of the occupation, and they were strongly supported by the regime. Among the more successful were Charles Péguy's *Mystère de la charité de Jeanne d'Arc* (The mystery of the charity of Joan of Arc), written in 1910 and adapted by his son (it was put on in Paris in June 1941); the oratorio *Jeanne d'Arc au bûcher* (Joan of Arc at the stake), with words by Paul Claudel and music by

Arthur Honegger, which toured the country in the summer of 1941, with a special train to transport the actors, orchestra members, and all their props, costumes, and instruments; George Bernard Shaw's *Saint Joan*, the first of the Joan plays during the occupation, opening in Paris in December 1940; and Claude Vermorel's *Jeanne avec nous* (Joan with us), which was completed in 1938 and began an eight-month Paris run in January 1942.[79]

A dramatic performance would occasionally incorporate lines that were unmistakably subversive of Vichy and sympathetic to the Resistance. Such was the case with René Herval's oratorio *Jeanne d'Arc triomphante* (Joan of Arc triumphant), which was performed in the cathedral of Rouen on May 30, 1943, the beginning of what was to prove the darkest period of the German occupation. The handling of the Joan story in Herval's work was entirely conventional, but the final chorus could only be understood as a summons to the French people to resist:

> Sweet France, the day has come
> When you will emerge from your suffering, to be born again.
> Thanks to the spirit that exalts you and brandished steel
> The enemy flees. Joan guides you,
> Joan whose intrepid heart
> Shines in battle with a divine fire.
> The God of the armies will lead you on as before,
> Invisible and strong, across the blazing plains.
> There will be fighting in the shadow of His sword,
> And you will see Victory surrounded by a golden halo
> In the rising dawn.[80]

But the Herval oratorio in its explicitness was an exception. Far more often, Vichy thought police and German censors had a hard time figuring out what a given play's real meanings—and a given theater audience's real reactions—were. Thus, Patrick Marsh, although acknowledging that Claudel, Péguy, and Vermorel's intentions are not clear in their plays, asserts confidently that "what is important about [the works of] all . . . three . . . is that they were taken by the audience to be an attack on the 'occupier'—obviously, in this case, the Germans; the circumstances surrounding their production turned them into 'pièces de circonstance' [plays that resonated with current circumstances] which had a very poignant message for contemporary French audiences."[81] Without questioning the last part of Marsh's claim, I must point out that the fact remains that some French viewers drew very different conclusions about the meanings of these plays.

The clearest illustration of this ambiguity was Vermorel's *Jeanne avec nous*. The play, which dealt with Joan's trial, imprisonment, sentencing, and execution, was praised in the collaborationist press, with Lucien Rebatet, who began his journalistic career with the *Action française* in the late 1920s and was a dedicated exponent of fascism and virulent anti-Semitism, hailing Vermorel's Joan as a "patroness of French Fascism."[82] But after the war's end, when *Jeanne avec nous* was again put on (in December 1945) and critics were free to say what they pleased about its political import, the play was widely viewed as the clearest instance of a Resistance drama. Georges Douking, who directed the 1942 production, had the English officers and soldiers in the play click their heels Nazi style, which may have been what Vermorel had in mind when he reported in December 1945 what Douking said about their project at the time: "'Even if it is only a dress-rehearsal, if we are still alive in three or four years, it will nevertheless not be bad to be able to say: well, we had the nerve to stage it in January '42 in Paris.'"[83] A large number of reviewers of the 1945 production were confident that the audiences of the earlier version could have had no trouble seeing that the real message of Vermorel's play was the indictment of an occupying power. And so the critics had a marvelous time mocking the simplemindedness of the German censors, one of them reconstructing what he imagined to be the German reasoning as follows: "Very good play. Play against English. A play for Joan of Arc is necessarily a play for Germans." One critic, who had also seen the 1942 production, insisted that the judges who condemned Joan in the play were instantly recognizable as stand-ins for Vichy. And Simone de Beauvoir, in her memoir *La force de l'âge* (1960, The prime of life), said that in applauding Joan's "proud response" to the English, "we demonstrated without ambiguity against the Germans and against Vichy."[84]

None of this is to suggest that Vermorel intended his play to have the political meanings assigned to it in the immediate postwar period.

In 1938, when he put the finishing touches to the play, the German invasion hadn't yet taken place, and because the playwright had the members of the French church address each other as "comrade," some reviewers thought that his original target may have been the Communists. Certainly, the French clerics who stood in judgment of Joan (with the exception of Martin Ladvenu, who often defended her during the trial) are portrayed as deeply unsympathetic, self-aggrandizing sorts, which could have been intended as a knock against the Communists. There are a number of indications, moreover, that Vermorel (like many others in prewar Europe) was not unsympathetic to fascism. Shortly before completing *Jeanne avec nous*, he had pressed for a Franco-German youth theater to foster improved cultural relations between the two countries.[85] Also, it has been pointed out that Vermorel contributed articles to the pro-Nazi newspaper *La Gerbe* not only as a preview to the opening of his play in 1942, but also as a critic who a year earlier had mounted a vigorous attack on surrealist and avant-garde theater.[86] Finally, in contrast with de Beauvoir's recollection, Vermorel wrote in December 1945 of the shiver that ran down his spine each time the *silence* of the audience drew attention to a daring allusion in the play, such as the English soldiers clicking their heels or the French priests addressing each other as "comrade."[87]

It is of course possible that Vermorel's views, like those of many of his compatriots, changed over time. It is equally possible that he remained deeply ambivalent from start to finish. This is especially apparent in the play's treatment of the Catholic Church. The church in general was a strong supporter of the Vichy regime during the war. Yet in Vermorel's play the clergy are quite willing to collaborate with France's archenemies, the brutal and bloodthirsty English. The church, moreover, is consistently portrayed in harshly negative terms, to the point where even historian Gabriel Jacobs, who is as skeptical as anyone regarding the reliability of the postwar political judgment of *Jeanne avec nous* as a Resistance play, acknowledges that Inquisition representative Jean Lemaître's long and detailed accounts of the physical torture inflicted on Joan "were too close to reality not to have been taken as an indictment of the methods of the Gestapo or the Milice."[88] And just to keep things from getting too simple, the real French church during World War II, in contrast to the church depicted in the play, venerated Joan of Arc, as did of course other supporters of Vichy, not to mention the Resistance headed by de Gaulle. The long and the short of it is that there was something for everyone in Vermorel's play, which, despite—or because of—its author's nervousness, may have been exactly the way he wanted it.

In the closing scene of the play, Joan is dead. The French and English principals have gradually assembled in the tribunal hall. They talk about Joan, what she represented and what she might become over time. The duke of Bedford addresses her: "Fifty years from now, if it comes to pass that people speak of you, in what strange image will you be cast? Who were you? Did you yourself know?" Two shutters softly open onto a French window, and "Joan" appears "with white flowers falling around her, her eyes closed, her hands joined, wearing a straight dress and a helmet. She is clad entirely in white." It is a statue, and to Bedford's question "Who is this woman?" the sculptor, smiling on his work, replies: "Faith. I have made her wearing this pure straight dress, like a stalk shooting up—but with a helmet on her head: the warrior Faith, the true Faith." But to the Inquisitor's question, "What did you think of Joan?" the artist (who has resumed his work) replies: "Joan? What Joan?" "Joan of Arc," Lemaître interjects. The man says: "Ah! Joan of Arc!" He makes a move with his chisel, then turns back toward the others, with an air of sincere ignorance: "Which Joan of Arc?"[89]

The questions with which Vermorel concludes his play focus on who *Joan* is—a sorceress in the service of the devil (as a number of the judges at her trial insisted) or, as she herself repeatedly claims and reiterates in a conversation in her prison cell with Lemaître, a good Christian obedient only "to the voices of my God." "He knows," she adds, "that men, even of the Church, are forgetful. Forgetful that they must above all serve truth, love. If He has chosen me to remind them of this, it is because He saw me as one who is fair and meek. 'Be good,' those were the first words I knew from Him."[90] Although the question of who Joan was might have been appropriate in the fifteenth century, in 1942, more than two decades after Joan had been declared a saint, it is hard to imagine French audiences having anything but affection, if not veneration, for their national heroine. The more meaningful question for wartime viewers of *Jeanne avec nous*, I would suggest, was not "Which Joan of Arc?" but "Which France?"—and to this question there was no single or simple answer.

THE DIMMING OF POPULAR MEMORY: JOAN OF ARC AFTER THE WAR

Joan of Arc is visually omnipresent in today's France. "A high percentage of churches," according to one observer, "have a statue or effigy of Joan somewhere; schools, colleges, streets and squares are named after her, as are religious groups, associations, clubs, cafés, hotels, restaurants, sweetshops and even an on-line dating service."[91] Although the image of Joan was actively exploited in the early postwar years, and in the 1980s the French Right, in the guise of Jean-Marie Le Pen's anti-immigration National Front, again took possession of her (mimicking its precursor, the Action française, in the 1920s and 1930s), Joan has seemingly retreated as a compelling figure in French life. In a poll taken not long after the war—in 1948—only 11 percent of those polled included her in a list of famous French men and women; by 1980, the number had dropped to 2 percent, and by 1989 to zero percent. It speaks worlds that, as one writer commented in 2006, "Marie Curie, a physicist who won two Nobel prizes and was an atheist, is now regarded as a more inspiring figure from the past."[92]

The most convincing explanation for this drop-off in interest is that Joan's star has tended to rise when France has been under mortal threat, when war has clouded the horizon and the country has been in need of a powerful emotional lift—a patriotic savior who can succeed against steep odds. But such concerns have been absent from French life for close to seventy years at this point, replaced by other French worries: the incorporation of Muslims into the population; provision of pensions for an aging population; working out a satisfactory relationship with Germany; the preservation of French culture, the French language, and French cuisine in a world in which American popular culture has become dominant; and the like—all topics to which the story of Joan of Arc has little or nothing to say.[93]

I began this chapter with an improbable comparison between the Joan of Arc story and the King Goujian story of ancient China. I end it in the same way. It will be recalled that once the political–military crises to which the Goujian story spoke were resolved and the collective national concerns that had previously dominated China's twentieth-century history were replaced after the 1980s by a dramatic expansion in the realm of private interests and worries, the aspects of the story that Chinese looked to for inspiration and psychological support in their daily lives also changed. A comparable shift seems to have taken place in regard to the Joan of Arc story—comparable but different. Although Joan's place in French popular culture—and indeed, with the occasional exception, in French politics—has faded,[94] she remains a topic of serious scholarly study in France and elsewhere. A great many leading Joan scholars have in recent decades been women—a fact that, although seeming natural enough to us, would have been a source of some surprise to Joan, in whose day few women were even literate. Also, many modern students of Joan, male as well as female, have taken special note of the ways in which the French heroine went against the conventions for women of her time, ironically becoming in the process a model for an expanded repertoire of behaviors for women in our own day, a popular focus (at least in the Anglo-American world) of college and university courses in women's and cultural studies.[95]

Nothing resembling this has happened in the case of the Goujian story in China. The point is not that there are no gender themes in the larger Goujian narrative; it does have such themes—some of them even pertaining to the role of women in war. In a play completed in November 1931, only months after the Mukden Incident that sparked the Japanese takeover of Manchuria, Zheng Dan, one of the more important female characters in the Goujian story, expresses anger and hatred toward the state of Wu and regret that she cannot join the Yue army: "Daughters can't serve as soldiers? Females aren't people? Females aren't one component of the citizenry? Females shouldn't be patriotic?"[96] But there is scant evidence that this aspect of the Goujian story caught hold during the war with Japan,[97] and in any case, in contrast to Joan of Arc, gender themes were far from being a key aspect of the makeup of Goujian himself.

Apart from specific content, the other way in which the Joan story differs from the Goujian story is in its geographical and conceptual reach. As noted earlier, the Goujian story did not migrate beyond the East Asian realm, whereas the story of Joan of Arc, above all perhaps in its gender ramifications, has never even at the very outset been an exclusively French possession and in modern times has extended quite literally around the world, Joan having by now become, as one writer put it, "a figure of universal significance as a feminist model, if not a model feminist."[98] It is on this basis, at least in theory, that Joan can contend with the likes of Marie Curie. But there are different kinds of feminist models, each appropriate to a particular set of historical and cultural requirements, and the probability of Joan of Arc's competing with the Marie Curies of the world, at least in France, will almost certainly depend on the French once again being exposed to serious military peril. It was war, after all, not science, that was Joan of Arc's métier. And the likelihood of France's being imperiled militarily any time soon seems lower now than at any time in the previous two centuries.

5

ARTFUL PROPAGANDA
IN WORLD WAR II

This final chapter, although addressing essentially the same historiographical issues taken up in the earlier chapters, differs from the earlier ones in a number of ways. For one thing, it deals with two core stories instead of one. The main reason for this is that the two films that form the chapter's principal content are closely related thematically and chronologically. Both Sergei Eisenstein's *Alexander Nevsky*, which began showing in the Soviet Union in late 1938 in the context of rising tensions with Nazi Germany, and Laurence Olivier's film treatment of Shakespeare's *Henry V*, released in the United Kingdom in November 1944, several months after the D-Day landing of Allied forces in northern France, were unabashedly political in nature, consciously designed to promote national cohesion and foster patriotic sentiment in their respective countries. A second reason for treating the two films together is that Olivier's *Henry V* was, as we shall see, directly influenced by Eisenstein's *Alexander Nevsky*.

Another way in which this chapter differs from the others is that it focuses on a close examination of specific versions of the two stories dealt with—renderings of the stories that, owing to the medium in which they were created (film) and the political environment in which they were realized (World War II), reached mass audiences overnight and did much to popularize the original stories from which the two motion pictures were derived. It did not hurt, of course, that although both movies were initially intended for propagandistic purposes and therefore warmly supported by the British and Soviet states, they were also of towering importance in the history of cinema and have been justly celebrated ever since for this reason.

SERGEI EISENSTEIN'S *ALEXANDER NEVSKY*

Nowhere is the murky relationship that often prevails between past story and present history more conspicuous than in Eisenstein's *Alexander Nevsky*. The film was ostensibly based on the historical Nevsky, a Russian prince who lived in the thirteenth century and whose attitude and actions were construed as a kind of template for the attitude and behavior Eisenstein (and his sponsor Joseph Stalin) wanted the inhabitants of the Soviet Union to emulate in the late 1930s. But the documentation Eisenstein had to work with in presenting the historical Nevsky was so meager—when the Film Committee gave him the choice of Nevsky or another Russian hero, he chose Nevsky "because nothing is known about him"[1]—that he was essentially free to shape the film's hero into the patriotic symbol of his imagining. This would not, moreover, be the first time that Nevsky's image was exposed to such manipulation. Medieval sources on him were not only scanty, but also from the very beginning heavily embroidered. The main source, the hagiographic *Life of Aleksandr Nevskiy*, was probably first produced in a monastic institution not long after Nevsky's death in 1263; it then went through numerous editions, each of which introduced changes reflecting the values and norms of the time and place in which the fresh rendering had been created. Thus, as for medieval hagiography in general, it was not a "life" in the modern biographical sense, but rather an idealized depiction of its subject, a sacred story "designed to teach the faithful to imitate actions which the community considered to be exemplary."[2] If there is still some question about the degree to which Josephus's account of Masada was distorted by the author's personal circumstances and agenda, there can be no doubt concerning the mythic content of the *Life of Aleksandr Nevskiy*; and we know from Eisenstein's own admission that the film version represented in effect a remythologization of the earlier mythified traditions surrounding Nevsky, a conscious reframing of the image of the hero so that it spoke unambiguously to what was taking place in Eisenstein's day. "*Alexander Nevsky*," one scholar has commented, "says much more to us about 1938 than it does about the thirteenth century."³ It will help to appreciate this reframing if, before getting to the film, we take a brief look at the historical Nevsky and his early mythologization.

THE HISTORICAL ALEXANDER NEVSKY

Russia in the first half of the thirteenth century was deeply fragmented politically and subjected to a number of military threats, the longest lasting and most devastating of which came from the Mongols, who subjugated a sizable portion of the country in 1237–1241, bringing a violent end to the Kievan Rus period of Russian history. In summarizing what we know with reasonable assurance about the historical Nevsky (1220–1263), we might find it helpful to look at him in terms of four involvements, which to some extent interacted with and shaped one another: (1) his relationship with the populace of Novgorod, a large and prosperous trading city straddling the Volkhov River in northwestern Russia; (2) his actions in defense of the Novgorod region against external threats; (3) his strategy for dealing with the Mongols; and (4) his relationship with the Russian Orthodox Church.

The first Russian prince of importance to rule under the Mongol sway, Nevsky began to exercise surveillance over Novgorod in 1233, when he was a youth of twelve or thirteen—initially together with his father, Yaroslav, and subsequently on his own when his father went to Kiev in 1236. In the chaos and confusion that accompanied the Mongol conquest, there was a great deal of rivalry and contention between Novgorod and other Russian principalities, most important Suzdalia to the southeast. The city of Novgorod was also riven by internal factional squabbles, making it a hard place to control. Although the reigning prince had substantial authority over its military, legal, economic, and administrative affairs, he had to share power with the *veche*, or town assembly, which placed severe restrictions on his actions.

More significant, perhaps, than the intramural rivalries among the Russian principalities were external threats coming from the west, mainly from the Lithuanians, Germans, and Swedes. When Yaroslav left for Kiev, he entrusted the defense of the frontiers of Novgorod and the nearby town of Pskov to his son. The most celebrated chapter in Alexander's defense of Novgorod involved two battles, one fought against the Swedes,

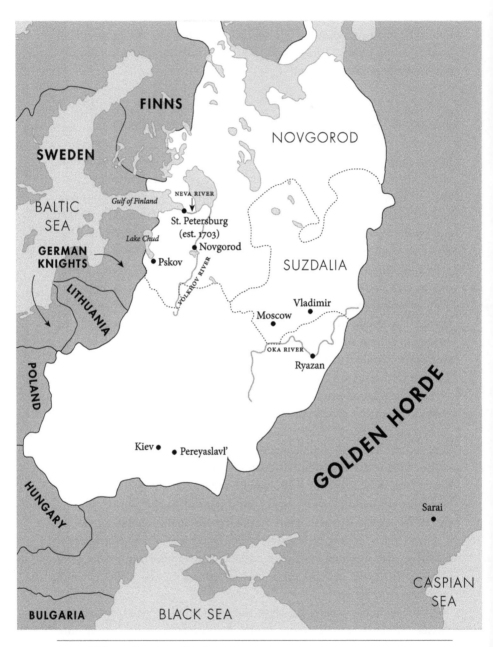

MAP 5 Thirteenth-century Russia.

the other against the German Knights (a merger of two Catholic groups, the Livonian Order of Swordbearers and the Teutonic Knights). The clash with the Swedes, which took place along the Neva River in 1240, led two centuries later to a chronicler's awarding of the sobriquet "Nevsky" to the victor. Although the Novgorodians welcomed Alexander's assistance in addressing the Swedish threat, it soon became clear that he had enemies in Novgorod as well as Pskov. When he returned to the city from the Neva, he had a falling-out with the citizenry (for reasons the sources do not make clear), causing him to leave the city in a huff and repair to his boyhood home in Pereyaslavl' (just southeast of Kiev). The German Knights, with the help of local inhabitants in southern Estonia and the prince-ruler of Pskov himself, took advantage of the situation to march on Pskov and occupy the town. The citizenry of Novgorod, now themselves fearful of a German attack, sent an urgent request to Alexander to return, which, after some foot dragging, he did in 1241. Once "the instigators of sedition" in the city had been hanged, the prince, along with his brother Andrei, marched on Pskov, which they retook with ease. Then, bent on maximizing their success, they crossed the frontier into Estonian–German territory, where they concentrated their forces on what some of the later sources say was the ice of Lake Peypus (or Peipus or Chud). The German Knights, with Estonian support, tried to break through the Russian lines with a wedge formation. But they were defeated (April 5, 1242) and later in the same year agreed to give up any Russian territory still in their hands and to exchange prisoners of war.[4]

"So ended," the British historian John Fennell tells us, "what many historians have called one of the great decisive Russian victories of the thirteenth century, the crushing of the crusade of the Teutonic Knights against Novgorod and Pskov, the rout of the Germans, the heroic defence of the western frontiers against papal aggression, the turning-point in relations between Russia and the West, and so on." Fennell disagrees sharply with this understanding, however, contending that this battle and the earlier one against the Swedes were "relatively minor victories" that were "blown up to epic proportions" in the *Life of Aleksandr Nevskiy* and later chronicle accounts.[5]

If Alexander's military feats are subject to controversy, so are his relations with the Golden Horde, the northwestern khanate of the Mongol Empire, established in the thirteenth century with its capital in Sarai (originally situated on the lower stretch of the Volga River). There is no question of Nevsky's willingness to submit to and cooperate with the Mongols. But was this cooperation an act of appeasement or betrayal, as Fennell insists, or was it a sagacious policy born of clear-sighted recognition of the power disparity between the Mongols and Russians, as many Russian scholars have contended?[6] In 1252, while Nevsky was in Sarai, the Mongols sent a force against his brother Andrei, who in 1248 had been made grand prince of Vladimir (the capital of Suzdalia, conquered by the Mongols in 1238).[7] Andrei, unhappy over his continued subjugation to the Mongols, was overpowered and fled the country, whereupon the Mongols appointed Alexander grand prince of Vladimir in his stead.[8] Nevsky remained in this position, which gave him virtual control over Novgorod and all the territories north of the Oka River,[9] until his death in 1263. During his tenure as grand prince, he repeatedly acted to defend the entire region against his longstanding adversaries to the west (the Germans, Swedes, and Lithuanians). At the same time, however, when Novgorodians resisted Mongol census takers and tax collectors, as they did a number of times, he could be brutal in enforcing Mongol policy— on one occasion, according to the *Novgorod Chronicle* entry of 1257, cutting off the noses and gouging out the eyes of some of the leading rebels. In seeming contradiction to this reaction to tax resistance—although without more evidence it is hard to say—when a number of major towns in Suzdalia drove out Mongol tax collectors in 1262, Nevsky journeyed to Sarai apparently to plea for clemency for them.[10]

There was an intimate connection between Nevsky's policy of accommodating Mongol overlordship and his relationship with the Orthodox Church, whose members in the thirteenth and fourteenth centuries "prayed for the well-being of the khan and followed a policy of accommodation with the Mongols to the point of establishing an episcopal see in Sarai [in 1261]."[11] According to Nicholas Riasanovsky and Mark Steinberg, "it was especially because of [Alexander Nevsky's] humble submission to the khan and his consequent ability to preserve the principality of Novgorod as well as some other Russian lands from ruin that the Orthodox Church canonized him [in 1547]."[12] Whatever the case, the appointed head of the Russian Church, Metropolitan Kirill, was a warm supporter of Nevsky, spending more time in Vladimir than in the metropolitan see of Kiev and delivering the oration at Nevsky's funeral in 1263. Because the Orthodox clergy were the only men in Russia who were spared taxation and conscription under the Mongols, argues Fennell, the church "could hardly be expected to do anything but afford Aleksandr all possible support in the pursuance of his pro-Tatar policy and to foster in his *Life* the image of him as the great champion of Orthodoxy in the face of papal aggression."[13]

THE EARLY MYTHOLOGIZATION OF NEVSKY

As should be plain from the preceding section, the mythologization of Alexander Nevsky began during his lifetime. But it became still more conspicuous after his death, when "his reputation grew to truly iconic status."[14] Mari Isoaho discusses the imbalance between the mythified treatment of Nevsky and historical reality in her fine study of the hagiographic *Life of Aleksandr Nevskiy*. This source, she points out, for the most part remains silent about what was truly important historically: a crucial event such as the Mongol conquest is thus virtually ignored in the *Life*, which concentrates instead on "extolling Aleksandr's glorious victories over the Swedes and the Teutonic Knights in the west."[15]

In his analysis of the stages through which the *Life of Aleksandr Nevskiy* passed, Donald Ostrowski presents a hypothetical reconstruction of a secular military tale, no longer extant, that he believes was written in the second half of the thirteenth century and served as the *Life*'s foundation. The text lionizes Alexander and celebrates in greatly exaggerated language his military achievements and glory. Thus, after he vanquished the Germans at Lake Chud and took "a multitude of prisoners," "the entire population" of Pskov "met him in front of the town glorifying lord Prince Alexander. And they began to hear his name throughout all countries, up to the sea of Egypt, to Mount Ararat, and on both sides of the Varangian Sea, and to Rome."[16]

Ostrowski believes that more than a century after this military tale was written, probably in the second half of the fourteenth century, an ecclesiastical redactor edited it, adding "pious sentiments and religious topoi" in an effort to transform the original text into a "saint's tale." Then, in the second half of the fifteenth century, the *Life* was edited again, introducing anti-Mongol interpolations.[17] This change reflected the new position of the Moscovite Church, which was now under the protection of the ruler of Moscow rather than of the Byzantine emperor and therefore was no longer obliged to follow the Byzantine Church's policy of collaboration with the Golden Horde.[18] The change was also nourished by the growth in the fifteenth century of an ideological movement that "glorified the Russian struggle against the Mongols."[19] In this new setting, the dominant image of Alexander was no longer the celebrated military hero of the original version of the *Life* or the saintly prince of the second version. Alexander was now reconfigured as a self-sacrificing ruler who in order to save his people and his country from utter devastation was prepared to go to Sarai and humble himself before the khan: "It is better that I should die alone for the Orthodox Christian faith before the godless tsar than spill the blood of innocent people and put the whole city in danger."[20]

The mythologization of Alexander Nevsky continued in later centuries. In one conspicuous instance, although the images and symbols that Peter the Great (r. 1682–1725) deployed to augment his power derived typically from the West, one Russian predecessor he made substantial use of was Nevsky. Peter emphasized his own similarity to Alexander's heroic conqueror image and reburied the latter's remains in a monastery bearing the Nevsky name in his new capital, St. Petersburg. Further links to Nevsky were the location of St. Petersburg at the mouth of the Neva River and the name of its main thoroughfare, "Nevsky Prospekt."[21]

EISENSTEIN'S BACKGROUND AS A FILMMAKER

Eisenstein's filmmaking career can be described as an ongoing tug-of-war between the genius of the true artist and a political environment (to which all Soviet creative talents were beholden) that went through unpredictable shifts over time and could sometimes get nasty. *Strike* and *Battleship Potemkin*, his earliest films, both made in the mid-1920s and built around the theme of class warfare, had strong backing from the state and won international critical acclaim. The response of the masses, however, was less clear-cut, leading one film critic to comment wryly that after watching *Potemkin*, "nobody went Bolshevik, but a lot of people left with some pretty revolutionary ideas about film making."[22] The international praise that *Potemkin* in particular attracted was transformative for the youthful Soviet director, who, after an abortive effort to get state funding for a film on the Chinese Revolution, was commissioned to work on two important domestic film projects.[23] When Mary Pickford and Douglas Fairbanks, on a visit to Moscow in the summer of 1926, invited Eisenstein to Hollywood to make a movie for United Artists (of which they, along with Charlie Chaplin, were co-owners), the filmmaker's reputation at home and abroad soared, prompting him years later, in a spirit of giddy self-congratulation, to write, "At twenty-seven, the boy from Riga became a celebrity. Doug and Mary travelled to Moscow to shake the hand of the boy from Riga—he had made *Potemkin*."[24]

In the summer of 1929, Eisenstein went abroad to study foreign cinematography. After almost a year in Europe, he finally got to Hollywood in June 1930 and began work on a number of projects there. Nothing much came of these efforts, however, and he was about to return to the Soviet Union when he received an invitation to do a film on Mexican history. Excited by this prospect, he left for Mexico in December 1930 and in the following year began work on *Que viva Mexico!* By late summer 1931, the top Soviet film bureaucrat Boris Shumyatsky, who had little sympathy with Eisenstein's international filmmaking frolics, wrote to him insisting that he return to the Soviet Union. Eisenstein ignored the request, but by year's end Stalin himself weighed in with a telegram to the Soviet director's main backer, the left-leaning novelist Upton Sinclair. When Sinclair withdrew his financial support, Eisenstein, his Mexican film unfinished, was forced to return to Moscow, where he arrived in spring 1932.

The Soviet Union that Eisenstein encountered on his return was a far cry from the one he had left almost three years earlier. The state's grip over cultural activities in particular had tightened dramatically. For the next few years, Eisenstein tried his hand at several projects, none of which reached fruition. The most prominent of them was *Bezhin Meadow* (1937), based on a Turgenev short story and centering on the theme of unquestioning loyalty to the state. As the filming approached completion, it was shown to Shumyatsky, who subjected it to multiple criticisms. Eisenstein, clearly upset, engaged a new scriptwriter, the famed short story writer Isaak Babel, changed some of the actors, and moderated the film's more experimental aspects. But despite these efforts to salvage the situation, in March 1937 the production was abruptly suspended by official decree; Shumyatsky published an article in *Pravda* lacerating it, and the film was later banned.[25]

Although Eisenstein, under severe pressure, published a self-criticism, "The Mistakes of *Bezhin Meadow*," in April,[26] he can only have felt that his career and possibly his very life were in jeopardy (the first Moscow show trials had recently taken place, resulting in the executions of sixteen "enemies of the state," including former Politburo members).[27] In desperation, at Babel's suggestion (Babel himself soon became a victim of the Great Purge*), he wrote Stalin directly asking for another chance and was offered two projects, one of which, as noted earlier, was Nevsky.[28] In early 1938, the film industry itself was targeted, and several major figures were placed under arrest, among them Shumyatsky, who in January lost his position as head of the all-powerful Film Committee and was executed six months later. Positively gleeful at the humiliation of his longtime bête noir, Eisenstein by this point was deep into the production of his new film.[29]

A short piece Eisenstein wrote in 1937 sheds much light on his attitude toward the making of *Alexander Nevsky*. He felt a strong connection with *Tales from History* by the children's writer Alexandra Ishimova, which the great Russian poet Alexander Pushkin had happened to be reading at the time he was killed in a duel exactly a hundred years earlier. Ishimova's work, Eisenstein tells us, had "a fair amount of 'ladies' handiwork' about it" and was of "doubtful veracity." But Pushkin, despite being mindful of the importance of historical accuracy, was "captivated" by the book. Eisenstein explains why:

> It is the remarkable depth of the author's love for the theme she has chosen that so charms. The theme is her homeland and her people. Her love for her homeland and the Russian people is the captivating thing which stands out from the pages of Ishimova's history. . . . The panoply of the materialist method alone is inadequate when it comes to history. . . . If it is not infused by a genuine love, fervour and the feeling of a blood tie with the past, our approach will be as infertile as any unscientific, speculative ramble into our past and just as remote from true Marxism-Leninism, which indissolubly interweaves angry passion or the thrill of battle with the subtlety of strictly scientific analysis. And that is why, when beginning to talk about one of our oldest national heroes, Alexander Nevsky, I find myself involuntarily turning to the pages of Ishimova's book.[30]

---

*The Great Purge was the succession of campaigns of political repression and persecution orchestrated by Stalin in 1937–1938.

Although enjoying ample freedom in reconfiguring history in his making of *Alexander Nevsky*, Eisenstein throughout the production was forced to work closely with Stalin-appointed hard-liners, whose job it was to keep him from the kinds of experimentation that had gotten him into trouble earlier in his career. The wonder is that, in spite of these political constraints, he was able in the end to put his signature stamp on the film and in the same breath win Stalin's enthusiastic approval.[31] It helped, of course, that the film had been commissioned by the state in the first place.[32] But it helped even more that, as Eisenstein himself put it in the title of a short essay dealing with *Nevsky*, "my subject is patriotism."[33] The rise of National Socialism in Germany in the 1930s and mounting apprehension in the Soviet Union concerning the exposure of its western borderlands forced a fundamental realignment in Soviet goals from world revolution to national defense. Class warfare might work for the 1920s, but for the late 1930s only national unity infused with patriotic fervor would do.

THE FILM

Nevsky was Eisenstein's first full-length sound film.[34] It also marked the beginning of a long and fruitful collaboration with the great Russian composer Sergei Prokofiev (1891–1953), who wrote the musical score not only for *Nevsky*, but also a few years later for *Ivan the Terrible*.[35] Viewers of *Nevsky* are reminded of the cruelty of Mongol subjugation in the desolate landscape with which the film opens: "Bones. Skulls. Scorched earth," Eisenstein elucidates. "The charred remains of human habitation. People led away to slavery in a distant land. Ruined towns. Human dignity trampled underfoot. Such is the terrible picture of the first decades of the thirteenth century in Russia that confronts us."[36]

Eisenstein doesn't waste any time in emphasizing what the main focus of the film will be. A scuffle takes place early on between a small band of Mongol warriors leading a group of Russian captives and Alexander with some fishermen followers in Pereyaslavl' (where he has gone as a result of a quarrel with the Novgorod city leaders). When the Mongols discover that the head fisherman is none other than the famous Nevsky, they invite him to join the Golden Horde as one of their commanders. Nevsky responds with the Russian proverb "It's better to die than to leave your homeland," and the Mongols depart. Alexander's face darkens with anger as he watches the Russian prisoners being led away to a life of slavery and suffering. But he makes it plain to his followers that the "Teutonic and Livonian Knights" (who, for the benefit of contemporary viewers unlikely to know who they were, are clearly identified in the film's opening captions as "the German aggressors") are the greater cause for concern and must be defeated first, after which "we shall take care of the Mongols."[37] Russian movie audiences in 1938 would have had little difficulty decoding this comparison between the Teutonic and Livonian Knights and the Mongols: Nazi Germany's threat to the motherland was far more pressing than the danger presented by the Japanese, then fighting in Manchuria.[38]

The scene shifts to Novgorod, the support of which, Nevsky had made clear in the previous scene, was needed if the Russians were to defeat the Germans. Eisenstein, determined to build Russian folk culture into the film, begins the scene with an entertaining episode involving two swaggering locals, Gavrilo and Buslai, who, the armorer Ignat tells his customers, had fought the Swedes on the Neva with Prince Alexander. Having nothing else to busy themselves with, Gavrilo and Buslai flirt with a lovely peasant lass named Olga. Both propose to Olga, who says she must have time to think about it. The assembly bell suddenly tolls loudly, summoning the inhabitants of Novgorod to drop what they are doing and gather at the Yaroslav court. A wounded Russian warrior from nearby Pskov announces to the crowd that the Germans ("like wild beasts") have taken his city and that the people, betrayed by the Pskov mayor (Tverdilo), have been treated with hideous brutality. Novgorod, he warns, will be next. The citizens of Novgorod debate how they should respond to the threat. Officials, merchants, and churchmen urge capitulation; Olga, condemning their self-seeking attitude, calls for resisting the Germans. A key issue is whether the principality of Novgorod should act on its own, doing whatever is in its own interest, or should consider itself a part of Greater Russia. The armorer Ignat, supporting the position taken by Olga, comes out strongly in favor of inviting Prince Alexander to return and lead them against the Germans. There is more squabbling, but finally the crowd is swayed and decides to summon Alexander.

We find ourselves next in Pskov, now under German occupation. The Teutonic Knights wear white robes and black helmets in the shape of inverted buckets, with narrow rectangular slits for eyes, making the

Germans faceless and thus accentuating their inhumanity. There are dead bodies on the ground from the fighting earlier. The church's presence is conspicuous, with priests in white habits holding large black crosses high above their heads. In front of the line of knights, bound and kneeling, are the defeated warriors of Pskov. Opposite them are a group of Pskovian women and children, the women weeping and cowering in fear. Tverdilo, the city's traitorous mayor, tells the crowd that the pope in Rome has appointed the master of the Teutonic Order to rule over the Russian realm. He asks them if they are ready to submit to Rome. One of the bound Pskov warriors, Pavsha, gray-haired and haggard from fighting, challenges Tverdilo, saying that Russia will never be ruled by Rome. Tverdilo, beside himself with rage, calls for the blasphemer's punishment. Pavsha's daughter, Vasilisa, runs up to him and says she will die with him. He pushes her off, saying, "Remember our blood! Avenge us!" German soldiers now proceed to slaughter the bound warriors and unarmed citizens of Pskov. Children and even naked infants are hoisted high in the air before being cast into the flames, while an evil-looking German monk in a black-hooded robe looks on approvingly. Then trumpets are sounded, and Pavsha is taken to the execution area, but before he is hanged, he shouts out to his fellow citizens, "Go to Pereyaslavl'! Call Alexander! Devastated Pskov is crying out for you, Alexander!"

The scene changes to Pereyaslavl', where two fishermen are mending their nets. A group of people from Novgorod appears and asks to see Alexander. When he appears, they tell him that the Germans have already taken Pskov (which Alexander is stunned to hear) and are rapidly approaching Novgorod. They ask him to be their leader, to rise for Novgorod, to which he responds somewhat testily (having been sent away from the city), "I shall rise to avenge the suffering of Russia." He adds that to take the offensive against the Germans, his personal guard will not suffice, and they will need to call on the support of the peasantry: "With their help, we shall surely defeat the enemy by spring." We next see Russian peasants armed with primitive weapons converging from all directions on Alexander, who is on horseback wearing a helmet and battle attire. As the throng of ordinary Russian folk swells, a chorus is repeated: "Arise you Russian people! In a just battle to the death! Arise, people free and brave!. . . . For the homes of our fathers, arise, you Russian people!"

We are now in Novgorod, where the first ranks of peasant volunteers come into sight and, with much whooping and singing, pour into the crowd of townspeople. Alexander mounts the assembly tribune. With his appearance, the crowd quiets down. Accenting the theme of national unity, he asks the people to fight not just for Novgorod, but for all of Russia: "Arise for the sake of our motherland, of our people! . . . Arise for the cities of Russia, for Kiev, Vladimir, and Ryazan! Arise for the sake of our fields, forests, and rivers, for the sake of our great people!" The people of Novgorod are stirred by his words. Carrying torches, they join in singing the same chorus heard in the previous scene. The armorers announce that they will quickly fashion spears and shields and axes for the peasant soldiers. Ignat places his military wares onto the stall and invites the crowd to take whatever they need for the impending battle. Vasilisa, responding to her father's last words to her, says she too wants to fight and is duly fitted with armor. Buslai and Gavrilo overtake Olga in the crowd and, with the urgency of impending battle, press her to come to a decision. She announces that she will wed the suitor who shows the greatest valor against the Germans.

Meanwhile in the German camp, the bishop is celebrating a religious rite. There is chanting in Latin. The black-hooded monk with the evil face is playing a field organ. Outside the tent, the German foot soldiers, clad in white robes with black crosses sewn on the left shoulder, kneel in the snow around the campfires and sing psalms. Word is suddenly brought to the grand master of the Teutonic Knights that Alexander has risen against the Germans and that a Russian advance party is trapped in the forest. The knights jump to their feet, put on their helmets, and grab their weapons. The bishop blesses the soldiers. They enter the dark forest ready to do battle. The Russian advance party, meanwhile, is making its way slowly through the thick snow, with Buslai and another warrior leading the way. The German soldiers surprise the Russians, and fighting breaks out.

On the other side of frozen Lake Chud, too far away to hear the noise of battle, the main body of Russian warriors awaits the return of the advance party. Many of them are sitting around the fire, where Ignat, with gleeful gesticulating, entertains them with the old folk tale "The Vixen and the Hare": "The hare skips into a ravine, but the fox follows him. The hare runs into the woods, but the fox stays on his tail. So the hare jumps between two birch trees. The fox comes after him and gets stuck! It's twisting and turning, but can't get free. What a calamity! The hare looks at her severely and says: 'Now I will violate your chastity.' 'No, neighbor, don't put me to such shame! Have pity,' cries the fox. 'I have no time for pity,' says the hare and violates her!"

All the listeners laugh heartily. Pacing back and forth, tense because of the advance party's failure to return, Alexander has overheard the tale in spite of himself. With a gleam in his eye, he exclaims, "Got her stuck between the trees, did he?" Ignat replies, "Yes, he did." "And violated her?" "He did!" There is more laughter.[39]

A Russian suddenly runs up to the gathering and, kneeling before Alexander, announces that Buslai has been taken prisoner. Alexander raises him up brusquely and exclaims, "Buslai, a prisoner? You lying dog! Buslai would never surrender!" He then strikes the man and promptly gives the order to his men to prepare to rescue the advance party, which they proceed to do.

The film cuts to Lake Chud, where the Battle on the Ice is shortly to begin. It is worth noting that this celebrated scene was shot in the summer prior to the rest of the film, the appearance of ice being created by covering a leveled field near the Mosfilm Studio with a thick layer of chalk and liquid glass (sodium silicate). ("The artificial winter," Eisenstein boasted, "was a success, complete and indisputable. No one saw the difference."[40]) Alexander and Gavrilo ride their horses on the icy surface. The prince observes that the ice is thin (it is early April already), but that it will pose a greater danger to the Germans owing to their heavier armor. As he details his strategy to his commanders, it becomes clear that he has been inspired by Ignat's recounting of the tale "The Vixen and the Hare." He knows that the Germans will attack in a wedge formation. He tells Buslai (who along with the advance party has been successfully rescued) that his job will be to position his men directly in the path of the oncoming German knights, where they will bear the brunt of the wedge. Two other Russian forces, one led by Alexander and one by Gavrilo, will then at Alexander's signal attack the Germans from the right and left flanks in a pincer movement, in effect squeezing the Germans between them, much as the birch trees trap the fox in Ignat's tale.[41]

The German warriors are massed on the western side of the lake with their accompanying cohort of Catholic clerics. War trumpets sound. The massive German force begins to cross the lake, the knights on horseback, clad in white with a black cross on the back and wearing their sinister-looking cross-slit helmets (some topped by large horns). The Russians wait patiently on their side of the lake, the foot soldiers holding long

FIGURE 5.1 Nikolai Cherkasov as Alexander Nevsky in Eisenstein's film of that title (Mosfilm Studio, 1938). (From the Harvard Theatre Collection, Houghton Library, Harvard University [call number: MS Thr 402].)

poles with hooks on the ends for yanking the Germans off their horses. Alexander orders Buslai to take his position at the center to absorb the wedge. Buslai and Gavrilo embrace. Buslai leaves. Alexander says to Gavrilo: "When the Germans hit Buslai, let the wedge stick in deep. And then we will hit them together from both sides." The German force arrives, the battle with Buslai's men is joined. Alexander, watching for the right moment from his flank , suddenly waves his sword in the air and shouts, "For Russia! For Russia!" Gavrilo repeats, "For Russia!"

The Battle on the Ice takes up a substantial part of *Nevsky*'s running time (roughly 30 minutes of the total 111). The air is filled with the sounds of swords clashing and warriors shouting, punctuated from time to time by the Germans' trumpets. In the initial clash, we see Russian foot soldiers using their hooked poles to pull German warriors from their horses. A fresh wave of Germans appears at one point, armed with crossbows. The Russian fighters use axes in addition to swords. Buslai and Gavrilo are seen fighting like tigers in close-up shots. After the fighting has gone on for some time, Alexander rides into the German lines and challenges the grand master to a duel. The warriors on both sides now become spectators. Alexander bests his German adversary, orders him bound as a prisoner, and shouts out, "We have carried the day!" The Russians now pursue the retreating Germans and, on reaching the other side of the lake, charge into the bishop's tent and attack the priests. The battle ends when the ice on the western edge of the lake, not strong enough to support the German soldiers' concentrated weight, breaks up, causing scores of Germans to be swallowed up in the dark waters.[42]

The noisy clamor of combat is now replaced by quiet. Alexander surveys the dead and wounded warriors strewn about on the remaining ice. High-pitched, mournful music is heard, contrasting sharply with the rousing, charged music that accompanied much of the fighting. Russian women with torches move about among the bodies searching for their loved ones. Buslai cradles Gavrilo in his arms, both of them badly wounded. Olga appears and joyously exclaims, "You are alive! Dear ones! Thank God, you are alive." She tells them that the Germans have been utterly defeated: "Spread to the four winds or sunk below the ice!" Buslai and Olga lift Gavrilo to his feet, and with Olga in the middle the three walk off slowly together.

The film's final sequence takes place in Pskov, where a large crowd of Pskov and Novgorod citizens have assembled. As the cathedral bells peal, Orthodox clerics file in, followed by the Russian dead, borne through the town on horse-drawn carts. The people drop to their knees, bowing deeply in respect. The fallen heroes are followed by the main German prisoners, including the grand master and the monk in black. Against a background of triumphal music, Alexander then appears, smiling broadly and waving at the crowd, patting little children, shaking the hands of older folks. After him come the victorious Russian cavalry and foot soldiers. Then, along with captured German knights, the traitor Tverdilo enters, wearing a harness and horse collar and pulling a wooden wagon. Standing on the steps of the cathedral, Alexander addresses the people and tells them they must always remember the Battle on the Ice. If they forget this victory over the Germans, they will become "like Judas, traitors in the eyes of all Russia!" He then takes on the task of dispensing justice. The German foot soldiers should be freed, he suggests, because they were forced to fight, but the German knights should be ransomed. As for Tverdilo, who is kneeling on the ground surrounded by townspeople, his fate, Alexander says, is for the people to decide. On hearing this pronouncement, the enraged citizens fall on the traitor and beat him to death.

Lovely Olga, driving a sled carrying the wounded Gavrilo and Buslai, approaches Alexander. She tells the prince that prior to the battle she had promised to marry the one who fought most bravely against the enemy and asks him to render a decision. Buslai interjects that, of the two of them, Gavrilo was the braver and therefore deserves Olga's hand. But the bravest of all, he exclaims, was Vasilisa, and it is she whom (with her unspoken consent) he would wed. The romantic concerns happily resolved, Alexander raises his goblet and calls on the crowd to celebrate. The film concludes with his patriotic injunction and oath: "Go and tell everyone in the foreign lands that Russia lives. He who comes to us as a guest, let him come with no reservation. But he who comes to us with a sword shall die by the sword. On this stands Russia, and on this she shall stand forever."

THE AFFINITY BETWEEN *NEVSKY* AND THE SOVIET UNION IN THE LATE 1930S

The main theme in *Alexander Nevsky* that summons to mind the Soviet Union's circumstances in the late 1930s is, of course, the menace of German military aggression on the country's western flanks. But several other themes were deliberately built into the film to close the distance between the thirteenth century and the Stalinist era in the twentieth. One is national unity. Russia in the first half of the thirteenth century, as indicated by the initial response to the German threat in Novgorod, was not a politically unified country. The film dramatizes this lack of political unity with the frequent references to treachery, the most striking instance of it by the mayor of Pskov, Tverdilo. These political problems of Alexander's day had clear echoes in problems that were conspicuously present in the 1930s, and Alexander's strong reaction to internal disloyalty and repeated and forceful emphasis on the unity of Russia were obvious allusions to Stalin's fear of spies and traitors and the high priority he placed on national cohesiveness in the face of the German threat.

More broadly, Alexander's flawless character as a leader—his great courage and unswerving confidence, his brilliance as a commander in wartime, and his popularity among the people—suggest "a thinly veiled representation of Stalin."[43] Eisenstein himself presented this comparison in an article that appeared in *Izvestia* on July 12, 1938. The correlation made between Alexander and Stalin in the article is unmistakable:

> The only miracle in the battle on Lake Peipus [Lake Chud] was the genius of the Russian people, who for the first time began to sense their national, native power, their unity: a people able to draw from this awakening self-awareness an indomitable strength; able to advance, from their midst, a strategist and commander of genius, Alexander; and with him at their head, to defend the motherland, having smashed the devious enemy on foreign territory and not allowed him to despoil by his invasion their native soil. "The swine were finally repulsed beyond the Russian frontiers," wrote Marx. Such will be the fate of all those who dare encroach upon our great land even now. For if the might of our national soul was able to punish the enemy in this way, when the country lay exhausted in the grip of the Tatar yoke, then nothing will be strong enough to destroy this country which has broken the last chains of its oppression; a country which has become a socialist motherland; a country which is being led to unprecedented victories by the greatest strategist in world history—Stalin.[44]

The original script for the film ended with Nevsky's being poisoned and dying.[45] But Stalin, wanting it to conclude with the dramatic entrance of the victorious Alexander into Pskov, scrapped this original ending, declaring: "The screenplay ends here. With the triumphal entrance into Pskov. Such a good prince cannot die!"[46] The inference was clear: Alexander in this scene is not only a prince and a saint, but also the beloved leader of his people, entering Pskov to the ringing of bells, much as Stalin himself wanted to be appreciated and acclaimed.

One reason Alexander was much loved by the ordinary people of his day was that he didn't put on airs and distance himself from them. This characteristic is seen in his interactions with the fishermen early in the film. It is seen in his closeness to the warrior Buslai, whom he knows well enough to be absolutely certain that he cannot possibly have allowed himself to be taken prisoner. It is seen in the confidence he shows in the peasants' ability to take a key part in the fight against the Germans. And it is seen in the strategic insight he draws from the armorer Ignat's narration of "The Vixen and the Hare." Eisenstein very consciously incorporated all of this into the film, of course. He deliberately has Alexander overhear Ignat's story and then interrogate him about it: "It was a good idea to show the close contact existing between the Prince and his warriors," Eisenstein commented. From Alexander's close questioning of Ignat, Eisenstein continued, his mind starts to work out "a plan for the complete encirclement of the Teuton horde. It was certainly not from the tale that his wise strategic move originated. But the graphic picture of the folk-tale gave him a valuable hint as he planned the arrangement of his troops."[47]

One other theme in *Nevsky* that virtually all Eisenstein scholars have taken note of and that reinforces the resonance between Alexander and Stalin as Russian national leaders is the film's severance of Russian nationalism from explicitly defined religious roots. Although the historical Alexander was a Christian prince who in 1547 was made a saint of the Russian Orthodox Church, the Alexander of the film is a thoroughly secular leader, and the thirteenth-century Russia he inhabits is, aside from elements in the occasional background shot (such as the crosses on top of the Novgorod cathedral's onion domes), one that has been almost completely shorn of Christian reference, evoking the stance Stalin himself adopted toward religion with his wholesale destruction of churches in the early 1930s.[48] However, Eisenstein lost no opportunity to emphasize the intimate relationship between the Catholic Church and the Teutonic Knights. The knights' battle dress and helmets are clearly marked with the symbol of the cross, and in every scene in which German warriors are shown, whether engaged in battle or in the slaughter of innocent children, their actions are accompanied by the blessings of the Roman Church's representatives. These representatives, moreover, as symbolized by the bishop and the monk in the hooded black robe, are depicted as evil-looking, malevolent figures rather than as agents of good, and, of course, in the climactic Battle on the Ice the side that has the church's support proves no match for the secularized Russians led by Alexander. None of this suggests, however, that Eisenstein's portrayal of Nevsky is entirely devoid of religious symbolism. Alexander's concluding words, that "he who comes to us with a sword shall die by the sword," echo the New Testament Book of Matthew—"All who draw the sword will die by the sword" (26:52)—and place Nevsky in the role of the Messiah,[49] which, understood in secular terms (as Stalin would have understood it in the 1930s Soviet Union), was essentially the part Eisenstein asked Nevsky to shoulder in the film. One scholar has gone so far as to find currents of Christian symbolism permeating *Nevsky*.[50] But this argument, in my view, is not convincing, and the symbols in any case are never made explicit, so what we end up with is a film that, in religion as in politics, reconfigures thirteenth-century Russia to make it speak unmistakably to the circumstances prevailing in the late 1930s Soviet Union.

THE RECEPTION OF *NEVSKY*

Alexander Nevsky rode the wave of historical spectacles—*Ivan the Terrible* was another instance—that became especially common in Soviet cinema starting in the latter part of the 1930s, as the state paid growing attention to reviving patriotism via appeals to the prerevolutionary national past. Premiering in Moscow in late November 1938, barely two months after the Munich Pact forced the capitulation of Czechoslovakia and left the Soviet Union all but alone in its antagonism toward Nazi Germany, the film was a huge box-office success, so much so that its folk-tale heroes, Buslai and Gavrilo, became characters in children's games and, according to some reports, Stalin went up to the director at the end of the opening and, slapping him on the back, declared, "Sergei Mikhailovich, you are a good Bolshevik after all!"[51] Eisenstein and the film's lead, Nikolai Cherkasov (who also played the title role in both parts of *Ivan the Terrible*), were decorated with the Order of Lenin in February 1939. The universal recognition of the film's political message was confirmed when, after the signing of the Molotov–Ribbentrop Nonaggression Pact of August 1939, it was hastily withdrawn from Soviet theaters as an anti-Nazi film but then no less hastily put back in circulation with the German invasion in June 1941. Nina Tumarkin notes the resonance between the military march (and leading Russian war hymn) "Sacred War," which only days after the German launching of Operation Barbarossa was played by an orchestra at the Belorusskii railroad station to fete troops leaving for the front, and the patriotic chorus heard in Novgorod ("Arise you Russian people!") as the inhabitants of the city prepare to go to war against the Germans in Eisenstein's film. The Orthodox Church had officially canonized the historical Alexander Nevsky for his military exploits, and within months of the German attack in 1941 he was canonized again, this time by

Joseph Stalin, who on November 7, 1941, the anniversary of the October Revolution (in the Gregorian calendar), made one of the more stirring speeches of his career: "Comrades, Red Army and Red Navy men, officers and political workers, men and women partisans! The whole world is looking upon you as the power capable of destroying the German invader robber hordes! . . . The war you are waging is a war of liberation, a just war. May you be inspired in this war by the courageous figures of our great ancestors, Alexander Nevsky, Dmitrii Donskoi, Kuzma Minin, and Dmitrii Pozharskii, Aleksandr Suvorov, Mikhail Kutuzov!"[52]

Alexander Nevsky rehabilitated Sergei Eisenstein's reputation. The film was widely praised both in the Soviet Union and in Europe and America.[53] Apart from being awarded the Order of Lenin, Eisenstein was made head of productions at the Mosfilm Studio in 1940 and the following year awarded the Stalin Prize. Prokofiev's score for the film and the cantata derived from it, which became one of the most acclaimed cantatas of the twentieth century, also merited a Stalin Prize in 1941, but politics got in the way. Mikhail Khrapchenko, the head of the Committee on Arts Affairs, felt that Prokofiev had been insufficiently patriotic.[54] When *Nevsky* returned to the screens after the German invasion, it was also shown in improvised cinemas to Soviet soldiers at the front. The film was, in one critic's judgment, "by far the greatest crowd-pleaser of Eisenstein's career." In its barely concealed reshaping of Alexander's life so that it spoke directly to contemporary Soviet concerns, it may also have been the most propagandized film the Soviet director ever made.[55] And there can be little doubt that, as in the case of Olivier's *Henry V* in England, to which I now turn, the heroic Nevsky depicted in the film exerted a far greater influence on Russian popular memory than did the image of the Russian prince found in the original historical sources.[56]

LAURENCE OLIVIER'S *HENRY V*

The temptation to deal with Laurence Olivier's film *Henry V* in the same chapter with Eisenstein's *Alexander Nevsky* was too great to resist. As noted earlier, both films were produced against the backdrop of German aggression in World War II and were expressly intended to bolster popular confidence in the eventual crushing of a hated adversary. Both films were also created in response to state initiative and were warmly applauded by the top political leadership in their respective countries of origin. The directors of the two movies called on the services of leading composers—Sergei Prokofiev in the Soviet Union and William Walton in England—to provide musical accompaniment for the cinematic action. And there was, as well, a tangible connection between the films: the key sequence in *Nevsky*, the Battle on the Ice, directly influenced the shooting of the dramatic highlight of Olivier's film, the Battle of Agincourt.[57]

Alongside these and other connecting links between the two pictures, there are also significant differences. For one thing, Olivier was given complete freedom to shape *Henry V* as he wished, whereas Eisenstein was constrained by government-appointed minders who watched every step he took in the film's production to ensure that he didn't indulge in excessive experimentation. However, Olivier's freedom of action was limited by one restriction that did not apply to his Soviet counterpart: the material he had to work with—a play by England's greatest cultural treasure—could be changed only so much without sinking the entire enterprise. It was understood that in transforming a drama written for the stage into a moving picture, extensive changes and cuts would have to be made, but Olivier nevertheless had to proceed with caution.

Last, there was a substantive difference between the motives guiding the two filmmakers: Eisenstein, aside from his artistic goals, was intent mainly on creating a patriotic film, for personal reasons but also, in light of the frightening experience he had just been through, because it was the safest course for him in terms of his political survival. Although patriotism was also of central concern to Olivier, it was only one factor shaping his vision. As Michael Anderegg has shrewdly observed, "Far from simply making a wartime propaganda film, Olivier was doing a number of different things in *Henry V*. He was honoring Shakespeare and simultaneously promoting himself as the world's premier Shakespearean actor. He attempted to balance theater and film, realism and artifice. He was making a Shakespeare film that at the same time commented on the challenges involved in making a Shakespeare film. In producing an art film aimed at a popular audience, he was promoting both Shakespeare and the British cinema."[58]

OLIVIER AND THE WAR EFFORT

After an acting career on stage and in film, including three sojourns in Hollywood, the last in the late 1930s, Olivier returned to England to take part in the war effort. Although he played in a few war films, his dream was to become a pilot (he had taken flying lessons in California before returning to England), and in mid-April 1941 he signed on with the Fleet Air Arm and was posted to the naval air station at Worthy Down, near Winchester. Despite his wish to be sent on flying missions, the Ministry of Information saw Lieutenant Olivier's talents as lying elsewhere and preferred to put him to use making patriotic speeches. A film clip of one such performance, at a Royal Albert Hall rally in January 1943 marking the twenty-fifth anniversary of the Red Army, which was then battling the Germans, ended with the following impassioned exhortation: "We will go forward, heart, nerve, and spirit steeled. We will attack! We will smite our foes! We will conquer! And in all our deeds in this and in other lands, from this hour on our watchwords will be urgency, speed, courage: urgency in all our decisions, speed in the execution of all our plans, courage in face of all our enemies. And may God bless our cause!"[59]

Many would agree that Olivier's "greatest contribution to the war effort," as one of his biographers put it, was his conversion of Shakespeare's *Henry V* into "a rousingly patriotic cinema epic."[60] Leslie Banks, who plays the part of the Chorus in the film, took the patriotism plaudit a step further: "Larry ended up fighting his war with the making of *Henry V*, and he won a more glorious victory than most of the field marshals of the British army."[61] But it took a while for the film to happen, and in the meantime the early period of the war was a time of disappointment and frustration for the actor. Doing *Henry V* on film wasn't originally Olivier's idea. The impetus came from Dallas Bower, a BBC producer. Bower had initially wanted to do a television adaptation of the play, but this idea didn't pan out.[62] With the outbreak of war, having meanwhile moved over to the Ministry of Information, he asked Olivier in 1942 to read the key speeches from *Henry V* in a radio version. An Italian producer, Filippo del Giudice, heard the broadcast and, aside from being captivated by Olivier's reading, decided that with its spectacular pageantry and patriotic subject matter, in particular the stunning English victory over the French at Agincourt in 1415, *Henry V* would make an ideal propaganda film. After convincing the Ministry of Information that "every care would be taken to stress the propaganda angle," del Giudice set about persuading Olivier.[63] Olivier had done an unsuccessful film version of *As You Like It* years earlier, and this experience, along with others' indifferent efforts to film Shakespeare's plays (which he found "absolutely appalling"), had persuaded him that "the Bard's works were best left to the stage."[64] Predictably, therefore, when del Giudice approached him, his first reaction was less than enthusiastic. But he talked it over with his close friend and fellow actor Ralph Richardson, who told him, "You *must* do it. But do it on your terms. Total artistic control. Write the script. And direct it yourself."[65] (Others also advised Olivier, as one of them put it, "to direct the bloody thing yourself."[66]) Olivier went back to del Giudice, fully expecting to be scoffed at because the production was bound to be hugely expensive and he had, up to that point in his career, never directed or written anything. To his great surprise, del Giudice quietly agreed, saying, "I do whatever you want." The only condition was a stipulation in Olivier's contract that, for an additional payment of £15,000 tax free, he agree not to produce, direct, or act in a film, in Britain or the United States, for a period of eighteen months from the release of *Henry V* to prevent him from doing anything that would compete with it.[67]

HENRY V AND AGINCOURT IN HISTORY

One of the hardest challenges facing Olivier was the transforming of Shakespeare's play into a film. But before I discuss this process, something must be said of the far steeper challenge the Bard himself had faced in transposing an actual historical episode into the spatially and temporally confining framework of a play. This was of course particularly true of the Battle of Agincourt. It was less true of the portrayal of Henry V, though this lesser difficulty didn't keep Shakespeare from taking considerable liberties anyway in his reconfiguring of the English king. The historical Henry V was already well established as an English national icon by the 1590s. Shakespeare added to the icon's worth "by putting his most patriotic speeches into Henry's mouth." He also made the king into a more likeable person, possessed of "a cheeriness that the real Henry never had."[68]

During Henry's childhood, there were times when it was not clear that he was ever going to become the king of England. Although he was born in 1386, it was not until 1399, when Richard II was ousted, that Henry's father acceded to the throne and he himself became the heir apparent. England was far from united during these years, and there was frequent fighting among different factions. There were also significant political differences between Henry and his father, resulting in Henry's being removed from the king's council on more than one occasion. It is possible that the tradition of Henry's youthful peccadilloes, immortalized by Shakespeare, was in part related to this unstable situation. It is also possible that the tradition was an imagined one from start to finish.[69] Whatever the truth, with his father's death in 1413, Henry became king and promptly made clear his intention to rule England as a united nation. When domestic threats emerged, he responded with firmness and ruthlessness. One early threat, for example, was a planned uprising by the Lollards,* which Henry learned about from informers in January 1414, shortly after his assumption of the kingship. The Lollard leader was alleged to have been John Oldcastle, who had previously been sentenced to death for his heresy but had escaped and was now scheming to assassinate the king and his brothers. Apart from being treasonous, this scheme was an act of personal infidelity because Oldcastle was a friend—the original, it has been argued, of Shakespeare's Falstaff[70]—who had fought alongside Henry on a number of past occasions. The plotters were rounded up, thirty-one of them hanged, and an additional seven burned at the stake for heresy. Although Oldcastle himself managed to escape again, he was apprehended in 1417 and executed by burning. Henry made no attempt to save any of these men. Indeed, "he declared in parliament that the intent of Lollardy was not only 'to adnull and subvert the Christian faith and the law of God' but also 'to destroy our sovereign lord the king himself.'" Heresy and treason had become intertwined in Henry's mind, contends Ian Mortimer, "and deviation in matters of faith was synonymous with political rebellion. Those who saw their faith as a justification for treason could expect no mercy."[71]

---

*The Lollards were followers of John Wycliffe, a prominent theologian who was dismissed from Oxford University in 1381 because of his heretical criticisms of the Roman Church.

Henry V's coldblooded actions, either in the administration of justice (as he saw it) or in contravention of contemporary military traditions, were well documented in his behavior away from England also. Determined to recover English sovereignty over the French, Henry sailed for France on August 11, 1415. During the Battle of Agincourt, fought on October 25, 1415, where he won his greatest victory, he gave the order to his soldiers to kill their prisoners (among whom were some of the most illustrious French aristocrats), an act generally seen as a violation of medieval Christian war etiquette.[72] In 1417, two years after the Battle of Agincourt, Henry renewed the war against France on a larger scale. Lower Normandy was swiftly conquered, and Rouen, cut off from Paris, was encircled in the summer of 1418. "This siege," according to one account, "cast an even darker shadow on the reputation of the king than his order to slay the French prisoners at Agincourt. Rouen, starving and unable to support the women and children of the town, forced them out through the gates believing that Henry would allow them to pass through his army unmolested. However, Henry refused to allow this, and the expelled women and children died of starvation in the ditches surrounding the town." The English finally conquered Rouen in January 1419 and soon were at the walls of Paris. Now, after lengthy negotiations, the Treaty of Troyes was signed (in May 1420), recognizing Henry as the heir and regent of France and disinheriting the dauphin Charles, actions that were soon sealed by Henry's marriage in June 1420 to Catherine of Valois, the daughter of the French king, Charles VI (see chapter 4). Although Henry returned to France once again, it turned out to be his final campaign because he died suddenly of dysentery in August 1422 at age thirty-six.[73]

As medieval battles go, Agincourt is fairly well documented. There is general agreement regarding its bare outlines, which a sizable number of contemporary chroniclers recorded. Although there are wild discrepancies in regard to the number of combatants, especially on the French side,[74] we have a reasonably accurate picture of the chronology; the precise location of the fighting has never been disputed; and the topography of the battlefield has not changed much over five centuries. There is a good bit of consensus also in regard to the battle's broad characterization. It was, the late John Keegan tells us, "a victory of the weak over the strong, of the common soldier over the mounted knight, of resolution over bombast, of the desperate, cornered and far from home, over the proprietorial and cocksure." These themes are captured in Shakespeare's play. But, Keegan adds, Agincourt was "also a story of slaughter-yard behaviour and of outright atrocity"—features that, although hinted at in the play, were harder to depict.[75]

In part, the "slaughter-yard behaviour" had to do with the conditions under which the battle was fought. The weather had been atrocious on the eve of the engagement, creating extreme muddy conditions. In accounting for the decisive English victory, Larissa Taylor, although acknowledging the mud, appears to assign primacy to Henry's talent as "one of the great military strategists of all time."[76] Others have put more emphasis on the mud. "Above everything else," writes Mortimer, "[Henry] was lucky that it rained so heavily at Agincourt on the night of 24 October. If it had not, the French wings might have been able to charge into the advancing English archers, scattering them before they could shoot enough arrows, thereby winning the battle for France and humiliating Henry and undermining his pretensions to be doing God's work."[77] The medieval military historian Clifford Rogers, after presenting a detailed and knowledgeable account of the battle, suggests a more complex set of reasons for the French defeat: "The French lost because of the fighting qualities of the English *and* the effectiveness of the longbow *and* the mud *and* their own errors" (which he spells out).[78]

As in all efforts to reconstruct the events of the past, the hardest of all to portray, for historians no less than for playwrights, is the sensory experience of the fighting: "what the Agincourt arrow-cloud can have looked, or sounded like; what the armoured men-at-arms sought to do to each other at the moment of the first clash; at what speed and in what density the French cavalry charged down; how the mêlée—the densely packed mass of men in hand-to-hand combat—can have appeared to a detached onlooker, say to men in the French third line; what level the noise of the battle can have reached and how the leaders made themselves heard—if they did so—above it."[79] Here, the filmmaker, with his modern cinematic technology, arguably operated at an advantage over the playwright. The most difficult task facing Olivier was not the depiction of the experience of battle (though of course this could be done only up to a point), but the reimagining of *Henry V* as a motion picture without in the process completely abandoning its original theatrical features and form.

MAKING A PLAY INTO A MOVIE

According to his own account, Olivier took his cue in wrestling with this issue directly from Shakespeare:

> The main problem I had was to find a style so that Shakespeare actors could do their stuff but still be acceptable to a cinema audience. I wondered at first how to begin the film. In the play Shakespeare complains about the confines of the Globe Theatre. He uses the Chorus to narrate and comment, showing his frustration that the Globe audience wasn't in France. I wondered how to present the Chorus. Have him as a voice-over perhaps? I realised I had to put him where Shakespeare put him—in the Globe. The play was telling me the style of the film.
>
> And so we have an Elizabethan actor challenging the very unruly audience to use their imaginations. And that would challenge the film audience, I felt. So I set the first few scenes in the Globe to get the audience used to the language, and enjoy the comedy of Falstaff, Nym, Bardolf [sic] and Pistol. I, as Henry, would be an actor waiting in the wings. I was getting the film audience to become restless and feel confined in the Globe, and then we leave the theatre, and Henry is saying, "Now sits the wind fair, and we will aboard. And we're off to France."[80]

Another challenge for Olivier (one that Eisenstein did not face) was the limited funding available for the production: "He couldn't afford to shoot miles of film, so he worked out every shot, every movement, every angle, and every cut. He wanted, wherever possible, to shoot in one take. He set himself an enormously difficult task as a first-time film director."[81] But, although the film still ended up costing £474,888 to make, more than any previous British picture, it established Olivier as "not just the best-known Shakespearean actor in the world, but the first director to ever successfully transfer Shakespeare to the cinema. And he had done it all virtually on his own, under his own artistic control."[82] As for del Giudice, although the funds he had raised to make the movie were insufficient, forcing him to relinquish controlling interest in his film company to J. Arthur Rank to obtain additional backing, when he saw the final version of the film, he remarked, "I was not exaggerating when I said this masterpiece will make film history and that millions will be talking about it for ages to come."[83]

THE FILM

In the film's original version (but not in the DVD versions available in Britain and the United States), its patriotic message is made clear from the outset with the following dedication:

> To
> the Commandos and Airborne Troops
> of Great Britain
> The spirit of whose ancestors it has been humbly attempted to recapture
> in some ensuing scenes
> This Film is Dedicated.[84]

As already noted, the film opens in the Globe Playhouse.[85] An aerial view of London is shown based on an engraving from 1600. The Chorus appears and, after introducing "the warlike Harry," hints at what is to come in regard both to the plot and to the setting in which the plot unfolds by suggesting the limitations of the Globe's physical space: "Can this cockpit hold the vasty fields of France? Or may we cram within this wooden O the very casques that did affright the air at Agincourt?" He then challenges the audience to let their imaginations roam free: "Think, when we talk of horses, that you see them, printing their proud hoofs i' th' receiving earth; for 'tis your thoughts that now must deck our kings, carry them here and there, jumping o'er times, turning th' accomplishment of many years into an hour-glass."

The scene shifts to an antechamber in King Henry's palace, where the archbishop of Canterbury and the bishop of Ely argue the justifications for an English invasion of France. This episode is much condensed from Shakespeare's original scene, and Olivier makes the clerics look quite foolish. Not wanting viewers of the film to get caught up in the ambiguous political motivations of the English, he shifts the focus to the provocation offered by an arrogant French envoy who, on being admitted to the king's presence, goads him with a present of tennis balls from the French dauphin—a clear allusion to Henry's "wilder days" when, heedless of his responsibilities as heir apparent, he caroused with the likes of Sir John Falstaff, a comic figure of ill repute. The English king is clearly stung by the French heir apparent's taunting. In language dripping with sarcasm, he thanks the dauphin for his present and then, springing to his feet, adds:

"When we have matched our racquets to these balls, we will in France, by God's grace, play a set. . . . And tell the pleasant Prince, this mock of his hath turned these balls to gun-stones, and his soul shall stand sore-chargèd for the wasteful vengeance that shall fly from them."[86] The Chorus appears and comments on the preparations being made for war. A boy displays a billboard to the audience indicating a change of scene to the Boar's Head tavern. This is followed by a comical epi-sode with Nym, Bardolph, and Pistol—all members of the band attached to Falstaff—as well as Pistol's wife, Mistress Quickly. The exchanges among them are punctuated frequently by audience laughter and applause (we are still in the Globe Playhouse). A boy appears on the balcony of the tavern and announces that Sir John is very sick. The three men and Mistress Quickly go quickly to Falstaff's bedside. The Chorus announces: "The King is set from London, and the scene is now transported, gentles, to Southampton. There is the playhouse now, there must you sit, and thence to France."[87] Although the setting is no longer the Globe, the use of artifice contin-ues as a model shot of Southampton in 1415 C.E. is shown on the screen. Aboard a ship, the archbishop of Canterbury is giving a benediction to the kneeling King Henry and his knights. Henry, acting the part of a compassionate monarch, orders that a man who the day before had denounced him be set free. Stepping ashore from the ship, he walks over to a table on the quay, where to the cheers of his soldiers he announces: "Let us deliver our puissance into the hand of God, putting it straight in expedition. Cheerly to sea the signs of war advance. . . . " With a seal, he stamps a paper on the table, then completes the rhyme, "No King of England, if not King of France." He turns and walks away, followed by Canterbury and the nobles.[88] The illusion that the action has returned to the Globe Playhouse is dis-solved as a real tavern (the Boar's Head) is shown. Through an upper-story window, the camera enters the room where Falstaff, in a state of delirium, struggles to sit up in bed and murmurs, "God save thy Grace—King Hal—my royal Hal, God save thee, my sweet boy." With a pained expression on his face, Falstaff then hears the voice (off-screen) of King Henry bluntly conveying to him (in lines taken from *Henry IV, Part Two*) the message that "Hal" is now a mature king and no longer the irresponsible lad of yore: "I know thee not, old man. . . . Presume not that I am the thing I was; for God doth know, so shall the world perceive, that I have turned away my former self, so shall I those that kept me company."[89] As Henry finishes speaking, Falstaff lies back on the bed and breathes his last.

The Chorus announces a scene shift to Southampton, where the English fleet is being made ready. A model shot of the ships becomes visible through the mist. The fleet sets sail, heading for Harfleur on the coast of Normandy (see map 4 in chapter 4).[90]

The next sequence takes us to the French palace. The French have learned of Henry's war preparations, and an old and frail King Charles VI, taking the English threat seriously, instructs the noblemen in his presence and the dauphin to ready France's defenses. The dauphin, smug and overconfident, agrees that the French side should prepare itself but minimizes the extent of the threat. The French constable states his belief that the dauphin is badly mistaken. King Charles, sharing the constable's conviction, reminds the assembled that Henry is of the same "bloody strain" as Edward, Black Prince of Wales, who at an earlier time brought so much grief to France.

At this point, trumpets sound, and it is announced that ambassadors from King Henry have arrived and wish an audience with the French monarch. Charles receives the envoys, headed by the duke of Exeter, who delivers a blunt statement of Henry's demand that Charles resign his crown and kingdom, which rightfully belongs to the English king and his heirs, but if he chooses not to acquiesce in Henry's demand, there will be bloody consequences. He then turns to the dauphin and informs him that King Henry has for him only "scorn and defiance, slight regard, contempt, . . . an if your father's highness do not, in grant of all demands at large, sweeten the bitter mock you sent his Majesty, he'll make your Paris Louvre shake for it." King Charles informs Exeter that the French will respond to the English demands on the following day. The ambassador presses him to do so "with all speed" lest King Henry come to France himself to question the delay. King Charles faints.[91]

The scene changes to English soldiers storming the beach at Harfleur. To spur them on, Henry delivers an impassioned speech ending with "God for Harry, England and Saint George!" The soldiers cheer in response and repeat the concluding charge. The siege commences. In short order, the walls of the town having been badly battered by English cannon fire, the governor of Harfleur announces to Henry, who stands outside the gates at the head of his army, that Harfleur surrenders because the dauphin has failed to respond to his call for help. Henry commands that the gates be opened. He then orders the duke of Gloucester to enter the town with his soldiers, fortify it against the French, but treat the population with mercy. Henry announces that he and the rest of the English force will remain in Harfleur overnight and then, because winter is approaching and many of the soldiers are ill, retire to Calais.*

After being apprised of the loss of Harfleur, the French court remains confident of its military superiority. King Charles orders that Henry be captured and brought to him as a prisoner. The French herald, Mountjoy, approaches Henry to deliver the French king's warning that England shall repent Henry's folly and that Henry should therefore consider his ransom. Henry tells the herald, "My ransom is this frail and worthless body; my army, but a weak and sickly guard. Yet, God before, tell him we will come on, though France herself . . . stand in our way." The king throws a purse of money to the herald for his labor.[92]

The French effort to persuade Henry to back down having failed, the armies of the two adversaries camp for the night, only fifteen hundred paces separating them. The camera zooms in on the camp of the French, where the mood is festive and celebratory. Certain of victory, the French are impatient for the day to come. The constable boasts of the superiority of his armor, the duke of Orleans and the dauphin of the excellence of their horses. They compete with each other in disparaging the enemy they will soon confront. "It is now two o'clock," ventures Orleans, "but, let me see—by ten we shall have each a hundred Englishmen."[93]

The atmosphere is very different in the English camp. The Chorus (off-screen) sets the tone: "The poor condemnèd English, like sacrifices, by their watchful fires sit patiently and inly ruminate the morning's danger." King Henry visits with his soldiers, "bids them good morrow with a modest smile and calls them brothers, friends and countrymen. A largess universal, like the sun, his liberal eye doth give to everyone, thawing cold fear, that mean and gentle all behold, as may unworthiness define, a little touch of Harry in the night." Henry borrows the cloak of the elderly Sir Thomas Erpingham and, now unrecognizable as king, moves about chatting and exchanging thoughts with his soldiers. He comes upon three

---

*Calais, on the northern coast of France, had been besieged and taken by King Edward III of England in 1347, early in the so-called Hundred Years War. Edward drove out the French inhabitants and peopled the port with English. It remained a part of England for the next two centuries, during which time it was viewed as the English gateway to France.

soldiers seated around a campfire. He sits down with them, and they talk. He tells the soldiers that he believes the king to be a man just like them. In contrast to the arrogance and flippancy that define the mood in the French camp, the thoughts of the English with whom the disguised Henry converses are very much focused on death. One of the soldiers, a sweet-faced country lad, speaking very deliberately, describes the terror common to all men on the eve of combat: "But if the cause be not good, the King himself hath a heavy reckoning to make, when all those legs and arms and heads chopped off in a battle shall join together at the latter day, and cry all, 'We died at such a place.' . . . I'm afraid there are few die well that die in a battle."

The soldiers move away, except for the country lad, who has fallen asleep on the ground. Henry, seated in the dark next to the sleeping youth and responding to the gloomy sentiments he has just heard, soliloquizes on the heavy burden of kingship: "Upon the King! Let us our lives, our souls, our debts, our careful wives, our children, and our sins, lay on the King! We must bear all. What infinite heartsease must kings forego that private men enjoy!" Erpingham sees the king and tells him his nobles are looking for him. Henry starts walking back to the camp. He hears prayers being chanted in one of the tents and, pulling back the flap, sees a service in progress. He turns to Erpingham and tells him to collect the nobles at his tent. He then kneels on the ground outside the tent and offers a prayer of his own. He bumps into Gloucester, who tells him the army awaits his presence. The king and Gloucester walk together up the hill.[94]

The English nobles are readying themselves fearfully for a battle in which, as one of them remarks, they are outnumbered five to one. Henry overhears the earl of Westmoreland expressing the wish that the English army were larger. Approaching the group, he remarks:

> If we are marked to die, we are enough to do our country loss; and if to live, the fewer men, the greater share of honour. . . . This day is called the Feast of Crispian: He that outlives this day, and comes safe home, will stand a-tiptoe when this day is named and rouse him at the name of Crispian. . . . Old men forget; . . . but he'll remember, with advantages, what feats he did that day. . . . This story shall the good man teach his son, and Crispin Crispian shall ne'er go by from this day to the ending of the world but we in it shall be remembered, we few, we happy few, we band of brothers. For he today that sheds his blood

with me, shall be my brother, be he ne'er so base. And gentlemen in England, now a-bed, shall think themselves accursed they were not here, and hold their manhoods cheap whiles any speaks that fought with us upon Saint Crispian's day.

Henry is surrounded by his army during this speech. The soldiers cheer their king, who announces to them, "You know your places. God be with you all!"

Final preparations for battle are now in progress on both sides. English soldiers are driving stakes into the ground with wooden mallets. The stakes are driven at an angle and their points resharpened in order to catch a charging French warhorse in the chest.[95] A soldier helps King Henry put on his chain mail. The dauphin is lowered by a winch onto his horse. The constable and another knight toast the dauphin and company with wine. Englishmen continue banging in stakes. Arrows are distributed to English archers. English soldiers are shown sharpening the stakes. Mountjoy, the

FIGURE 5.2 Laurence Olivier as Henry V delivering the "band of brothers" speech on the eve of the Battle of Agincourt in his film *Henry V* (United Artists, 1944). (From the Harvard Theatre Collection, Houghton Library, Harvard University [call number: TCS 37].)

French herald, rides into the English camp and is escorted to King Henry, now on his horse in full armor. Representing the constable, Mountjoy asks the king one more time if he is prepared to offer terms for his ransom "before thy most assurèd overthrow." "I pray thee," Henry responds, "bear my former answer back." The English soldiers cheer. The music begins. "Come thou no more for ransom, gentle herald, they shall have none, I swear, but these my bones, which if they have as I will leave 'em them, shall yield them little. Tell the Constable." Mountjoy promises to do so and bids Henry farewell. As the king leaves, the herald calls after him: "Thou never shalt hear herald any more."[96]

In the Battle of Agincourt, which now commences, the French cavalry, like the Teutonic Knights in *Nevsky* heavily armored and wearing creepy-looking helmets, are at one end of the field, a line of English archers,

FIGURE 5.3 The English side's unarmored archers let fly their arrows at Agincourt in Olivier's film *Henry V* (United Artists, 1944). (From the Harvard Theatre Collection, Houghton Library, Harvard University [call number: TCS 37.)

many wearing neither armor nor helmet, at the other. The French cavalry charge forward. At a signal from Henry, the English let fly their arrows. Two additional lines of English archers fire. Many of the arrows strike their targets. The music resumes. The French chargers are in complete disarray. The English archers keep firing. A second wave of French cavalry charge forward while the first wave retreats, causing the two waves to become entangled with each other. The English archers continue firing while running forward. French infantrymen become enmeshed with the cavalry. A third wave of French cavalry charge, English archers retreating. English infantrymen jump Robin Hood–like from the branches of trees and attack the advancing cavalry with their knives. English and French infantrymen engage in hand-to-hand fighting. King Henry leads a flank attack with his knights. He commends the English side for having done well but acknowledges that the French still hold the field.

The French knights are nevertheless distraught. The dauphin and the duke of Orleans cannot believe the English show of strength. A party of marauding French knights rides into the English camp. One knight cuts down a tent and kills a boy; another sets fire to a tent in which another dead boy is seen. The French knights ride away. Henry on foot sees the dead boy and exclaims, "I was not angry since I came to France until this instant." The king mounts his horse and rides full tilt back to the battle-field, where he challenges the French constable. With his sword, Henry knocks the constable's sword out of his hand. The constable then hits Henry's hand with his mace, causing the king's sword to go flying. Henry now strikes the constable on the chin with his mailed fist. The constable falls to the ground and lies there. As English soldiers gather around the constable's body, Henry rides up to the English herald: "Take a trumpet, Herald. Ride thou unto the horsemen on yon hill; if they will fight with us, bid them come down, or void the field; they do offend our sight."

No sooner has Henry issued these instructions than the French herald appears. It is now the English king's turn to mock: "God's will, what mean's this, Herald? Com'st thou again for ransom?" "No, great king," Mountjoy replies, "I come to thee for charitable licence, that we may wander o'er this bloody field to book our dead and then to bury them. The day is yours." As the king takes off his helmet, a castle appears in the distance. The music starts. Henry asks the name of the castle and is told that it is called Agincourt. Henry: "Then call we this the field of Agin-court, fought on the day of Crispin Crispianus." Mountjoy kneels and kisses the English king's hand. A loud chorus of men's voices is heard.

The camera slowly pans the desolate battlefield strewn with the bodies of both French and English soldiers, a riderless horse roaming among the dead. The English herald presents Henry with a paper indicating that French losses in the battle total ten thousand; he then presents a second paper giving the English losses at "but five-and-twenty score." Henry gives thanks to God and calls out, "Let there be sung *Non Nobis* and *Te Deum*"—the chanting of the soldiers begins as he mounts his horse— "And then to Calais and to England then where ne'er from France arrived more happier men." The English army is shown walking in procession toward Agincourt village.[97]

The film's penultimate scene takes place in the French palace, where King Henry and the French royals agree on the desirability of changing "all griefs and quarrels" between them into "love," the English king asks the French to acquiesce fully in "all our just demands," and, as was the common practice of the day, King Henry woos Princess Catherine with the aim of cementing the bond between the two royal houses. The wooing, despite Henry's fractured French and Catherine's even more fractured English, is successful and blessed by King Charles: "Take her, fair son, that the contending kingdoms of France and England, whose very shores look pale with envy of each other's happiness may cease their hatred; that never war advance his bleeding sword 'twixt England and fair France." All assembled say "Amen!" Celebratory choral music is heard. The film ends with a return to the Globe Playhouse. Henry and Catherine are crowned and, to the accompaniment of audience applause, seated side by side on adjacent thrones. The Chorus enters and supplies a formulaic wrap-up. As at the beginning of the film, we see an image of London in 1600 with the Globe Playhouse in the foreground. A playbill flutters down from the sky and, striking the camera lens, announces the cast and credits.[98]

THE RESONANCE BETWEEN OLIVIER'S *HENRY V* AND BRITAIN IN THE LATTER STAGES OF WORLD WAR II

The most conspicuous link between Olivier's film and the British situation in late 1944 is arguably the film's dramatic echoing, only months after D-Day, of the landing on the beaches of northern France. This connection had already been made with the original Shakespeare play. When a landing craft of the East Yorkshire Regiment neared the beach at

La Brèche in early June 1944, Major "Banger" King read *Henry V* aloud to his men: "On, on you noble English! Whose blood is fet from fathers of war-proof."[99] What Olivier's film did was strengthen the association between *Henry V* and the war. World War II had been a grim experience for the British, and in November 1944, when *Henry V* opened in London, the terror was anything but over. The optimism created by the June invasion had been tempered by military setbacks in Europe, and in the period between June 1944 and March 1945 London and the southern areas of the country were menaced by Hitler's "vengeance weapons," the V-1 "flying bombs" and V-2 rockets (first launched in September), which resulted (according to one count) in more than 8,000 civilians killed, some 22,000 seriously wounded, and 25,000 houses in the London region destroyed or damaged beyond repair.[100] In these circumstances, Olivier's film offered the British, at an especially vulnerable moment in their experience of the war, the possibility of a dramatic turnabout and glorious ending.

Beyond this, the King Henry portrayed in the film measured up well against English notions of the ideal warrior and compassionate leader of his people. As has often been pointed out, the Henry of Shakespeare's play, his bright qualities darkened by periodic acts of coldness and cruelty, is far more complex psychologically than Olivier's Henry. In the play, Henry, while in Southampton before departing for France, condemns his boyhood friend Scroop and two others to death for treasonous plotting; later, standing outside the gates of Harfleur, he promises the most vicious actions against the town's population if the governor does not surrender immediately to the English, threatening his soldiers' defilement of their "shrill-shrieking daughters," their "fathers taken by the silver beards and their most reverend heads dashed to the walls," their "naked infants spitted upon pikes whiles the mad mothers with their howls confused do break the clouds"; and on the eve of the engagement at Agincourt, he orders the execution of Bardolph, another companion of his carefree youth, for having robbed a church.[101] Winston Churchill, who had earlier encouraged Olivier to make a movie of *Henry V*, was uncomfortable with these three scenes, so they were removed from the final film. (Two other parts of the original play that were omitted, because retaining them would have compromised the film's patriotic spirit, were Henry's controversial order to kill the French prisoners and the final speech of the Chorus, which states that those running the country during the infancy of

Henry V's son and successor, Henry VI, eventually "lost France and made his England bleed."[102]) The problematic scenes duly excised, the prime minister, who with his wife and daughter had a private showing of the picture at his official country residence at the time of its London release in late November 1944, "went into ecstasies about it," according to his private secretary.[103] As Douglas Brode has observed, the film's Henry "is what Churchill requested: the fantasy hero figure England needed during its darkest hour. Olivier had fashioned the right film and Henry for that moment in time."[104]

Olivier's idealized Henry is also reflected in his depiction of Agincourt. Much as in Eisenstein's Battle on the Ice, Olivier's Agincourt has a David-and-Goliath quality about it. The French, like the Teutonic Knights, are heavily armored, smugly confident of victory against the ragtag English, and quite capable of committing atrocities in the process (the savage killing of noncombatant pages in the English camp). The English, in contrast, although greatly outnumbered, manage to pierce the French armor (literally as well as figuratively) with their Robin Hood bows and arrows and, as in the Battle on the Ice in *Nevsky*, bring the battle to a successful conclusion when their heroic Henry bests the French constable in one-on-one combat.[105] Brode offers an illuminating comparison between Olivier's Agincourt and that of Kenneth Branagh, who refilmed Shakespeare's play in the very different social/historical setting of the late 1980s. Where Branagh, his views shaped by the lingering influence of the Vietnam tragedy and the folly of the more recent Falklands War, portrays a somberly realistic Agincourt, evoking the muck and squalor of the trench warfare of World War I, Olivier's romanticized Agincourt, in both the fighting itself and the "band of brothers" speech on the battle's eve, is "imbued with the 'good war' sensibility of World War II,"[106] another war men might "think themselves accursed" for not having been part of.

There is an irony here too delicious to be passed over. Olivier not only romanticized the film he made, he also (years later) romanticized the making of it: "There we were, a band of artists and technicians, humble in our souls because Hitler was killing our countrymen, imbued with a sense of history, gallantry overcoming wartime shortages and problems."[107] But apart from the fact that the Agincourt battle was filmed in Ireland, where a supply of able-bodied men was ready at hand owing to Ireland's neutrality in the war, many of the extras hired for the rest of the shooting (which took place in Denham, England) were

English, American, or Australian troops who had evaded military service. As Anthony Holden remarks in his biography of Olivier, "A less patriotic band would have been hard to find."[108]

As an expression of British patriotism during the war, the film *Henry V* had one problem. The French, for all their less than admirable qualities as displayed in the film—a representation of the French national character that some French bitterly protested[109]—weren't convincing stand-ins for Nazi Germany. In Eisenstein's *Nevsky*, the presentation of patriotism is two dimensional, focused equally on the depravity of the German aggressors and the glorious spirit of a unified Mother Russia. A case can of course be made for the fact that in June 1944, when D-Day took place, although all of France was by this point under German occupation (the southern part of the country having been occupied in late 1942), day-to-day administration of the country was still in the hands of the collaborationist Vichy regime. But this argument is less than convincing, especially when, following England's triumph, Henry marries the daughter of the French king and the English and French thrones are joined—a harmonious dénouement that would have been unthinkable between the Russians and the Germans in *Alexander Nevsky*. Michael Anderegg suggests one way out of this dilemma: "As in Shakespeare's day, England and France were 'friendly enemies,' and a plan by England to invade France, for Henry as well as for Churchill, could be dressed up as a desire to rescue her from wrongful imprisonment."[110] The weight of the patriotism motif in Olivier's *Henry V*, in any case, need not rest on the nature of the enemy. The film is a celebration of the spirit of the British people, of the country's military performance against steep odds, and, of course, of England's greatest poet—all factors capable of inspiring British patriotic feeling.[111]

THE RECEPTION OF *HENRY V* AND THE IMPORTANCE OF TIMING

While still showing in London (where it had an eleven-month run), *Henry V* in the spring of 1945 went on general release in England. It proved a big hit for school outings, helping a generation of schoolchildren "to see Shakespeare through new, and more receptive, eyes." It also made film-going a more up-market activity than it had been previously, research showing that as many as half the people who saw it were not regular patrons of the cinema. A major ingredient in the success of *Henry V* was undeniably William Walton's score, which was modeled on the music Prokofiev had composed for *Nevsky*. The British composer groused about the difficulties he encountered—"How does one distinguish between a crossbow and a long bow musically speaking?"[112]—but Olivier praised the final score as "the most wonderful I've ever heard for a film. In fact," he went on, "for me the music actually made the film. The charge scene [at Agincourt] is really made by William's music."[113] The movie's American premiere was in Boston in April 1946, where it played to full houses for eight months. In New York, it had a run of forty-six weeks, setting a record for a British film and earning for Olivier the New York Film Critics Award for Best Actor of 1946. In March 1947, Hollywood also responded, giving the English actor a Special Academy Award for producing, directing, and starring in a film that had made movie history and in the process greatly raised the standing of the British motion picture industry in the United States. Olivier graciously presented the Oscar to Filippo del Giudice, telling him not inaccurately, "Without you *Henry V* would never have been made."[114]

The box-office success of *Henry V* was in large measure a consequence of the moment in time at which it was presented to the public. If England had not been in the midst of its "most terrible war" in 1944,[115] the film would certainly have been treated respectfully by audiences, and it would have made its mark in the history of the cinema regardless of the number of individuals who viewed it, but its popular appeal would have been far narrower. And the same is true of *Alexander Nevsky*: if it had opened not in 1938 but a half century later, when World War II was long over and Germany was no longer perceived as an aggressor nation, it wouldn't have had the impact it had in the Soviet Union. Timely alignment between story and history, between a narrative and a contemporary historical situation that invites those experiencing it to attach special import to that narrative, was crucially important.

Such alignment, via a process of analogical transference, can very often (perhaps typically) be achieved long after an original historical episode has passed. I will give three examples.

Arthur Miller once observed in regard to his 1953 drama *The Crucible*: "I can almost tell what the political situation in a country is when the play is suddenly a hit there—it is either a warning of tyranny on the way or a reminder of tyranny just past."[116] The reason for Miller's observation is that although his play deals with the late-seventeenth-century witch hunt in Salem, Massachusetts, it is also a thinly disguised reflection of the playwright's outrage at the witch hunt of his own day, McCarthyism, thus making it serviceable as a metaphor for political oppression wherever or however it might occur.

Much the same point can be made about Lillian Hellman's *The Lark*, her adaptation of the French playwright Jean Anouilh's *L'Alouette* (1953), which deals with the fifteenth-century story of Joan of Arc and portrays Joan "as a simple individual conscience struggling against blinkered ideology and all-powerful institutions." Hellman, herself a victim of McCarthyism—along with her longtime companion Dashiell Hammett, who was later sent to prison, she had been called to testify before the House Un-American Activities Committee in 1952—refused to cooperate with the authorities' demand that she divulge the names of associates in the theater who may have had ties to the Communist Party and was as a result placed on the Hollywood blacklist. Her reworking of Anouilh's play predictably put strong emphasis on its heroine's courage, refusal, and defiance; and her political intent was not lost on the audiences in New York City who flocked to its 229 performances in 1955 and 1956, thrilled apparently to see the staging of a drama that showcased a young woman who courageously resisted being trampled under by illegitimate authority, clearly alluding to the American demagoguery of the day.[117]

The third example brings us back to World War II. In late summer 2009, to coincide with the seventieth anniversary of Britain's declaration of war against Germany, Decca released an album titled *We'll Meet Again: The Very Best of Vera Lynn*, which brought together original recordings of songs such as "The White Cliffs of Dover" and "We'll Meet Again," which had won the hearts of British soldiers and bucked up the spirits of anxious loved ones back home during the war. Dame Vera, widely known in that earlier era as the "Forces' Sweetheart," was ninety-two years old in 2009 when her album made the Top 20, and she thought it "hilarious" that she was "back in the charts, . . . higher than U2 and Eminem," which she said she hadn't even heard of until that moment. To explain her success, she said, "Our boys are away again," referring to the British soldiers fighting in Iraq and Afghanistan, "and the music is significant again. And it's a bit of nostalgia, too."[118] The message in the album isn't one of heroic triumphalism, as in Olivier's *Henry V*; it is, much more, one of recovering in a new war context the sentiments of enduring meaning that had originally been voiced in an old one.[119]

Certainly, the opportune alignment of the patriotic thrust of *Henry V* and the historical circumstances prevailing in Europe at the time of its release was a prime factor in the film's popular triumph. But we must not forget that Olivier's film was not just about patriotism, as noted earlier. This is apparent from the reviews, which although almost always drawing attention to the wartime environment in which it was produced, regularly supplemented this connection with a discussion of the film's other virtues. Thus, the American critic James Agee in *Time* magazine noted the setting in which Olivier made *Henry V* and suggested that "in appearance and in most of what they say, the three soldiers with whom Henry talks on the eve of Agincourt might just as well be soldiers of World War II." But Agee also described the film as the "perfect marriage of great dramatic poetry with the greatest contemporary medium for expressing it."[120] Ivan Butler, writing in the magazine *Cinema in Britain*, alluded to the patriotism theme but also noted other aspects of the movie's timeliness: "Olivier's *Henry V* burst like a rising sun on the cinema screen at the end of 1944: seldom can a film's timing have been more apt. The word of the day was 'breakthrough'—for the war, for the Britain of the future—and for Shakespeare on the screen."[121] And the influential (and often controversial) British theater critic Kenneth Tynan commented that "Larry didn't realize it at first, because he was so close to it and so exhausted, but he had created what was perhaps the first true work of art that had ever been put on film."[122] In other words, Olivier's *Henry V* had enduring importance in the history of cinema, as did Eisenstein's *Alexander Nevsky*. But the emotional impact of the film at the moment when it was first shown was intensified many times over by what was then going on in the world—and this is exactly the way it was planned.

CONCLUSION

Again and again in this book, I have emphasized the importance for communities in crisis of a story that alludes to (or even occasionally defines) the core themes of the crisis. In each instance, although the story claims to have its origins in a long-ago time, a major part of its allure derives from its metaphoric evocation of what is taking place in the historical present. The stories I have dealt with have been widely accepted as "true" among the community's members, even though in every case the picture that the stories present of individuals and actions from a much earlier period diverges, often quite sharply, from the picture of what really happened produced by critical historical scholarship. The stories, in other words, form a vital part of the community's cultural endowment—what historians often refer to as its "collective" or "popular memory"—as distinguished from its history in a more formal academic sense, and as such they often do more to shape the community's sense of what happened in the past than historians' careful reconstructive efforts. The story of King Goujian would certainly not have had the impact it had on Chinese in the twentieth century had it not been for an influential historical novel on the story (*Wu Yue chunqiu*) written in the Eastern Han dynasty more than five centuries after the historical Goujian lived. And without Shakespeare—and later Olivier—it is doubtful whether the historical Henry V and Battle of Agincourt would figure as large as they do in the modern consciousness of the British people.[1] The British-born historian Simon Schama goes so far as to argue that Shakespeare's histories were not just the making of the Bard, but the making of the English, too. Here is what he has to say about *Henry V* and World War II:

> Shakespeare awakened the historian in me. He seemed to deliver a certain idea of England at a time when all that was left otherwise was tea and cricket. In 1955, just 10 years after the war, it was as though the Bard had scripted Churchill; that the original "happy few" were prototypes for the boys who flew in Spitfires. What now looks like the shamelessly chauvinistic film version made by Olivier in 1944 as a morale booster for D-Day made perfect sense to us even after the war had ended. Hadn't we all been in it together, Exeter, Harry the King, George the King, Winston, Dunkirk, the Blitz, Normandy? "We band of brothers, for he who today sheds his blood with me shall be my brother"! We needed the pennants of Agincourt and the Crispin–St Georgery of it all, for London was still a sooty pea-soup fog-shrouded place; bombed out buildings in the city and East End sticking up like stumps of blackened teeth.[2]

There is a deeply paradoxical aspect to the process of matching ancient story to present history. Although the story initially appeals because of its central themes, it never lines up exactly with what is transpiring in the historical present, which leads to its being tweaked or even substantially modified so that it speaks to the present situation more unambiguously and serves its inspirational function with greater efficacy. In some instances, the story is even consciously rewritten, with a view less to making it fit than to actually reshaping the present environment. In such cases—the Joan of Arc story under Vichy is a prime example—practically all that remains of the original narrative is the name of its title character. Although this mythologization and even fictionalization of the past is disturbing to many historians, at least in their capacity as historians, for most folks it is not a matter of great moment because they don't generally have the time, the inclination, or the specialized training to unearth the cold facts concerning what really happened in the remote past and are content to live in a world of stories that support—rather than challenge—their strongly held beliefs and emotional preferences.[3] This predisposition, I would suggest, is likely to be especially pronounced in crisis situations.

STORY AND HISTORY: MATCHING AND ADAPTATION

As will be seen from a brief recapitulation of the process of story adaptation (in some instances outright manipulation) undergone in each of the examples I have dealt with, the overall process was reasonably consistent, although there were interesting variations from case to case. The most distinctive example, perhaps, is the Battle of Kosovo (1389), widely perceived as the central event in Serbian history and eventually serving as the cornerstone of Serbian national consciousness. The differences between the mythology and the actual historical circumstances surrounding the battle are sizeable. In terms of its military consequences for the fate of the early Serbian state, Kosovo was not nearly as important as the battle of the Maritsa River valley (1371), which preceded it, or the events of 1459, seventy years later, when Serbia finally succumbed to the Ottoman Turks. Although remembered by Serbs as a calamitous defeat, the Battle of Kosovo seems in fact to have been fairly inconclusive. The myths and legends that grew up around it were fashioned in epic poems and folk ballads soon after its end and were given a strongly Christian reading by the Serbian Orthodox Church (most conspicuously in the Christ-like characteristics invested in the Serbian leader, Prince Lazar, who chose a kingdom in heaven over a kingdom on earth, opting to die heroically rather than live in shame). A core theme in the Kosovo myth is the tension between loyalty and betrayal, as epitomized in the figures of Miloš Obilić and Vuk Branković. This tension reflected the historical reality that after the crushing Serbian defeat of 1371, numbers of Serbs went over to the Ottoman side and very probably, in sharp refutation of the legend, fought alongside the Turks in the Battle of Kosovo. Also subversive of the legendary account, modern scholars have questioned whether the historical Vuk Branković, the very picture of evil in Serbian popular memory, actually betrayed the Serbian side in the battle and whether Miloš Obilić, the iconic representative of Serbian loyalty, even existed historically.

By the time we get to the nineteenth century and the first stirrings of nationalism among the Serbian people, the Kosovo myth, embodying considerable departures from what is believed to have transpired historically, was already firmly in place. But this did not keep its mythic character from continuing to develop, as two celebrated figures from the world of Serbian letters, Vuk Karadžić and Petar Petrović Njegoš, adapted it to the new tide of nationalism. Karadžić, with his published compilations of Serbian epic ballads, transformed the stories of Lazar and the Battle of Kosovo from oral lore into coherent written narratives that supplied Serbian national ideology with its mythical foundations and rendered Serbian epic traditions accessible to recently literate elements among the Serbs themselves, furnishing their new nationalist faith with the folk ingredients it had previously lacked. Njegoš, through his enormously influential poetic drama *The Mountain Wreath*, introduced into Serbian nationalism a strain of rhetoric marked by uncompromising violence, departing in flagrant fashion from the actual history of Muslims in Montenegro (which was far less bloody) and incorporating a vision of Christianity in which nothing was holier than taking revenge against one's enemies. The nationalism-inflected Kosovo story with which Serbs became armed in the course of the nineteenth century was both a reflection of the growing importance of nationalism in Europe in general at the time and a vital source of Serbian thinking and behavior in response to that nationalism.

Psychiatrist Vamik Volkan usefully views the Battle of Kosovo as an example of what he calls a "chosen trauma," a concept that he also applies to other famous battles, such as the Battle of Bilá Hora (White Mountain) near Prague in 1620, which the Czechs still actively commemorate despite their having been decisively defeated in it by the forces of the Hapsburg Empire, and the U.S. Seventh Cavalry Regiment's massacre of Lakota Indians at Wounded Knee in 1890—an event that the descendants of the Native Americans killed there continue to memorialize to this day.[4] The concept of chosen trauma refers to "the shared mental representation of a large group's massive trauma experienced by its ancestors at the hands of an enemy group, and [to] the images of heroes, victims, or both connected with it. Of course," Volkan tells us, "large groups do not intend to be victimized, but they *'choose'* to mythologize and psychologize the mental representation of the event." Thus, "the *'reality'* of what happened during . . . [the Battle of Kosovo] did not matter to the next generations of Serbian people. What mattered for the next generation of Serbs was the evolution of the mental representation of this battle as a chosen trauma."[5]

In certain respects, the encounter between Jewish warriors and the armies of Rome at Masada in 73 C.E. may also be viewed as a chosen trauma. What we know concerning what actually happened at Masada is of questionable reliability. In writing *The Jewish War*, Flavius Josephus presumably made up the speeches by the Sicarii leader Elazar ben Yair, in which the justification for mass suicide (better to die as free men than live as slaves) was presented to the defenders, and much of the rest of what Josephus tells us about the event is tainted by the fact that he had long since betrayed the Jewish cause and gone over to the Roman side. Unlike the Battle of Kosovo, the fall of Masada, rather than being promptly memorialized in folk ballads and epic poetry, rapidly faded from Jewish consciousness. Even after the tenth century, when a Hebrew adaptation of *The Jewish War* appeared in Europe, Masada appears to have had little impact on medieval Jewish readers; there certainly is no indication that the fortress's fall to the Romans in 73 C.E., little known within the larger Jewish community even at the time, was remembered by later generations of Jews as a central trauma in Jewish history.

In fact, it was not until many centuries later—when significant numbers of Jews journeyed to Palestine in the years after World War I in response to the call of Zionism, the desperate situation of the Jewish population in eastern Europe in the 1920s, and new restrictions on foreign entry into the United States—that the Masada story began its migration from the outer fringes of Jewish history to the very center of Jewish national consciousness. The early Jewish settlers in Palestine faced a daunting array of problems. Many of them had been traumatized by their experiences in Europe. Many were desperately poor. They often found it difficult to adjust to the very different physical environment of Palestine, added to which many settlers did not speak or understand modern Hebrew. And from the beginning there had been friction between the new Jewish migrants and the Arab population long resident in the area. Jews hailed the publication of a modern Hebrew translation of *The Jewish War* in 1923, which reinforced in their minds the legitimacy of their presence in Palestine. But, as we have seen, the ancient events at Masada took up only a very small part of Josephus's work. In the bleak circumstances the settlers faced in the 1920s, it was Yitzhak Lamdan's poem *Masada* (1927), with its powerful evocation of the predicament facing the Jewish defenders of the ancient fortress as a metaphor for the tension between desperation and hope felt by so many early-twentieth-century Jews in Palestine, that really established Masada as a chosen trauma in the Jews' minds. The poem became an immediate sensation, capturing in heart-rending allegorical language the settlers' overriding concern with survival in a desolate and unwelcoming environment.

The poem, which eventually became required reading in Hebrew schools, departed in important respects from Josephus's account of what happened at Masada in 73 C.E. It was about a psychological, not a military, encounter. And its central theme was not mass suicide in preference to enslavement. Rather, although hardly an optimistic poem, it held out a slender reed of hope that the Jewish people, in rebelling against the fate that had dogged their history from the beginning, would on this occasion for once find a more promising path.

The focus on survival that was the central significance of Masada for Jewish settlers in the 1920s did not, however, remain unchanged. As the story became more deeply ingrained in Jewish popular memory, it acquired new metaphoric meanings in response to the evolving circumstances of the Jewish population first in Palestine and later in Israel. The growth of a modern welfare state in the decades after the 1920s, the intensification of Arab nationalism, and the steadily increasing proportion of native-born Jews in the Jewish community as a whole resulted in a situation completely different from that of the earlier generations of settlers. When young Jews read Lamdan's poem, they were less sensitive than their parents and grandparents to the feelings of gloom and uncertainty, ambiguity and fear, contained in it and much more inclined to see its central message as one of heroic defiance, proudly symbolized in the phrase "Never again shall Masada fall!"

The full emergence of Masada as a patriotic symbol came in the early 1940s with the Nazi persecution of the Jews in Europe and the threat to the British Mandate posed by the advance of Field Marshal Rommel's forces toward Egypt. In this environment, youth groups held up the courageous defenders of Masada (along with more recent examples of Jewish heroism) as models for young Jews to emulate. Special emphasis, interestingly, was laid on the Masada defenders "dying holding their weapons," thereby passing over the most troubling aspect of Josephus's account. This emendation of the original narrative came to be widely accepted prior to the establishment of the State of Israel. And after 1948, when the young state was threatened by hostile Arab countries, a large part of the Jewish population saw Masada as a political metaphor for Israeli militancy vis-à-vis its neighbors. This attitude persisted, although it became increasingly negative over time, suggesting a situation that Jews must never allow to occur again in their history. In the meantime, the hold of the original Masada myth-story—secular, patriotic, and heroic—on

Israelis' imaginations began to weaken in the late 1960s and early 1970s. Among the factors that encouraged this process of attrition were the increasing commercialization of the Masada site as it was reconfigured for tourism, Israel's demonstrated military supremacy in the Middle East, the rethinking of Israeli attitudes toward the Holocaust, increasing divisions within Israeli society, and a growing chorus of criticism of the appropriateness of the Masada heroic myth to Israeli national goals.

The stories of King Goujian and Joan of Arc, although vastly different from each other in specific content, bear certain similarities that prompted me to situate them close together in the book. The most obvious similarity is that the top wartime political leaders of the countries in which these stories circulated—Chiang Kai-shek, Charles de Gaulle, and Philippe Pétain—identified strongly with the stories' protagonists.

Another similarity is that the ambiguity and structural complexity of both the Goujian and Joan of Arc stories were sufficient to invite people in different historical situations to fasten upon different aspects of the original story. Thus, in the case of the Goujian narrative, Chiang Kai-shek and the Nationalists stressed the core theme of humiliation and revenge in the ancient saga as a result of the Japanese military threat they faced in the 1920s and 1930s. But after 1949, when the main threat to the Nationalists' survival on Taiwan was not a foreign nemesis but the People's Republic of China with its vastly greater population, territory, and resources, the part of the story that fixed the Nationalists' attention was the fact that the state of Yue, despite the great disparity in wealth and power between it and the state of Wu, was able to completely obliterate Wu after twenty years of patiently building up its population and military strength. Readers will recall a further example of the effect of situational change on the reading of the Goujian story. As long as Chiang Kai-shek was alive, much effort was spent in Taiwan fashioning a close identification between the Nationalist leader and an idealized Goujian, but once Chiang passed from the scene in 1975, the brutal Goujian, who in the original historical narrative emerged after his triumph over Wu, was restored to the story, both in Taiwan and in the People's Republic, sometimes (at least in the People's Republic after Mao Zedong's death, which took place a year after Chiang's) as a means of critiquing the tragic flaws of the now deceased leader.

The adaptation of the Joan of Arc story during World War II was more complicated owing to the fact that both Charles de Gaulle and

Philippe Pétain, the two main French political leaders during the war, strongly identified with Joan even though they were on opposite sides of the conflict. In the hands of a leader such as de Gaulle, the meaning of the Joan story was fairly straightforward: just as Joan of Arc had devoted her brief life to bringing an end to foreign occupation of France in the fifteenth century, de Gaulle led the resistance to the German occupation during the war. Pétain also identified with this core theme in the Joan narrative, but his was a more literal identification: as an ally of France's German conquerors, the Vichy leader was free to target the English specifically as the object of Joan of Arc's enmity and to portray himself, because he had made peace with the Germans (thereby saving France from utter devastation), as a Joan-like savior of France in the 1940s. If the latter identification strikes us today as somewhat strained, it seemed far less so to many French people in the immediate aftermath of the swift German victory in spring 1940. In other respects, to be sure, Vichy's reinvention of Joan of Arc as an example for French youth in an environment heavily imbued with fascist values and as a model of conventional female domesticity praised more for her sewing than for her military prowess must have struck a hollow note among many of Joan's twentieth-century compatriots. Nevertheless, although Vichy's efforts to align the Joan of Arc story with the Pétain government's values and goals were forced, to say the least, the fact that the Pétainists saw such alignment as important was in itself of great significance. It spoke to the desirability, shared by many in France at the time, of having Joan of Arc on (and by) their side during a moment of severe national crisis, regardless of what she was said to represent.

If the Kosovo mythology and (to a lesser degree) the evolving account of the Masada story may be viewed as chosen traumas, this was hardly true of the Eisenstein and Olivier films dealt with in chapter 5, both of which constructed past events in triumphant rather than traumatic terms. Also, in contrast to the operation of the Kosovo and Masada myths, the utility of the two films as exercises in political propaganda created in response to a specific military peril was sharply bounded in time: once the war against Germany ended, their value as propaganda ended as well. In other regards, however, particularly in the ways in which they shaped the popular memories of the citizens of the Soviet Union and Great Britain during World War II and even after, Eisenstein's *Alexander Nevsky* and Olivier's *Henry V* embodied some of the same characteristics as the Kosovo and Masada legends.

The central theme of *Nevsky*—the threat of German attack against western Russia and the need for a united Russian response to it—pointed unambiguously to the situation the Soviet Union faced in the late 1930s, and where the historical materials at his disposal did not adequately support other areas of resonance between thirteenth-century Russia and the Soviet Union of the 1930s, Eisenstein did not hesitate to make them do so. The idealization of the historical Alexander as a brilliant military strategist and beloved leader of the Russian people was clearly intended to build support for Stalin's wartime leadership, and the film's portrayal of a Russian nationalism shorn of its religious foundations was much more symptomatic of the Soviet Union of the 1930s than anything that existed in Alexander's day, when nationalism as such was still centuries away and a spirit of religion permeated Russian life.

Eisenstein, in his reshaping of the persona of Alexander, dealt with a figure who had been heavily mythologized already in the thirteenth century, with the result that the cinematic Nevsky he created may be said to have been two removes from the Nevsky of history. Olivier did something similar in his handling of Henry V. There historically really was an English king named Henry V, and there really was a Battle of Agincourt in 1415 in which the English army under Henry's outstanding military leadership defeated the far more powerful forces arrayed against them in France. But Shakespeare's play *Henry V*, although building on these and other historical details, was a work of fiction from start to finish, and Olivier, in turn, although using Shakespeare's play as his point of departure, made further changes (some at the suggestion of Churchill himself) in order to enhance the film's value as British propaganda in the final stages of the war against Hitler. The English invasion of northern France and its eventual military triumph were the common threads in all of the versions (including the original historical account), although the resonance with the D-Day landings of June 1944, only months before the film's release, was much strengthened for contemporaries by the fact that France was under German occupation at the time. But apart from these points of correspondence, Olivier's Henry V was made into a heroic figure of fantasy proportions, not only a brilliant commander on the battlefield, but a man of warmth and compassion, with most of the character defects and acts of brutality distinguishing the historical Henry and to some degree reflected in Shakespeare's rendering of the king either played down or removed entirely. Closely paralleling Eisenstein's idealization of Alexander Nevsky, Olivier's calculated reshaping of Henry V was intended not only to send the British prime minister into ecstasies, but also to make the British public proud to be British, in both of which goals it was a rousing success.

THE FUNCTION OF STORIES IN TIME OF CRISIS

What I have called the power of story, although bearing a special relationship to history (in French and German, the same words, *histoire* and *Geschichte*, are used for both *story* and *history*),[6] permeates virtually all human activities. Journalists live and die by the stories they uncover, analyze, and report to their readers, listeners, or watchers. Politicians use stories to frame the messages they want prospective voters to absorb, to establish a favorable image of themselves (and, no less commonly, an unfavorable image of a rival),[7] and to connect with their audiences.[8] Educational theorists have for some time held the view that "humans are storytelling organisms who, individually and socially, lead storied lives," so that "the study of narrative . . . is the study of the ways humans experience the world."[9] A fourth-year medical student says that fairy tales helped her understand the suffering of her patients; a historian of science argues that stories help us make sense of complicated experiences such as illness and suffering; in the field of psychology, stories play a vital healing role in a range of talk therapies; and according to a Columbia University ad announcing a Graduate Program in Narrative Medicine, "The care of the sick unfolds in stories. The effective practice of healthcare requires the narrative competence to recognize, absorb, interpret, and act on the stories and experiences of others. Medicine practiced with narrative competence is a model for humane and effective healthcare."[10] Story takes a fundamental part in the law and in legal processes of all sorts.[11] It is a vital element in all religious writings and rituals. Myths, children's stories, fairy tales, and legends have been scrutinized for the insights they offer into how corporations and other large organizations operate.[12] Although creative writers earn a living by making up stories, all of us frame our experiences in narrative form when relating them to ourselves or to others. Indeed, one neuroscientist has recently argued that the "fabrication of stories is one of the key businesses in which our brains engage,"[13] and another has described the storytelling function of the brain's left hemisphere—it "takes what information it has and delivers a coherent tale to conscious awareness"—as never stopping, except perhaps during deep sleep.[14] Clearly, the utilization, creation, telling, and remembering of stories are an essential part of what it means to be human.

If this is indeed so, a plausible answer to the question Jerome Bruner poses concerning human beings' "seemingly innate addiction" to story[15] may well be that, like walking erect on two legs, having an opposable thumb, and thinking that babies are cute,[16] our reliance on story is a direct consequence of biological evolution, that without our ability to frame virtually all the things we think, dream, desire, do, and experience in narrative form we would not be able to function—or at least not in ways recognizable to us today. There is a strong possibility, in short, that our brains' capacity to organize nearly everything that happens in our lives in narrative terms, thereby introducing intelligibility (including an understanding of cause and effect) into what would otherwise be unmanageable chaos, gave human beings at some point in the remote past an incalculable survival advantage over those species that could not do this or did it less well.[17]

The fact that story is ubiquitous and "takes the same basic form across cultures"[18] does not mean, of course, that all stories are alike or that they perform the same kinds of functions in the lives of all individuals and societies. Although focusing in some instances on individuals (King Goujian and Joan of Arc), in other instances on important battles (Masada and Kosovo), and in yet other instances on a combination of the two (Nevsky and the Battle on the Ice, Henry V and Agincourt), the stories dealt with in this book possess a common and quite specific set of characteristics. However much modified, mythologized, distorted, and misrepresented over the centuries, none of the stories was *totally* fabricated: they all had roots in actual historical occurrences and may thus be referred to as "history stories." Although oral transmission played an important part in keeping some of the stories alive (the Battle of Kosovo being a prime example), they were also without exception eventually set down in one or another form of writing, circulated for centuries (although sometimes with considerable interruptions, as in the case of Masada), and were known far and wide in the countries of their origin. All of the stories, moreover, with the partial exception of Masada, had named human protagonists and more often than not supplied cognitive models that people, individually or collectively, could readily relate to and measure their own thoughts and actions against. And, finally, it is noteworthy that the stories I've dealt with were in every instance revived and popularized in the twentieth century in response to societal crises pertaining mainly to war or the threat of war and sooner or later in this setting received strong support from the state.

Crises—and I include here not only external threat and war, but also disease, drought, famine, and other calamitous events—have throughout history also commonly elicited stories of a very different nature from those dealt with in these pages. The stories I have in mind here—rumors and other forms of "improvised news"[19] that pass rapidly from mouth to mouth—emanate largely from oral tradition; generally speaking, they are extremely simple in structure; they tend to be local or regional in reach, although occasionally extending farther; they frequently target specific scapegoats; and rather than being stories that exist simply in people's heads, they have often (although by no means always) called for—and resulted in—collective action. Examples of stories of this sort include the widespread charge among Chinese in drought-plagued North China at the time of the Boxer Uprising (1899–1900) that foreigners were putting poison in village wells and the rumors of chinless ghosts and talking toads (who forecast that old people would die unless they ate a toad within a specified period of time) that were rife in eastern China in the aftermath of the devastating famine spawned by the Great Leap Forward of 1958–1960.[20] In both cases, the rumors incorporated death-related symbols in response to historical episodes that were themselves deeply marked by death and the fear of death. In other words, despite the differences between these "rumor stories" and the "history stories" recounted in the chapters of this book, they all share one key characteristic. Much of the power of both types of stories derived from their capacity to speak metaphorically to what was happening—or had only recently happened or was threatening to happen in the near future—to people in the historical present.

This symbolic parallelism between story and historical setting is a fundamental reason for the pervasive appeal of each story explored here. The right story in such circumstances hammers away at a particular theme or set of themes very clearly and compellingly, thus challenging people to see through the clutter of their everyday lives and recognize what is truly important to them at a particular historical moment. In this process, it helps if the story in question is one that has been drummed into their minds from childhood on. This education can be a very personal thing. For example, when I think of such qualities as persistence, determination, the refusal to be defeated by seemingly insurmountable obstacles, my mind often goes back to *The Little Engine That Could*, a story narrated by Paul Wing on an RCA record I listened to repeatedly as a boy. But in many other instances, including all of the stories dealt with in this book, the narratives, rather than being personal, are collective in nature, shared in common with other members of the community, almost all of whom were introduced to them from a very early age.

The Israeli philosopher Avishai Margalit, in discussing his notion of a "community of memory," asserts that "human beings . . . lead collective existences based on symbols that encapsulate shared memories."[21] These shared memories—not the past itself, Ernest Renan long ago cautioned, but the stories we tell one another about the past—are what bind national communities together in the present, becoming a part of the "rich legacy of memories" such communities hold in common.[22] In other words, the power of the stories discussed here, although deriving in substantial measure from their metaphoric embodiment of what was taking place in the historical present, also fed on the fact that the stories constituted a vital part of a shared (or popular) store of memories (sometimes referred to as a form of folk knowledge) that fostered group coalescence and made it possible for the members of the group to think of themselves and behave as a community.[23] Bruner has similar things to say about the relationship between "common stories" and the human groups or communities in which they circulate. The sharing of such stories, he states, "creates an interpretive community" that is critically important "for promoting cultural cohesion."[24] Or as Jonathan Gottschall has pithily put it, "Story is the glue of human social life—defining groups and holding them together."[25] What all these individuals are apparently suggesting is that some form of symbolic sharing (whether in the form of stories or memories) is absolutely key both to a culture's objective existence and to an individual's subjective sense of belonging to that culture.

Objectively, as the China historian Mark Elvin puts it, "shared stories . . . define the space" in which a particular human group operates— "its conceptualized physical landscape."[26] Subjectively, common stories and memories are the very stuff out of which the imagined communities

Benedict Anderson describes are formed. Although Anderson's notion of "imagined communities" is applicable to a variety of communal realms—religious, cultural, and so on—he uses it primarily to refer to nations (a particular kind of political community). A nation, according to him, is "imagined" "because the members of even the smallest nation will never know most of their fellow-members, meet them, or even hear of them, yet in the minds [sic] of each lives the image of their communion." A nation is imagined as a "community" because, despite the differences prevailing within it, it "is always conceived as a deep, horizontal comradeship."[27] The stories that circulate among the members of such a community, I would add, constitute at all times a special cultural language for discussing matters of immediate concern; and in time of peril more than ever, they supply a floor of reassurance that individual fears and worries about what is happening—or what may happen—are shared in common by other members of the community.

In addition to the horizontal comradeship Anderson refers to, there is also a vertical dimension to the stories that circulate in and to some extent define a national community. This dimension ties the community's members to a shared—or at least a partially shared—past. It fleshes out the sense of identity of the community members by telling them where they have come from and where they might be headed. Although the horizontal and vertical dimensions of national narratives seem starkly dissimilar, the former operating spatially and the latter temporally, they are not infrequently merged. Ger Duijzings thus writes of the Kosovo epic that it "offers Serbs a mental framework; it clearly fits Durkheim's notion of *collective representations*, which are sanctioned and enacted in rites that figure prominently in public debate and are used for demarcating the boundaries of the group. As in other national myths the Kosovo myth establishes continuity with the past and projects a predestined future. As a narrative it formulates certain values and oppositions which are fundamental to the community and are personified in the main characters of the story."[28]

It should be clearer at this point why the members of a national community instinctively turn to certain kinds of stories when the community's survival is at stake. Personal stories—the primary concern of many writers on narrative, based on the premise that stories are a fundamental part of the way in which individuals process experience and understand the world[29]—won't do in such situations. Instead, collective stories—stories that are widely known within a community, that are part of its heritage—are needed. But not just any old collective stories: the biblical story of Moses and Joshua cited in the preface, for example, would be out of place in this context. Instead, the needed stories must be closely aligned in content and structure with the crisis in which the community is embroiled. This is what Margalit is getting at when he writes: "Why did Stalin, an arch-manipulator, when locked in a war of life and death with the invading Nazis, invoke the national memories of great patriots from czarist Russia rather than working-class memories that he was ideologically supposed to represent? Stalin invoked the memory of Alexander Nevsky, who defeated the Teutonic knights (in the thirteenth century), rather than the memory of Karl Marx, and of Ivan the Terrible, who defeated the Tartars at Kazan in the sixteenth century, rather than Friedrich Engels."[30]

Beyond being attracted to collective narratives that bear a metaphoric likeness to the crisis a community is undergoing, the members of that community are also drawn to stories that show a way out of the crisis and are therefore a source of sorely needed hope and encouragement. Sometimes finding the right story is a fairly straightforward process. King Goujian, Nevsky, and Henry V, against long odds, triumph resoundingly over their enemies and thus promise a good outcome to the crisis facing people in the historical present. Although Joan of Arc does not live to see the English driven from France, she rises to the challenge posed by the English occupation and sets the pattern that Charles VII consummates two decades after her death. So, again, the Joan tale is a basically optimistic story, although not quite as uncomplicated as the Goujian, Nevsky, and Henry V narratives. The Masada and Kosovo stories, as tales of defeat rather than triumph, must undergo considerably more manipulation before they can function properly as motivational vehicles. The Masada narrative begins in the 1920s as a symbol of the Jews' hope for simple survival in their new home, but over time it evolves by stages to stand eventually for "the determination of a people to be free in its own land."[31] And, in certain respects resonating with Masada, the Kosovo legend as reworked in the nineteenth century arms Serbs with the confidence needed to wipe out their enemies and achieve their nationalist dreams.

POPULAR MEMORY AND CRITICAL HISTORY: CONCLUDING THOUGHTS

According to Roger Chartier, although history is "one among many forms of narration, . . . [it] is nevertheless singular in that it maintains a special relationship to truth. More precisely, its narrative constructions aim at reconstructing a past that really was."[32] No one ever said this was easy. But, as Georg Iggers puts it, there remains a fundamental difference between postmodern theories that deny "any claim to reality in historical accounts and a historiography that is fully conscious of the complexity of historical knowledge but still assumes that real people had real thoughts and feelings that led to real actions that, within limits, can be known and reconstructed."[33] As the preceding chapters make amply clear, this view of history's aim is sometimes accompanied, compromised, or even completely displaced by other aims, the common element of which is their structuring of the past in such a way that it lends support to present purposes and aspirations. A concern for veracity may be part of the process—or it may not. But, either way, a truthful picture of the past is not the thing that is of paramount concern. What is of the utmost importance is framing the past interpretively in such a way that it makes the present, the desired present, seem to evolve directly or at least plausibly from it—or, to state it somewhat differently, constructing a narrative that, although professing to square the present with the past, in fact does the very reverse in redefining the past so as to accommodate a preferred present.

Memory plays an essential part in this process of working out a satisfactory relationship between past and present. It is the mental faculty of retaining and recalling the past. But it is a faculty that functions in a wide range of ways.[34] Memory can operate comprehensively or selectively, more or less accurately, more or less honestly. It is always accompanied, moreover, by forgetting and invariably supplemented by invention.[35]

Although the rewriting of the Masada and Kosovo stories (not to mention the Joan of Arc story under Vichy) may seem particularly blatant, the fact is that all of the stories dealt with in this book and a great many other "history stories" not included here have undergone a comparable rewriting process. And this reworking doesn't seem to matter to most people, even if they suspect (as some of them surely must) that the stories have been doctored over time. "If," writes David Lowenthal, "Oliver Goldsmith was appalled by the 'ecclesiastical beggars' who rattled off lies and legends as facts at Westminister Abbey's Poets' Corner, most viewers neither seek objective veracity nor mind if it is absent. Echoing Washington Irving's indulgence of spurious Shakespeare relics at Stratford in 1815, they are 'ever willing to be deceived, where the deceit is pleasant, and costs nothing. What is it to us, whether these stories be true or false, so long as we can persuade ourselves into the belief of them?' "[36]

What is the basis for this indifference to truth? I hinted at an answer to this question in the preface. I want, at this point, to enlarge upon that answer.[37] J. H. Plumb maintained in his 1969 book *The Death of the Past* that "the past," by which he meant what I have called "popular" or "folk" or "collective memory," should never be confused with critical history. "True history," he wrote, is at bottom "destructive," its role being "to cleanse the story of mankind from those deceiving visions of a purposeful past." The French historian Pierre Nora, in his celebrated seven-volume work *Les Lieux de mémoire* (Realms of Memory, 1984–1992), made much the same point when he wrote that "[m]emory is always suspect in the eyes of history, whose true mission is to demolish it, to repress it." He did not, however, think that this was a good thing at all and so, along with his collaborators, set about reconstructing as many sites as possible that were evocative of French collective memory. Lowenthal, although using the term *heritage* for collective memory in his book *Possessed by the Past* (1996), fully agrees with Nora, contending that "heritage, no less than history, is essential to knowing and acting" and arguing that, "by means of it, we tell ourselves who we are, where we came from, and to what we belong." (The connection Lowenthal draws between heritage and identity is beautifully captured in an exchange between the novelist Jonathan Safran Foer and his six-year-old son, to whom he often read children's versions of Old Testament stories. After hearing about the death of Moses for the umpteenth time—"how he took his last breaths overlooking a promised land that he would never enter"—the son asked if Moses was a real person. "I don't know," Foer told him, "but we're related to him."[38])

The American historian Bernard Bailyn also addressed the uneasy relationship between history and memory with great eloquence at a 1998 conference on the Atlantic slave trade that almost broke up when many of the black scholars in attendance as well as others reacted heatedly to the cold, statistically grounded scholarly presentations on the trade. Bailyn drew a sharp contrast between critical, scientific historical writing, which is all head and no heart and keeps its distance from the past it is bent on recovering, and memory, whose relationship to the past is more like an embrace. Memory, he contended, "is not a critical, skeptical reconstruction of what happened. It is the spontaneous, unquestioned experience of the past. It is absolute, not tentative or distant, and it is expressed in signs and signals, symbols, images, and mnemonic clues of all sorts. It shapes our awareness whether we know it or not, and it is ultimately emotional, not intellectual."

Although all these writers accentuate the contrast between critical history and popular memory—a contrast I have repeatedly emphasized in these pages—this distinction is not, in fact, the whole story. The truth is that there is a great deal of overlap—or blurring of boundaries— between academic history and the history stories dealt with here, which is a prime reason for the confusion that exists between the two in many people's minds. Popular memory, as we have seen again and again, often has a genuine historical component. There really was a battle between the Serbs and Turks in Kosovo in 1389; a confrontation at Masada in 73 C.E. between a small group of Jewish warriors and a vastly stronger Roman force; a thirteenth-century Russian named Alexander Nevsky, whose army defeated a threatening German force on Russia's far western flank; a battle at Agincourt in 1415 in which a weaker English army led by Henry V defeated a much larger French force; a Chinese king, Goujian, who ruled a state called Yue in the latter part of the Zhou dynasty and eventually triumphed over his rival; and a plucky French maid called Joan of Arc who fought the English occupiers of northern France and was burned at the stake in 1431. How is a person untrained as a historian—or how is even a historian if he or she happens to be unfamiliar with the aspect of the past covered in the story—to know which parts of the stories dealing with such people and events are authentic and which are the product of inventive minds? People today constantly confront this problem when they see historical dramatizations in film or on TV or the stage or when they read historical fiction based on a core of actual historical persons and events.[39]

This is one side of the problem. Another is that although serious historians strive, along the lines suggested by Chartier and Iggers, to reconstruct a past that really was, they can never fully succeed in this venture.

Where full and reliable data are lacking (which is generally the case), they habitually make inferences, some of which are later shown to be wrong. Moreover, historians are never entirely impervious to the collective memory of the society in which they themselves live, which means that even as they do their best to identify and undermine the mythic aspects of our knowledge of the past—a sacred part of their responsibility as historians—they inevitably introduce into their accounts new myths (although they may not think of them as such) that are reflective of the values and thought patterns that happen to be important to people in their own day. This is what we mean—part of it at any rate—when we say that each generation makes its own history. It is what the sociologist Barry Schwartz means when he says that the remembering of Abraham Lincoln (and presumably of other important historical figures) must be regarded "as a constructive process as opposed to a retrieval process"—that, within limits, each generation of Americans has had its own Lincoln who differed in major or minor ways from the Lincoln of earlier generations.[40] And if we shift from heroic individuals to complex, large-scale events, it is what the documentary filmmaker Ken Burns means when he writes of Americans' propensity to periodically rethink the meaning of the Civil War.[41]

What this complicated relationship between critical history and popular memory suggests is that Bernard Bailyn's comment at the Atlantic slave trade conference would perhaps benefit from a slight shift of emphasis. At the moment when he made his remarks—to say nothing of the sensitivity of the issue to which they were addressed—it must have seemed necessary and desirable to draw the line between critical history and popular memory hard and fast. But although it is true that good history writing is always attentive to the distance of the real past from the present—David Lowenthal, in another of his works, famously referred to the past as a "foreign country"[42]—it is not true that such writing is always all head and no heart. Bailyn himself seems to acknowledge as much when he asserts that "perhaps history and memory . . . may act usefully upon each other."[43] I would reframe this assertion in stronger language and ask whether it is not inevitable that they interact in this way. According to J. H. Plumb, the distinguished French historian Marc Bloch "possessed the power to abstract himself from any preconceived notions about the past and to investigate an historical problem with detachment. And yet, detached as he was, his imagination, his creative invention, his sense of humanity infused all that he did."[44] This "infusion," in my judgment, is what good historical scholarship should aspire to. But it would be a mistake to believe that it can ever give us the past as it really was. Despite the most painstaking efforts to reconstruct such a past, efforts I wholeheartedly applaud, the questions historians ask—and that guide our research and writing—will unavoidably be informed in substantial measure by the present in which we, like everyone else, live, with all its values, assumptions, anxieties, foibles, and mythic preferences. And this circumstance more or less ensures that the product of our efforts will embody a tension between the past as it really was and the past we seek to illuminate and understand.

NOTES

PREFACE

1. Paul A. Cohen, *Speaking to History: The Story of King Goujian in Twentieth-Century China* (Berkeley: University of California Press, 2009).
2. The Obama talk is excerpted in David Remnick, "The Joshua Generation: Race and the Campaign of Barack Obama," *New Yorker*, November 17, 2008, 69–70; for more on the trope of Moses and Joshua from the time of the early black church in America through that of the civil rights movement, including a comparison between Jewish slavery in Pharaoh's Egypt and black slavery in the American South, see David Remnick, *The Bridge: The Life and Rise of Barack Obama* (New York: Vintage Books, 2011), 18–19, 21–23, 25, 454, 470, 560.
3. Quoted in Kevin Sack, "After Decades, a Time to Reap," *New York Times*, November 5, 2008.
4. Jerome Bruner, *Making Stories: Law, Literature, Life* (Cambridge, Mass.: Harvard University Press, 2002), 27.
5. There are of course exceptions to this assertion, a few of which I touch on in my discussion of popular memory in the conclusion.
6. Bruner, *Making Stories*, 27.

1. THE BATTLE OF KOSOVO OF 1389 AND SERBIAN NATIONALISM

1. Avishai Margalit, *The Ethics of Memory* (Cambridge, Mass.: Harvard University Press, 2002), 96–98.
2. Tim Judah, *Kosovo: War and Revenge*, 2nd ed. (New Haven, Conn.: Yale University Press, 2002), 5–8; Tim Judah, *The Serbs: History, Myth, and the*

Destruction of Yugoslavia (New Haven, Conn.: Yale University Press, 1997), 27–28; Olga Zirojević, "Kosovo in the Collective Memory," in Nebojša Popov, ed., *The Road to War in Serbia: Trauma and Catharsis* (Budapest: Central European University Press, 2000), 189; Lene Kühle and Carsten Bagge Laustsen, "The Kosovo Myth: Nationalism and Revenge," in Tonny Brems Knudsen and Carsten Bagge Laustsen, eds., *Kosovo Between War and Peace: Nationalism, Peacebuilding, and International Trusteeship* (London: Routledge, 2006), 23; Wayne S. Vucinich, "Introduction," in Wayne S. Vucinich and Thomas A. Emmert, eds., *Kosovo: Legacy of a Medieval Battle* (Minneapolis: University of Minnesota, 1991), ix–x. For details on what is known about the Battle of Kosovo, see Thomas A. Emmert, *Serbian Golgotha: Kosovo, 1389*, East European Monographs no. 278 (New York: Columbia University Press, 1990), 42–60, and "The Battle of Kosovo: Early Reports of Victory and Defeat," in Vucinich and Emmert, *Kosovo*, 19–40.

3. Zirojević, "Kosovo in the Collective Memory," 189. There is a general consensus on this point. Noel Malcolm judges the battle to have had "a status unlike that of anything else in the history of the Serbs" (*Kosovo: A Short History* [New York: New York University Press, 1998], 58); see also Miranda Vickers, *Between Serb and Albanian: A History of Kosovo* (New York: Columbia University Press, 1998), 15, and Vucinich, "Introduction," ix–x. As a further indication of the importance of the Battle of Kosovo, both as history and as legend, a conference specifically devoted to it was held at Stanford University in June 1989 on the eve of the battle's six hundredth anniversary. The conference papers were published in Vucinich and Emmert, *Kosovo*.

4. Zirojević, "Kosovo in the Collective Memory," 195. For excerpts of writings from the years immediately after the Battle of Kosovo that portray Lazar as a Christ-like figure, see Vasa D. Mihailovich, "The Tradition of Kosovo in Serbian Literature," in Vucinich and Emmert, *Kosovo*, 142–47.

5. Zirojević, "Kosovo in the Collective Memory," 190; Kühle and Laustsen, "The Kosovo Myth," 25; Robert D. Kaplan, *Balkan Ghosts: A Journey Through History* (1993; reprint, New York: Vintage Books, 1994), 38.

6. Vickers, *Between Serb and Albanian*, 9–12.

7. Malcolm, *Kosovo*, 62–63.

8. Quoted in Judah, *The Serbs*, 35; for the full text of the epic song "The Prince's Supper," from which this excerpt is taken, see Anne Pennington and Peter Levi, trans., *Marko the Prince: Serbo-Croat Heroic Songs* (London: Duckworth, 1984), 14–15.

9. Michael A. Sells, "Religion, History, and Genocide in Bosnia-Herzegovina," in G. Scott Davis, ed., *Religion and Justice in the War Over Bosnia* (New York: Routledge, 1996), 24.

10. Judah, *Kosovo*, 7–8; Judah, *The Serbs*, 30–32, 36; Zirojević, "Kosovo in the Collective Memory," 205. Malcolm gives an informed account of the Vuk Branković betrayal question (*Kosovo*, 65–68).

11. Zirojević, "Kosovo in the Collective Memory," 193.

12. Vucinich, "Introduction," ix–x.

13. Kühle and Laustsen, "The Kosovo Myth," 23–24; Sells, "Religion, History, and Genocide," 24.

14. Zirojević, "Kosovo in the Collective Memory," 199–201.

15. Julie A. Mertus, *Kosovo: How Myths and Truths Started a War* (Berkeley: University of California Press, 1999), 10–11. Noel Malcolm makes a similar point in regard to the Serbian/Montenegrin conquest and de facto annexation of Kosovo in 1912. From the Albanian point of view, this action represented the imposition of colonialist rule, whereas in Serbian eyes it was understood as "a war of liberation to release a captive population (the Serbs of Kosovo) from an alien imperial power (the Turks). . . . The trouble . . . was that both of these conflicting conceptual models . . . were simultaneously true" (*Kosovo*, xlvi–xlvii). For a detailed scholarly discussion of the early peopling of the Kosovo area, see Malcolm, *Kosovo*, chap. 2.

16. Judah, *Kosovo*, 3. See also Vickers, *Between Serb and Albanian*, 6–7, and Gale Stokes, *The Walls Came Tumbling Down: The Collapse of Communism in Eastern Europe* (New York: Oxford University Press, 1993), 230.

17. Malcolm, *Kosovo*, 55–57; Vickers, *Between Serb and Albanian*, 9–11.

18. Vickers, *Between Serb and Albanian*, 18.

19. Ibid., 18–19; Malcolm, *Kosovo*, 111, 139–40.

20. Malcolm, *Kosovo*, 194–96, 199–200, 228.

21. Vickers, *Between Serb and Albanian*, 19.

22. Ibid., 23–24, 26–27; Malcolm, *Kosovo*, 127, 172–75.

23. Malcolm, *Kosovo*, xliv–xlvi, 139–41; Vickers, *Between Serb and Albanian*, 26–27.

24. Mihailovich, "The Tradition of Kosovo in Serbian Literature," 141–42.

25. Radmila J. Gorup, "Kosovo and Epic Poetry," in Vucinich and Emmert, *Kosovo*, 118.

26. Quoted in Mihailovich, "The Tradition of Kosovo in Serbian Literature," 145.

27. Vickers, *Between Serb and Albanian*, 15–16, 25–26; quotations from Mihailovich, "The Tradition of Kosovo in Serbian Literature," 141.

28. Pertinent here is the contrast Bernard Lewis draws between a *primary epic*, which emerges "spontaneously among a people still living amid or soon after the events which it celebrates," and a *secondary epic*, which is "more contrived, more literary, composed at a more advanced state of civilization or a higher social level, and often by the direction of a patron or even a ruler seeking to

serve some purpose" (*History: Remembered, Recovered, Invented* [New York: Simon and Schuster, 1987], 44–45). The secondary epic is nicely exemplified by Vuk Karadžić and Petar Petrović Njegoš's literary activities, which are discussed in the text.

29. Popović's play is discussed in Mihailovich, "The Tradition of Kosovo in Serbian Literature," 147–48, the quoted passage on 148.

30. Ger Duijzings, *Religion and the Politics of Identity in Kosovo* (New York: Columbia University Press, 2000), 184.

31. Ibid., 184–85; Judah, *The Serbs*, 34, 55; Duncan Wilson, *The Life and Times of Vuk Stefanović Karadzić, 1787–1864: Literacy, Literature, and National Independence in Serbia* (Oxford: Clarendon Press, 1970), 195–96; Kühle and Laustsen, "The Kosovo Myth," 24. On Grimm, in particular his relationship to Karadžić and to the emergence of nationalism in nineteenth-century Europe, see Joep Leerssen, *National Thought in Europe: A Cultural History* (Amsterdam: Amsterdam University Press, 2006), 122–26, 179–85, 197–200.

32. Judah, *The Serbs*, 61–62.

33. Vasa D. Mihailovich, "Introduction," in P. P. Njegoš, *The Mountain Wreath*, trans. and ed. Vasa D. Mihailovich (Irvine, Calif.: Schlacks, 1986), ix–x. See also Kaplan, *Balkan Ghosts*, xliii; Judah, *The Serbs*, 36, 63; Kühle and Laustsen, "The Kosovo Myth," 24; Duijzings, *Religion and the Politics of Identity in Kosovo*, 188.

34. Duijzings, *Religion and the Politics of Identity in Kosovo*, 188; Zirojević, "Kosovo in the Collective Memory," 197–98; Mihailovich, "Introduction," ix–x; Judah, *The Serbs*, 64–65. The reference to Albanians is in Njegoš, *The Mountain Wreath*, 101; on page 85, there is an implied reference to Albanian converts to Islam.

35. Njegoš, *The Mountain Wreath*, 1. I have changed "Karageorge" to the more commonly used "Karadjordje."

36. Ibid., 11.

37. Ibid., 65.

38. Ibid., 31.

39. Ibid., 86–87.

40. Vladika Danilo founded the Petrović Njegoš dynasty in 1697 and ruled until 1735.

41. Njegoš, *The Mountain Wreath*, 87–88.

42. Ibid., 94–102, quotations from 94–96.

43. Mark Mazower, *The Balkans: A Short History* (New York: Modern Library, 2002), 153–54.

44. Ibid., 150, 174 n. 8.

45. Judah, *The Serbs*, 77.

46. Duijzings, *Religion and the Politics of Identity in Kosovo*, 188 n. 13.

47. This point is stressed in Malcolm, *Kosovo*, xlvi, 228.

48. Dimitrije Djordjević, "The Tradition of Kosovo in the Formation of Modern Serbian Statehood in the Nineteenth Century," in Vucinich and Emmert, *Kosovo*, 318. For detailed accounts of the near obsession with Kosovo mythic traditions that marked the final decades of the nineteenth century, see ibid., 317–20, and Emmert, *Serbian Golgotha*, 124–33.

49. Djordjević, "The Tradition of Kosovo," 320.

50. Quoted in Emmert, *Serbian Golgotha*, 133–34.

51. I draw here again on Vasa Mihailovich's periodization in "The Tradition of Kosovo in Serbian Literature," 141, 152. See also Zirojević, "Kosovo in the Collective Memory," 206.

52. Djordjević, "The Tradition of Kosovo," 321.

53. Judah, *Kosovo*, 18–22. In Malcolm's judgment, the policies imposed by the Serbian and Montenegrin governments following their conquest of Kosovo in 1912 "created systematic hostility and hatred on a scale that the region had never seen before" (*Kosovo*, xlvi).

54. Mihailovich, "The Tradition of Kosovo in Serbian Literature," 153.

55. Mihailovich sees the reemergence of heightened Serbian attention to Kosovo mythology as having its inception during the 1960s in the context of growing ethnic strains between Albanians and Serbs; it was still, according to this author, very much in evidence at the time he wrote his article in 1991 (ibid., 141–42, 153).

56. For Yugoslav political developments between 1918 and 1980, I have relied on the convenient summation in Mertus, *Kosovo*, 285–92; Kosovo census data giving the proportions of different ethnic groups for select years between 1948 and 1991 are in ibid., 316. On later emigration of Serbs from Kosovo, see ibid., 122–33, and Judah, *Kosovo*, 44–45.

57. Judah, *Kosovo*, 38–42; Mertus, *Kosovo*, 17–93.

58. Mertus, *Kosovo*, 135–41, quotation from 141; Judah, *Kosovo*, 48–50.

59. Milošević's comments to the crowd are quoted in Judah, *Kosovo*, 53.

60. Ibid. See also Mertus, *Kosovo*, 142–43, and Stokes, *The Walls Came Tumbling Down*, 233.

61. Stokes, *The Walls Came Tumbling Down*, 233.

62. Mertus devotes an entire chapter of her study to the massacre (*Kosovo*, 135–73); see also Judah, *Kosovo*, 54.

63. Stokes, *The Walls Came Tumbling Down*, 234–35.

64. The English translation is in Mertus, *Kosovo*, 184.

65. This excerpt from Milošević's speech is taken from the text compiled by the National Technical Information Service, U.S. Department of Commerce, at http://www.slobodan-milosevic.org/spch-kosovo1989.htm (accessed October 31, 2009).

66. Mertus, *Kosovo*, 185; Duijzings, *Religion and the Politics of Identity in Kosovo*, 198.

67. Translated in Zirojević, "Kosovo in the Collective Memory," 207.

68. See, for example, Judah, *Kosovo*, 56–57; Stokes, *The Walls Came Tumbling Down*, 235–36.

69. This point is made in Judah, *Kosovo*, 59.

70. Ibid., 265–312, passim.

71. Steven Erlanger, "Showdown in Yugoslavia: Overview; Milosevic Concedes His Defeat; Yugoslavs Celebrate New Era," *New York Times*, October 7, 2000; Roger Cohen, "Crisis in the Balkans: The Indictment; Tribunal Is Said to Cite Milosevic for War Crimes," *New York Times*, May 27, 1999; Roger Cohen, "To His Death in Jail, Milosevic Exalted Image of Serb Suffering," *New York Times*, March 12, 2006; "Kosovo MPs Proclaim Independence," *BBC News*, February 17, 2008, http://news.bbc.co.uk/2/hi/7249034.stm; Dan Bilefsky, "Kosovo," *New York Times*, February 17, 2008; Steven Woehrel, "Kosovo: Current Issues and U.S. Policy," *Congressional Research Service*, August 19, 2009, http://www.fas.org/sgp/crs/row/RS21721.pdf; Dan Bilefsky, "Kosovo's Declaration of Independence Is Within Law, U.N. Rules," *New York Times*, July 23, 2010; "International Recognition of Kosovo," *Wikipedia*, http://en.wikipedia.org/wiki/International_recognition_of_Kosovo (accessed April 23, 2013).

72. Yosef Hayim Yerushalmi, *Zakhor: Jewish History and Jewish Memory* (Seattle: University of Washington Press, 2002), 113.

73. Ibid., 36, 62, 73, quotation from 36.

74. Gabrielle M. Spiegel, "Memory and History: Liturgical Time and Historical Time," *History and Theory* 41 (May 2002): 149–62, quotation from abstract on 149. Spiegel acknowledges Yerushalmi's influence on her own work.

75. E. E. Evans-Pritchard has useful things to say about this timelessness of myth: "[Myth] is not so much concerned with the succession of events as with the moral significance of situations, and is hence allegorical or symbolic in form. It is not encapsulated, as history is, but is a re-enactment fusing present and past. It tends to be timeless, placed in thought beyond, or above historical time; and where it is firmly placed in historical time, it is also, nevertheless, timeless in that it could have happened at any time, the archetypal not being bound to time or space" (*Anthropology and History: A Lecture* [Manchester, U.K.: Manchester University Press, 1961], 8, cited in Duijzings, *Religion and the Politics of Identity in Kosovo*, 193).

76. Stokes, *The Walls Came Tumbling Down*, 230–31; Zirojević, "Kosovo in the Collective Memory," 208, Čolović quoted on 208–9. See also the illuminating discussion in Duijzings, *Religion and the Politics of Identity in Kosovo*, 192–202.

77. Karadžić was initially charged with two counts of genocide and other crimes committed in the war in Bosnia in 1992. In 2012, a lower court dropped one of the genocide charges. On July 11, 2013, however, appeals judges at a UN war crimes tribunal in The Hague reinstated the dropped charge, reversing the lower court's decision. A verdict in Karadžić's trial is not expected before 2015. See Marlise Simons, "Genocide Charge Reinstated Against Wartime Leader of the Bosnian Serbs," *New York Times*, July 12, 2013, and Associated Press in The Hague, "Radovan Karadzic Genocide Charge Reinstated by UN Judges," *The Guardian*, July 11, 2013.

78. Aleksandar Hemon, "Genocide's Epic Hero," *New York Times*, July 27, 2008. Proud of being a poet himself, Karadžić claimed, according to Duijzings, to have "common blood and genetic traits with 'the most famous' Karadžić, Vuk Karadžić" (*Religion and the Politics of Identity in Kosovo*, 198 n. 20). See also Jack Hitt, "How Did a Serbian War Criminal Hide from the World as a Bioenergy-Channeling, Alternative-Medicine-Peddling, Bearded, and, Well, Nutty Guru? Radovan Karadzic's New-Age Adventure!" *New York Times Magazine*, July 26, 2009, and Marlise Simons, "Indicted Ex-leader of Bosnian Serbs Calls Atrocities 'Myths,'" *New York Times*, March 3, 2010.

79. At a giant rally in Belgrade on November 19, 1988, Milošević stated: "Every nation has a love which eternally warms its heart. For Serbia it is Kosovo. That is why Kosovo will remain in Serbia" (quoted in Judah, *Kosovo*, 55).

80. Bilefsky, "Kosovo's Declaration of Independence."

81. Although many Serbs viewed with ambivalence the arrest of the former Bosnian Serb military leader and wanted war crimes suspect Ratko Mladić on May 26, 2011, polls indicate that the status of Kosovo remains a key Serbian concern. See Steven Erlanger, "Arrest Follows Serbia's Uneven Path to Break with Its Past," *New York Times*, May 28, 2011, and Charles Simic, "The Bright Side of the Balkans," *New York Review of Books*, August 18, 2011, 59.

82. Quoted in Judah, *The Serbs*, 37. For interesting commentary on the "sacred soil" notion, as applied by Serbs to Kosovo and by Jews to Eretz Israel, see Leerssen, *National Thought in Europe*, 183.

83. Elie Wiesel, "For Jerusalem," *New York Times*, April 18, 2010, bold and full capitalization in original.

84. A letter sharply critical of Wiesel's idealized portrayal of Jerusalem, signed by one hundred Jewish residents of Jerusalem, including prominent intellectuals and academics, was published in the *New York Review of Books*, May 27, 2010, 57.

85. "Vuk Jeremić of Serbia President of Sixty-Seventh Session of General Assembly," http://www.un.org/News/Press/docs/2012/bio4405.doc.htm (accessed November 18, 2012).

86. Nicholas Kulish, "Recasting Serbia's Image, Starting with a Fresh Face," *New York Times*, January 16, 2010; Zeljko Pantelic, "Major Powers Warn Serbia to Cool Down Kosovo Rhetoric," February 9, 2010, http://waz.euobserver.com/887/29432.

87. Thus, once the history of Texas was resolved as far as Mexican and U.S. boundary claims were concerned, the story of the Alamo lost much of its resonance in the contemporary world. See Edward M. Bruner and Phyllis Gorfain, "Dialogic Narration and the Paradoxes of Masada," in Edward M. Bruner, ed., *Text, Play, and Story: The Construction and Reconstruction of Self and Society*, 1983 Proceedings of the American Ethnological Society (Washington, D.C.: American Ethnological Society, 1984), 70–71.

88. The European Union does not require Serbia to recognize Kosovo as an independent state (several current union members, including Spain and Cyprus, do not), but it does expect candidates for membership to have normal relations with neighbors (Matthew Brunwasser, "Support Slips for Serbian Autonomy in a New Country," *New York Times*, October 2, 2011).

89. For details of this agreement, see Dan Bilefsky, "Serbia and Kosovo Reach Agreement on Power-Sharing," *New York Times*, April 20, 2013; Vanessa Mock and Gordon Fairclough, "Serbia, Kosovo Advance Toward Bloc," *Wall Street Journal*, April 22, 2013, http://online.wsj.com/article/SB10001424127887324874204578438123563817706.html.

90. Quoted in Mock and Fairclough, "Serbia, Kosovo Advance Toward Bloc." See also the laudatory editorial "Moving Past the Last Balkan War," *New York Times*, April 25, 2013.

91. Catherine Ashton, "A Different Balkan Story," *International Herald Tribune*, April 26, 2013.

92. Bilefsky, "Serbia and Kosovo Reach Agreement on Power-Sharing." For an early report on some of the difficulties encountered in implementing the agreement, see Dan Bilefsky, "In Kosovo, Ethnic Barriers Linger as a New Approach Is Taking Effect," *New York Times*, June 12, 2013.

2. THE FALL OF MASADA AND MODERN JEWISH MEMORY

1. Lewis A. Coser, "Introduction: Maurice Halbwachs 1877–1945," in Maurice Halbwachs, *On Collective Memory*, trans. and ed. Lewis A. Coser (Chicago: University of Chicago Press, 1992), 32.

2. Yael Zerubavel, *Recovered Roots: Collective Memory and the Making of Israeli National Tradition* (Chicago: University of Chicago Press, 1995), 62; Bernard Lewis, *History: Remembered, Recovered, Invented* (New York: Simon and Schuster, 1987), 5–6; Nachman Ben-Yehuda, *The Masada Myth: Collective*

Memory and Mythmaking in Israel (Madison: University of Wisconsin Press, 1995), 228.

3. I have used the G. A. Williamson translation of *The Jewish War*, first published in 1959 and put out in a revised edition, with a new introduction, notes, and appendixes by E. Mary Smallwood (London: Penguin, 1981).

4. For details concerning the improvements made by Herod, including the building of a stone wall surmounted by seventy-five-foot-high towers on the Masada summit, see Solomon Zeitlin, "Masada and the Sicarii," *Jewish Quarterly Review*, New Series, 55, no. 4 (1965): 301.

5. See Smallwood's illuminating appendix A ("Bandits, Terrorists, Sicarii, and Zealots") in Josephus, *The Jewish War*, 461–62. In this appendix, she suggests a basis for the later confusion between the Sicarii and the Zealots, another Jewish faction that appears to have been no less violent and brutal than the Sicarii. On this question, see also Zeitlin, "Masada and the Sicarii," 315–17, and "The Sicarii and Masada," *Jewish Quarterly Review*, New Series, 57, no. 4 (1967): 263–64.

6. Josephus, *The Jewish War*, 398–99.

7. Ibid., 266–67.

8. Ibid., 399–403.

9. Ibid., 403–5, quotation from 404.

10. Smallwood, in her introduction to *The Jewish War*, states that by Josephus's day Greek had "been the *lingua franca* of Asia Minor, Syria and the eastern part of north Africa for over three centuries, and the educated Latin-speaking Italian, if not bilingual, was at least competent in Greek" (14).

11. Ibid., 14–15.

12. The battle of Jotapata is covered in detail in Josephus, *The Jewish War*, 200–216. Josephus's escape, the tension between him and his men in the cave, the collective suicide, and the Jewish commander's surrender to Vespasian are dealt with in ibid., 216–22, quoted passage from 217–18.

13. Josephus attributed this reprieve to divine providence or sheer luck. The Slavonic version of *The Jewish War* states explicitly what even the least cynical reader would surely suspect—namely, that Josephus "counted the numbers cunningly and so managed to deceive all the others" (*The Jewish War*, 470, see also 440 n. 19).

14. Zerubavel, *Recovered Roots*, 62.

15. Josephus, *The Jewish War*, 318. For a sampling of Josephus's appeals to the Jews to surrender, see ibid., 318–23, 344–45.

16. Smallwood, introduction to ibid., 13.

17. The point is made in both Zerubavel, *Recovered Roots*, 62, and Coser, "Introduction," 33. See also Barry Schwartz, Yael Zerubavel, and Bernice M. Barnett, "The Recovery of Masada: A Study in Collective Memory," *Sociological Quarterly* 27, no. 2 (Summer 1986): 161 n. 1.

18. Lewis, *History*, 6; Ben-Yehuda, *The Masada Myth*, 213; Coser, "Introduction," 33.

19. Zionism, to a considerable extent, represented Jewish intellectuals' self-conscious emulation of European nationalist movements. See Amos Elon, *The Israelis: Founders and Sons* (New York: Penguin, 1983), 60–62.

20. Three recent studies of the Dreyfus Affair are reviewed in Robert Gildea, "How to Understand the Dreyfus Affair," *New York Review of Books*, June 10, 2010, 42–44.

21. For a graphic account of the horrific circumstances in which most Jews lived in eastern Europe in the late nineteenth and early twentieth centuries, even quite apart from the devastations (the Russian term was *pogrom*) that were periodically directed against them, sometimes with government support, see Elon, *The Israelis*, 49–56. By 1887, according to Elon, a government inquiry commission stated that "90 percent of the Jews are a proletariat of such poverty and destitution as is otherwise impossible to see in Russia" (52).

22. Ibid., 59–60.

23. Zerubavel, *Recovered Roots*, 13–14.

24. Ibid., 63.

25. For an especially insightful probing of the different readings (or, as the authors would say, "tellings") of the Masada story, see Edward M. Bruner and Phyllis Gorfain, "Dialogic Narration and the Paradoxes of Masada," in Edward M. Bruner, ed., *Text, Play, and Story: The Construction and Reconstruction of Self and Society*, 1983 Proceedings of the American Ethnological Society (Washington, D.C.: American Ethnological Society, 1984), 56–79. As Yael Zerubavel observes, competing narratives sometimes coexisted, each satisfying a different group's or situation's needs. She calls this coexistence "the multivocality of commemorative narratives" ("The Death of Memory and the Memory of Death: Masada and the Holocaust as Historical Metaphors," *Representations* 45 [Winter 1994]: 91). Although putting less emphasis on the contemporaneity of competing narratives, I make a similar point in my book *Speaking to History: The Story of King Goujian in Twentieth-Century China* (Berkeley: University of California Press, 2009), xviii.

26. Leon I. Yudkin, *Isaac Lamdan: A Study in Twentieth-Century Hebrew Poetry* (London: East and West Library; Ithaca, N.Y.: Cornell University Press, 1971), 3–4. Elon describes the conditions in Palestine encountered by the first Jewish migrants: "Dressed in rags, they frequently went hungry, were regularly stricken down by attacks of typhoid and malaria, and were often forced to defend their farms against armed Arab neighbors. . . . They colonized hard, arid, seemingly impossible desert and mountain regions. Some worked as organizers of a clandestine defense force; some ran an underground route for illegal immigrants in defiance of British immigration regulations. Others

tirelessly toured Jewish communities abroad to collect the huge funds necessary to finance it all" (*The Israelis*, 12–13; see also 3, 82–105). The living conditions of both Jews and Arabs throughout Palestine toward the end of World War I were equally horrific. See the description in Tom Segev, *One Palestine, Complete: Jews and Arabs Under the British Mandate*, trans. Haim Watzman (New York: Holt, 2001), 19–22.

27. Schwartz, Zerubavel, and Barnett, "The Recovery of Masada," 153; see also the appendix, 161.

28. Mark Mazower, *Dark Continent: Europe's Twentieth Century* (New York: Vintage Books, 2000), 41–42, 51.

29. Ibid., 60, emphasis in original. Mazower notes that "the 1924 Romanian citizenship law made 100,000 Jews inside Romania stateless" (63).

30. Interestingly, Jewish socialist parties, even those that were strongly supportive of Jewish nationalism, also made a point of their staunch anti-Zionism. Historical perspectives on organized socialism's rejection of Zionism are detailed in Jonathan Frankel, *Crisis, Revolution, and Russian Jews* (Cambridge: Cambridge University Press, 2009), 157–80.

31. Yudkin, *Isaac Lamdan*, 4–9; Elon, *The Israelis*, 136.

32. A photoreproduction of Balfour's letter is given in "Balfour Declaration of 1917," *Wikipedia*, http://en.wikipedia.org/wiki/Balfour_Declaration_of_1917 (accessed July 24, 2010); see also Yudkin, *Isaac Lamdan*, 6–8. A recently published study by Jonathan Schneer suggests that British maneuvering at the time was somewhat more complicated than previously believed, but in the end the Balfour Declaration clearly supplied the diplomatic foundation for the State of Israel (*The Balfour Declaration: The Origins of the Arab–Israeli Conflict* [New York: Random House, 2010]).

33. The numbers of Jews leaving Palestine reached crisis proportions during the years immediately preceding the Great Depression. In 1926, for every 100 Jews who entered Palestine, 56.3 left; in 1927, 186.9 left for every 100 who entered; and in 1928, for every 100 entrants, 99.5 left (Schwartz, Zerubavel, and Barnett, "The Recovery of Masada," 161). For the problems facing Jewish settlers in 1920s Palestine, see ibid., passim, and Yudkin, *Isaac Lamdan*, 8–10; and on the fanatical insistence on communicating in Hebrew, see Elon, *The Israelis*, 110–11.

34. The point is made persuasively in Schwartz, Zerubavel, and Barnett, "The Recovery of Masada," 151–52, 159.

35. Lewis, *History*, 8.

36. For a careful study of the pogroms in the Ukraine in 1917–1921, see Henry Abramson, *A Prayer for the Government: Ukrainians and Jews in Revolutionary Times, 1917–1920* (Cambridge, Mass.: Ukrainian Research Institute and Center for Jewish Studies, Harvard University, 1999), 109–40. Abramson

makes it clear that the number of deaths resulting from the pogroms in the Ukraine immediately following the Revolution of 1917 was far greater than the number resulting from the Russian pogroms of the early 1880s or from the Kishinev pogrom of 1903. He puts the estimate of deaths very conservatively at fifty to sixty thousand (110).

37. These immigration waves are often referred to by the Hebrew term *aliya*, which implies a spiritual "ascent." The First and Second Aliyas took place in the years between the Russian pogroms of the early 1880s and the outbreak of World War I, when Palestine was still under Ottoman rule. The Third Aliya, which began shortly after the end of the war, had greater legitimacy in terms of international law as a result of the establishment of the British Mandate. The fourth wave of Jewish immigration to Palestine occurred during the latter part of the 1920s; it was followed in the 1930s by a fifth wave, but the rise of Nazism resulted in such a large number of Jewish migrants between 1933 and 1936 that the British had to severely restrict further migration. Distinctive characteristics of the different *aliyas* are noted in Yudkin, *Isaac Lamdan*, 8–10; Elon, *The Israelis*, 80, 90–91, 103, 107, 109, 132, 135–36, 145, 283–84; and Segev, *One Palestine, Complete*, 225.

38. Yudkin, *Isaac Lamdan*, 10; Lamdan's literary and journalistic involvements are detailed in ibid., 11–17.

39. Yudkin gives a full translation of *Masada* in ibid., 199–234.

40. Ibid., 199.

41. Ibid., 200–206.

42. Ibid., 209.

43. Ibid., 212–15.

44. Ibid., 220–22.

45. Ibid., 223. The parallels between the Masada of the first century and that of the early twentieth century are nicely drawn in Schwartz, Zerubavel, and Barnett, "The Recovery of Masada," 155–56.

46. Yudkin, *Isaac Lamdan*, 227–28.

47. This phrase traditionally adorned Hebrew books in medieval times (Yudkin, *Isaac Lamdan*, 233).

48. Ibid., 233–34.

49. The fear that they would not be able to adapt to Palestine engendered for many prospective Jewish migrants deeply conflicted feelings. These feelings are nicely exemplified in letters that the writer J. C. Brenner wrote between 1906 and 1909, when after much hesitation he finally decided to leave for Palestine as part of the Second Aliya (Elon, *The Israelis*, 108–9).

50. Schwartz, Zerubavel, and Barnett, "The Recovery of Masada," 159.

51. Robert Alter claimed that as of 1973 *Masada* had gone through "a score or more" of printings ("The Masada Complex," *Commentary* 56 [July 1973]: 22).

According to Zerubavel, the poem had by 1995 gone through eleven editions (*Recovered Roots*, 116, 274 n. 7). Citing a Hebrew-language Tel Aviv University master's thesis (1985) by Tamara Blaushild, Nachman Ben-Yehuda claims that Lamdan's poem became an integral part of the curriculum in Israeli schools in the late 1930s and early 1940s, peaked in influence in the 1950s, and underwent a decline in popularity in the late 1960s (*The Masada Myth*, 222–23).

52. Although my emphasis here is clearly on Lamdan's poem, Alter argues that Josephus's work, as an example of the power of literature to generate myth, is as much "literature" as Lamdan's (*The Masada Complex*, 24).

53. Schwartz, Zerubavel, and Barnett, "The Recovery of Masada," 149; see also Coser, "Introduction," 33.

54. Elon, *The Israelis*, 13–14.

55. Quoted in Segev, *One Palestine, Complete*, 175. Segev supplies a detailed account of the disturbances, which eventually also involved armed Jewish rioters seeking revenge and resulted in the deaths of forty-seven Jews and forty-eight Arabs (175–83).

56. Details of this disturbance are given in ibid., 314–27.

57. Among these refugees were an estimated sixty thousand German Jews (known among their non-German coreligionists by the mildly derogatory name "Yekkes"), who migrated to Palestine during 1933–1939 under the aegis of the so-called Haavara (Transfer) Agreement concluded in August 1933 between the German Ministry of the Economy and Zionist representatives from Germany and Palestine. One of the more bizarre chapters in German–Jewish relations in the immediate prewar years, the agreement was seen as being in the interests of both sides and had the support of Hitler himself. It enabled Jews to leave Germany for Palestine with a portion of their assets and was framed in such a way that it encouraged the export of German goods to Palestine in the hopes (only partly realized) of breaching the foreign Jewish economic boycott of Germany and ensuring a steady flow of foreign currency into the Reich (see Saul Friedländer, *Nazi Germany and the Jews*, vol. 1: *The Years of Persecution, 1933–1939* [New York: HarperCollins, 1997], 62–63).

58. Elon, *The Israelis*, 148–86.

59. Ben-Yehuda, *The Masada Myth*, 222–23.

60. Zerubavel, "The Death of Memory and the Memory of Death," 79.

61. The effort to spread anti-Semitic ideas among Arabs and other Muslims of the Middle East and North Africa as an instrument of Nazi war strategy is studied in Jeffrey Herf, *Nazi Propaganda for the Arab World* (New Haven, Conn.: Yale University Press, 2009). Suggestive of the tenor of the propaganda themes Herf explores are the following: "Kill the Jews before they kill you," "The Jews kindled this war in the interest of Zionism," "The Americans, the British, and the Jews are all conspiring against Arab interests."

62. Ibid.; Zerubavel, *Recovered Roots*, 72; Ben-Yehuda, *The Masada Myth*, 131–32.

63. The article appeared in the February 1942 issue of *Bamaale* and is quoted in Ben-Yehuda, *The Masada Myth*, 73–74. The Tel Hai skirmish between Jews and Arabs took place at an isolated Jewish settlement in the Upper Galilee on March 1, 1920. Six Jews were killed, including their commander, Yosef Trumpeldor, who previously had made a name for himself as a military hero (he lost an arm fighting in the Russo-Japanese War of 1904) and Zionist activist. Trumpeldor, minutes before dying from his wounds, was reported to have responded to a doctor's query with the words, "Never mind, it is worth dying for the country." The incident had a huge impact on the then still minuscule Jewish population of Palestine, and both Trumpeldor's last words (soon changed to "It is good to die for our country") and the incident quickly became the stuff of legend (Zerubavel, *Recovered Roots*, 39–47; Segev, *One Palestine, Complete*, 122–26).

64. Zerubavel, "The Death of Memory and the Memory of Death," 76–77; Zerubavel, *Recovered Roots*, 70.

65. Ben-Yehuda, *The Masada Myth*, 154–55, emphasis in original.

66. The writer Amos Oz, who was only a boy at the time, describes in moving language the emotions that overcame Jews in Jerusalem when the UN vote was announced. See *A Tale of Love and Darkness*, trans. Nicholas de Lange (Orlando, Fla.: Harcourt, 2004), 356–59.

67. Elon, *The Israelis*, 191–96; Tom Segev, *1949: The First Israelis* (New York: Free Press, 1986), 3–42; Segev, *One Palestine, Complete*, 500–519; "1948 Arab–Israeli War," *Wikipedia*, http://en.wikipedia.org/wiki/1948_Arab%E2%80%93Israeli_War#UN_Partition_Plan (accessed September 12, 2010); Oz, *A Tale of Love and Darkness*, 359–85.

68. "Israel Defense Forces," *Wikipedia*, http://en.wikipedia.org/wiki/Israel_Defense_Forces (accessed September 13, 2010).

69. Lewis, *History*, 4–5.

70. Ben-Yehuda, *The Masada Myth*, 147–52. Part of the swearing-in ceremony involved a reading aloud of an excerpt from Elazar ben Yair's speeches to the Masada defenders. For interesting commentary on the induction ceremony, see Baila R. Shargel, "The Evolution of the Masada Myth," *Judaism* 28 (1979): 363.

71. On Yadin's mythologization of Masada, see Zerubavel, *Recovered Roots*, 65–66, 198–200; Alter, "The Masada Complex," 19, 21; Shargel, "The Evolution of the Masada Myth," 364–68; Ben-Yehuda, *The Masada Myth*, 63–68. Ben-Yehuda has taken a particular interest in the politicization of Yadin's excavations; see his works *Sacrificing Truth: Archaeology and the Myth of Masada* (Amherst, N.Y.: Humanity Books, 2002), and "The Politics–Archaeology Connection at Work," in Philip L. Kohl, Mara Kozelsky, and Nachman Ben-Yehuda, eds.,

Selective Remembrances: Archaeology in the Construction, Commemoration, and Consecration of National Pasts (Chicago: University of Chicago Press, 2007), 247–76. On Yadin's own popularization of the excavations, see his book *Masada: Herod's Fortress and the Zealots' Last Stand*, trans. Moshe Pearlman (New York: Random House, 1966).

72. Zerubavel, *Recovered Roots*, 129–30.

73. Yael Zerubavel, "The Politics of Remembrance and the Consumption of Space: Masada in Israeli Memory," in Daniel J. Walkowitz and Lisa Maya Knauer, eds., *Memory and the Impact of Political Transformation in Public Space* (Durham, N.C.: Duke University Press, 2004), 246; see on the facing page a photograph of President Bill Clinton visiting Masada with his family in December 1998, accompanied by Israeli prime minister Binyamin Netanyahu and his wife.

74. Zerubavel, "The Death of Memory and the Memory of Death," 89–90.

75. Peter Beinart, "The Failure of the American Jewish Establishment," *New York Review of Books*, June 10, 2010, 18. The second poll, according to an Education Ministry official, constituted "a huge warning signal in light of the strengthening trends of extremist views among the youth" (ibid.).

76. See Yadin, *Masada*, 164–67, 181–91, for descriptions of these finds, along with photographs.

77. Zerubavel, "The Politics of Remembrance and the Consumption of Space," 244, 248–49. Zerubavel notes the irony that "whereas the religious argument was at the center of the earlier opposition to the secular interpretation of Masada, some Orthodox and Ultra Orthodox circles now embrace the place for its religious symbolic value" (248–49). Elaborating on this view, Omer Bartov points out that the religious and right-wing nationalist transformation that has taken place in Israel in recent years has been accompanied by a reemergence of apocalyptic and messianic notions, even among some of the country's military leaders. For such individuals, in his view, Masada has become a symbol of dying in the name of God (*kiddush ha-Shem*), a concept that goes beyond nationalism and prefers loyalty to faith and perceived destiny over loyalty to the state and its institutions or even the majority opinion (personal communication to the author, March 14, 2012). Supporting Bartov's point is a recent article by David Remnick in which he notes that the Israeli military "is becoming more and more heavily populated by religious Zionists. . . . In 1990, only two per cent of the infantry's officer training corps was religious; now the figure is forty-two per cent" ("The Vegetarian: A Notorious Spymaster Becomes a Dissident," *The New Yorker*, September 3, 2012, 27).

78. Zerubavel, "The Politics of Remembrance and the Consumption of Space," 242–44, 248.

79. Elon, *The Israelis*, 241–42, 325–26, quotation from 241.

80. In a speech given at Duke University on September 29, 2010, U.S. secretary of defense Robert M. Gates said that although veterans from Iraq and Afghanistan were embraced upon their return home, "for most Americans the wars remain an abstraction—a distant and unpleasant series of news items that do not affect them personally" (quoted in Elisabeth Bumiller, "Gates Fears Wider Gap Between Country and Military," *New York Times*, September 30, 2010).

81. George Packer, "The Unconsoled: A Writer's Tragedy, and a Nation's," *The New Yorker*, September 27, 2010, 50–61.

82. Elon, *The Israelis*, 6–7, 25–26, Dayan quotation from 26.

83. Israeli casualties in the Yom Kippur War were 2,688 killed and 7,250 wounded. The recently declassified and released confidential discussions held by Israel's top leaders in the first days of the 1973 war are highly revealing and created quite a stir among the Israeli public; for a summation of their contents, see Ethan Bronner, "Transcripts on '73 War, Now Public, Grip Israel," *New York Times*, October 11, 2010. For more on the war itself, see Mitchell Bard, "The 1973 Yom Kippur War," http://www.jewishvirtuallibrary.org/jsource/History/73_War.html (accessed September 20, 2010); "Yom Kippur War," *Wikipedia*, http://en.wikipedia.org/wiki/Yom_Kippur_War (accessed September 20, 2010).

84. The Yavneh tradition is often coupled with that of Masada as two alternative responses to situations in which Jewish life and culture are under dire threat. During the destruction of Jerusalem in 70 C.E., Rabbi Yohanan ben Zakkai, wishing to preserve Jewish traditions at a time when there was no longer a viable priesthood in Jerusalem, appealed to the Romans to let him establish a center of Jewish learning in the small coastal town of Yavneh. Ever since, the Yavneh and Masada metaphors, socially represented by the scholar and the warrior, have symbolized the choice between accommodation of the powers that be in order to ensure the cultural survival of Judaism or militant, nationalist-inspired resistance at the risk of extinction. See Lewis, *History*, 20–21; Ben-Yehuda, *The Masada Myth*, 48–49, 230–31; Bruner and Gorfain, "Dialogic Narration and the Paradoxes of Masada," 68–69.

85. The first comment is in a letter written by Dan Ben-Amos and dated February 18, 1983; the second comment comes from a letter written by Don Handelman and is dated March 6, 1983. The two letters are reproduced in Bruner and Gorfain, "Dialogic Narration and the Paradoxes of Masada," 76–79. Ben-Yehuda, in basic agreement with the second letter writer, feels that although the demythologization of Masada was in the making for a long time, what really triggered it was the Six-Day War, which among other things made it possible for Israelis to visit sites that were previously inaccessible to them, such as the Western Wall (*The Masada Myth*, 254–55).

86. Alter, "The Masada Complex," 23–24.

87. Thus, Israel, in the fighting that took place in Lebanon in the summer of 2006, could eliminate 90 percent of Hezbollah's fighting capacity, but Hezbollah could "still declare victory," claiming "that it fought the mighty Israeli army to a draw" (Steven Erlanger, "The Long-Term Battle: Defining 'Victory' Before the World," *New York Times*, August 3, 2006).

88. Alter, "The Masada Complex," 24.

89. Israel has neither confirmed nor denied the assumption that it has developed a serious nuclear weapons capacity, which was significantly enhanced in the aftermath of the Yom Kippur War (Joseph Lelyveld, "The Alliance That Dared Not Speak Its Name," *New York Review of Books*, October 28, 2010, 32). For Israel's longstanding policy of "opacity" in regard to its nuclear program, see Avner Cohen, *Israel and the Bomb* (New York: Columbia University Press, 1998).

90. Moshe Dayan, *Moshe Dayan: Story of My Life* (New York: Morrow, 1976), 450.

91. Shargel, "The Evolution of the Masada Myth," 370.

92. Zerubavel, "The Death of Memory and the Memory of Death," 86–89, quotations from 88; see also Zerubavel, *Recovered Roots*, 192–95, and "The Politics of Remembrance and the Consumption of Space," 245–46.

93. Ben-Yehuda, *The Masada Myth*, 126, 159–60, 200–201, 231, 250, 253–58; Zerubavel, "The Politics of Remembrance and the Consumption of Space," 248.

94. Elon notes the irony that although "Zionist dreamers envisaged a safe haven in Israel for persecuted Jews everywhere, . . . in Israel today [around 1970], Jews, as Jews, live in greater danger of their lives than anywhere else in the world" (*The Israelis*, 224). He devotes an entire chapter of his book (chapter 9) to this danger. See also David Grossman's remarkable novel *To the End of the Land*, trans. Jessica Cohen (New York: Knopf, 2010), which on one level is a monument to the suffocating omnipresence of war in Israeli life.

95. Ben-Yehuda, *The Masada Myth*, 255–56.

96. Ibid., 311.

97. "My paramount object in this struggle," Lincoln wrote Horace Greeley on August 22, 1862, "*is* to save the Union and is *not* either to save or destroy slavery. If I could save the Union without freeing *any* slave, I would do it" (letter included in *The People Shall Judge: Readings in the Formation of American Policy*, 2 vols. [Chicago: University of Chicago Press, 1949], 1:768–69, emphasis in original). For a riveting account of Lincoln and his wife's seemingly inconsistent (at least to us today) attitudes toward black people, focusing first on the relationship between Mrs. Lincoln and her black dressmaker, Elizabeth Keckley, and then on Mr. Lincoln's morally complicated dealings with the black abolitionist Frederick Douglass, see David Remnick, *The Bridge: The Life and Rise of Barack Obama* (New York: Vintage Books, 2011), 564–72.

98. Ben-Yehuda, *The Masada Myth*, 14, 21. The only thing that would keep the veracity of Josephus's work from being of little or no consequence, according to Ben-Yehuda, would be if "an empirically substantiated claim that Josephus Flavius's work is fatally flawed or totally fabricated" were to be made, something that thus far has not happened (325 n. 4). Ben-Yehuda also contends that "we simply must take Josephus's version as our baseline. When I refer to Josephus's historical narrative as truth this is exactly what I have in mind—a historical baseline. While it is possible that Josephus's version is a myth too, in my opinion that claim is quite fantastic. The chances that Josephus lied and cheated his own Roman masters as well as those who were actually involved in the events, and fabricated on a mass scale a siege that never was, people who never existed, an event that never took place, and the like, do not seem very high. . . . As a historical source, Josephus unquestionably provides a problematic account, but it is the only historical account we have. Historically speaking, then, it is the closest thing to truth that we have about the Jewish Great Revolt and the Masada campaign" (*Sacrificing Truth*, 33). We see here the fatal flaw in Ben-Yehuda's approach. He concedes that Josephus's account has problems, presumably meaning that it contains distortions and very possibly fabrications. But for it to be a "myth," it would have to be a *complete* fabrication, the chances of which "do not seem very high." My rejoinder to this assertion is that the same argument might be made with respect to the Masada story as it circulated in Palestine and Israel in the twentieth century. This story, too, was not totally made up—nobody (and this includes Ben-Yehuda) has yet attempted to make such a claim, at least to my knowledge. What, then, is the justification, in terms of Ben-Yehuda's own understanding of "myth" (as complete fabrication), for his consistent identification of the Masada narrative as a myth?

99. In *Recovered Roots*, Zerubavel has a brief discussion of some of the criticisms leveled at Josephus's account (197–200). See also Alter, "The Masada Complex," 21, 24; Shargel, "The Evolution of the Masada Myth," 360; Zeitlin, "Masada and the Sicarii," 305; Zeitlin, "The Sicarii and Masada," 254, 258; and the wide-ranging discussion of Josephus as a historian in Jack Pastor, Pnina Stern, and Menahem Mor, eds., *Flavius Josephus: Interpretation and History* (Leiden: Brill, 2011). I have found the most detailed, comprehensive, and persuasive reconstruction of what happened at Masada to be Shaye J. D. Cohen, "Masada: Literary Tradition, Archaeological Remains, and the Credibility of Josephus," *Journal of Jewish Studies* 33, nos. 1–2 (1982): 385–405. With respect to the mass suicide in particular, Cohen concludes, on the basis of both literary and archeological evidence, that although "at least some of the Sicarii killed themselves rather than face the Romans," this fact was "exaggerated and embellished." There was no mass suicide, and what suicides there were did not take place in anything like the fashion described by Josephus

(see especially 401–5). For a concise summary of Cohen's argument, see Neil Asher Silberman, *Between Past and Present: Archaeology, Ideology, and Nationalism in the Modern Middle East* (New York: Holt, 1989), 96–99.

100. Roland Barthes gives an illuminating account of the ways in which myth goes beyond a simple distinction between true and false in *Mythologies*, trans. Annette Lavers (New York: Hill and Wang, 1972), see especially the final section, "Myth Today," 109–59.

101. Marilynne Robinson, "Writers and the Nostalgic Fallacy," *New York Times Book Review*, October 13, 1985, 34.

102. Richard Slotkin, *Gunfighter Nation: The Myth of the Frontier in 20th-Century America* (New York: Atheneum, 1992).

103. The quotation is from Jill Lepore, *The Whites of Their Eyes: The Tea Party's Revolution and the Battle Over American History* (Princeton, N.J.: Princeton University Press, 2010), quoted in Gordon S. Wood, "No Thanks for the Memories," *New York Review of Books*, January 13, 2011, 40.

104. For insightful commentary on modern Chinese historical consciousness and the retrospective importance of the Opium War as "the beginning of a prolonged process of enforced 'modernization,'" see Jiwei Ci, *Dialectic of the Chinese Revolution: From Utopianism to Hedonism* (Stanford, Calif.: Stanford University Press, 1994), 25–27, 248–49 n. 1.

105. Wood, "No Thanks for the Memories," 41.

3. CHIANG KAI-SHEK, CHINESE NATIONALIST POLICY, AND THE STORY OF KING GOUJIAN

1. Although many of the details in this chapter are drawn from my book *Speaking to History: The Story of King Goujian in Twentieth-Century China* (Berkeley: University of California Press, 2009), in particular chapters 1–3, the thematic emphasis on Chiang Kai-shek's multifaceted relationship with Goujian and his story given here is substantially different from the focus in that book.

2. See Cho-yun Hsu, "The Spring and Autumn Period," in Michael Loewe and Edward L. Shaughnessy, eds., *The Cambridge History of Ancient China: From the Origins of Civilization to 221 B.C.* (Cambridge: Cambridge University Press, 1999), 564–65; Mark Edward Lewis, "Warring States Political History," in Loewe and Shaughnessy, *The Cambridge History of Ancient China*, 601. The dating of *The Zuo Tradition* and *Discourses of the States* differs from one source to another. David Schaberg spells out in detail the difficulties involved in the appendix "Orality and the Origins of the *Zuozhuan* and *Guoyu*" in his book *A Patterned Past: Form and Thought in Early Chinese Historiography* (Cambridge, Mass.: Asia Center, Harvard University, 2001), 315–24.

For the late fourth century B.C.E. dating, I rely on Stephen Owen, ed. and trans., *An Anthology of Chinese Literature: Beginnings to 1911* (New York: Norton, 1996), 77.

3. Schaberg, *A Patterned Past*, 329 n. 36. See also Chu Binjie and Wang Hengzhan, "Lun xian Qin lishi sanwen zhong de xiaoshuo yinsu" (A discussion of fictional elements in pre-Qin historical prose), *Tianzhong xuekan* 10, no. 2 (1995): 42–48.

4. For an account of the process by which stories became elaborated in early China and continued to grow and change thereafter, see Owen, *An Anthology of Chinese Literature*, 88. Owen singles out as a prime example Wu Zixu, who happens to figure in important ways in the Goujian story.

5. Gu Xijia, "Xi Shi de chuanshuo, shishi ji qita" (Legend, historical fact, and other matters pertaining to Xi Shi), *Minjian wenxue luntan* 1 (1998): 33–39; Gong Weiying, "Lishishang zhen you Xi Shi ma?" (Did history really have a Xi Shi?), *Anhui shixue* 6 (1986): 61–62.

6. Joan of Arc, as we shall see in chapter 4, provides an extreme example of this phenomenon. Indeed, Mary Gordon suggests that there are as many renderings of her story in fiction, film, drama, and television as there are storytellers (*Joan of Arc: A Life* [New York: Lipper/Viking, 2000], 148–65).

7. For more on *The Annals of Wu and Yue*, see Cohen, *Speaking to History*, 242–43 nn. 4 and 6.

8. For a fuller account of the Goujian story as it was known in antiquity, see ibid., chap. 1.

9. A biography of Zheng (under the name Cheng Ch'eng-kung) is in Arthur W. Hummel, ed., *Eminent Chinese of the Ch'ing Period (1644–1912)*, 2 vols. (Washington, D.C.: U.S. Government Printing Office, 1943–1944), 1:108–10. For a 1930s children's story recounting Zheng's liberation of Taiwan from the Dutch, see "Zheng Chenggong," in *Xiaoxuexiao chuji yong guoyu duben* (Chinese primer for lower primary students), 8 vols. (Taiyuan: n.p., 1936), 7:40–41. A fuller five-part account of Zheng's heroic achievements is in the Beiping newspaper *Shibao* (Truth Post), March 17–22, 1934.

10. A biography of Qi (under the name Ch'i Chi-kuang) is in L. Carrington Goodrich and Chaoying Fang, eds., *Dictionary of Ming Biography, 1368–1644*, 2 vols. (New York: Columbia University Press, 1976), 1:220–24; an extended discussion of his career is given in Ray Huang, *1587, a Year of No Significance: The Ming Dynasty in Decline* (New Haven, Conn.: Yale University Press, 1981), 156–88; for a children's story about Qi Jiguang's apotheosis as nationalist hero, see Jiafan [pseud.], "Guang bing" (Qi Jiguang's cakes), *Ertong shijie* 22, no. 18 (1928): 2–4.

11. Late Qing revolutionaries transformed Shi Kefa into an exemplar of racial nationalism (Ko-wu Huang, "Remembering Shi Kefa: Changing Images of

a Hero in Late Imperial and Early Republican China," paper presented at the annual meeting of the Association for Asian Studies, Boston, March 23, 2007). There is a biography of him (under "Shih K'o-fa") in Hummel, *Eminent Chinese of the Ch'ing Period*, 2:651–52. For an appraisal of Wen Tianxiang's heroism, see Frederick W. Mote, "Confucian Eremitism in the Yuan Period," in Arthur F. Wright, ed., *The Confucian Persuasion* (Stanford, Calif.: Stanford University Press, 1960), 233–34.

12. Frederick W. Mote, *Imperial China, 900–1800* (Cambridge, Mass.: Harvard University Press, 1999), 305; Robert Ruhlmann, "Traditional Heroes in Chinese Popular Fiction," in Wright, *The Confucian Persuasion*, 154. For an overview of writings from the 1930s and 1940s portraying Yue Fei as a national hero, see Sun Jiang and Huang Donglan, "Yue Fei xushu, gonggong jiyi yu guozu rentong" (Narratives of Yue Fei, public memory, and national identity), *Ershiyi shiji* 86 (December 2004): 91–92. On the promotion of Yue Fei as a patriotic symbol after the Mukden Incident of September 18, 1931, see Huang Donglan, "Yue Fei miao: Chuangzao gonggong jiyi de 'chang'" (The Yue Fei temple: The creation of a public commemoration "site"), in Sun Jiang, comp., *Shijian, jiyi, xushu* (Event, memory, narrative) (Hangzhou, China: Zhejiang Renmin, 2004), 168, 172.

13. Mote, *Imperial China*, 305.

14. At the fourth national congress of the Guomindang in November 1931, Chiang made a point of urging those in attendance to emulate Yue Fei in his loyalty and devotion to the national cause (Sun and Huang, "Yue Fei xushu," 96).

15. For the locus classicus of *guochi* and a brief account of the difference between its ancient and modern meanings, see Dai Yi's preface in Zhuang Jianping, comp., *Guochi shidian* (A dictionary of national humiliation) (Chengdu, China: Chengdu, 1992), 1.

16. In a frequently reprinted biography of Zheng Chenggong written by a Chinese student in Japan at the turn of the twentieth century, the "constantly recurring theme," according to Ralph Croizier, is "patriotic inspiration and national shame." Echoing the complaints of a small number of late Qing intellectuals, Croizier adds that in the writings of student nationalists at the time, Zheng's "heroic patriotic deeds and spirit are contrasted with the shameful inertness of contemporary Chinese" (*Koxinga and Chinese Nationalism: History, Myth, and the Hero* [Cambridge, Mass.: East Asian Research Center, Harvard University, 1977], 51–53).

17. On the relationship of Chinese nationalism to the Twenty-One Demands, see Zhitian Luo, "National Humiliation and National Assertion: The Chinese Response to the Twenty-One Demands," *Modern Asian Studies* 27, no. 2 (1993): 297–319. The Japanese side of the Twenty-One Demands is dealt with in Marius B. Jansen, *Japan and China: From War to Peace, 1894–1972*

(Chicago: Rand McNally, 1975), 209–23; for Yuan Shikai's response, see Ernest P. Young, *The Presidency of Yuan Shikai: Liberalism and Dictatorship in Early Republican China* (Ann Arbor: University of Michigan Press, 1977), 186–92.

18. Tom Mitchell, "Chiang: The Patriot," *South China Morning Post*, January 3, 2001, 13.

19. Photographs are in Zhongguo Geming Bowuguan (Museum of the Chinese Revolution), comp., *Huangpu junxiao shi tuce* (An illustrated history of the Whampoa Military Academy) (Guangzhou, China: Guangdong Renmin, 1993), 59, 60, 78, 79.

20. News account in *Shenbao*, May 10, 1928. Although a multiplicity of national humiliation days were eventually recognized and observed in China, there was initially only one National Humiliation Day, sometimes identified as May 7, sometimes as May 9. For a full discussion of the confusion over the correct date, see Paul A. Cohen, "Remembering and Forgetting National Humiliation in Twentieth-Century China," *Twentieth-Century China* 27, no. 2 (2002): 26–27 n. 13.

21. Chiang Kai-shek did not seek this confrontation, and, defying strong anti-Japanese sentiment within the party and military establishment (not to mention the Chinese public at large), he ordered the withdrawal of Chinese forces from Ji'nan (Parks M. Coble, *Facing Japan: Chinese Politics and Japanese Imperialism, 1931–1937* [Cambridge, Mass.: Council on East Asian Studies, Harvard University, 1991], 19–21).

22. *Shenbao*, May 9, 1929.

23. Ibid., May 10, 1929.

24. Ibid., May 9, 1931.

25. See the second foldout, entitled "Guochi zhonglei biao," in *Guochi tu* (National humiliation illustrated) (Shanghai: Shangwu, 1931 or 1932).

26. This assumption would not, of course, apply to the crown of thorns, which many Chinese at the time probably would not have been able to decipher.

27. Howard Gardner, *Leading Minds: An Anatomy of Leadership* (New York: Basic Books, 1995), 9–10, 14, 20, 290, and passim. I am grateful to Grace Huang for bringing Gardner's work to my notice.

28. In a fine article that illuminates the Chiang–Goujian connection and is the basis for part of the ensuing discussion, Yang Tianshi notes that because Chiang was a Zhejiang native, he knew the Goujian story well ("Lugouqiao shibian qian Jiang Jieshi de dui-Ri moulüe: Yi Jiang shi riji wei zhongxin suo zuo de kaocha" [Chiang Kai-shek's Japan strategy prior to the Marco Polo Bridge incident: An examination based mainly on Mr. Chiang's diary], *Jindaishi yanjiu* 2 [2001]: 8). My own research indicates that the Goujian story was widely disseminated throughout China during the republican era (and before)

and would likely have been well known to Chiang regardless of his personal geographical origins.

29. Chiang's attraction to and identification with Goujian is emphasized in a number of papers by Grace Huang, including "Laying on Brushwood and Tasting Gall: Jiang Jieshi's (Chiang Kai-shek's) Response to the May 3rd Tragedy," paper presented at the New England regional meeting of the Association for Asian Studies, Cambridge, Mass., October 25, 2003; "Avenging National Humiliation: Chiang Kai-shek's Response to the Japanese Occupation of Manchuria," paper presented at the annual meeting of the American Political Science Association, Chicago, September 3, 2004; and "Speaking to Posterity: Shame, Humiliation, and the Creation of Chiang Kai-shek's Nanjing Era Legacy," *Twentieth-Century China* 36, no. 2 (2011): 149, 154–55, 157–58, 160, 166–67.

30. The version I have seen is the vernacular one: He Jinghuang, "Yue wang Goujian" (King Goujian of Yue), *Zhejiang qingnian* 1, no. 4 (1935): 49–55. The Nanchang Field Headquarters' connection with the compilation is spelled out in an editorial note (ibid., 49). I am grateful to Robert Culp for bringing this publication to my notice.

31. Hans van de Ven, "New States of War: Communist and Nationalist Warfare and State Building (1928–1934)," in Hans van de Ven, ed., *Warfare in Chinese History* (Leiden: Brill, 2000), 366–71.

32. Yang, "Lugouqiao shibian qian Jiang Jieshi de dui-Ri moulüe," 10. See also Cohen, *Speaking to History*, 258 n. 89.

33. Shu Yin, "Zai wutaishang de rensheng (shang): Wo de juzuo he yanxi shenghuo" (A career on the stage [part 1]: My life in drama and acting), *Xin wenxue shiliao* 4 (1996): 56–57.

34. Entry dated September 20, 1931, quoted in Yang, "Lugouqiao shibian qian Jiang Jieshi de dui-Ri moulüe," 8. After meeting with a Japanese military officer on January 30, 1934, Chiang wrote in his diary: "His contemptuousness was plainly visible in his expression. If we don't forbear and put up with temporary difficulties [*woxin changdan*], how are we to revive the nation?" (quoted in ibid.).

35. Diary entry dated September 28, 1931, quoted in Yang Tianshi, "Jiuyiba shibianhou de Jiang Jieshi" (Chiang Kai-shek after the September 18 incident), in Yang Tianshi, *Jiang shi midang yu Jiang Jieshi zhenxiang* (The secret files of Mr. Chiang and the truth about Chiang Kai-shek) (Beijing: Shehui kexue wenxian, 2002), 352.

36. Diary entry dated February 14, 1934, quoted in Yang, "Lugouqiao shibian qian Jiang Jieshi de dui-Ri moulüe," 8.

37. Diary entry dated February 15–16, 1934, quoted in ibid., 9.

38. Jay Taylor, *The Generalissimo: Chiang Kai-shek and the Struggle for Modern China* (Cambridge, Mass.: Harvard University Press, 2009), 109, 136. Taylor argues that Chiang's philosophical and emotional preoccupation with the idea

of shame fit in well with the Christian emphasis on sin and atonement, but he adds that "the practice of Job-like perseverance in the face of suffering, difficulty, and death" was also consistent with Chiang's ascetic, neo-Confucian outlook (ibid., 91).

39. Diary entry dated February 15–16, 1934, quoted in Yang, "Lugouqiao shibian qian Jiang Jieshi de dui-Ri moulüe," 9–10.

40. Quoted in Chiang Kai-shek, *China's Destiny and Chinese Economic Theory*, with notes and commentary by Philip Jaffe (London: Dennis Dobson, 1947), 123.

41. Jiang Jieshi [Chiang Kai-shek], *Zhongguo zhi mingyun* (China's destiny), in *Xian zongtong Jiang gong quanji* (The complete works of the late president Mr. Chiang), 3 vols., comp. Zhang Qiyun (Taibei: Zhongguo wenhua daxue, 1984), 1:149. In subsequent years, Chiang regularly alluded to the Goujian story in his speeches. See, for example, "Nuli wancheng xunzheng daye" (Work hard to bring to fruition the great cause of political tutelage) (May 17, 1931), in ibid., 1:618–19; "Jiao yang wei" (Moral instruction, material support, strict discipline) (February 12, 1934), in ibid., 1:804–5.

42. Chiang's talk is excerpted in Zeng Die, "Yue wang Goujian zuo feiji" (King Goujian of Yue taking an airplane), *Ren yan* 1, no. 1 (1934): 19.

43. Lloyd E. Eastman, "Nationalist China During the Nanking Decade, 1927–1937," in John K. Fairbank and Albert Feuerwerker, eds., *The Cambridge History of China*, vol. 13: *Republican China, 1912–1949* (Cambridge: Cambridge University Press, 1986), part 2, 160–62.

44. Lloyd E. Eastman, *The Abortive Revolution: China Under Nationalist Rule, 1927–1937* (Cambridge, Mass.: Harvard University Press, 1974), 28.

45. Zou Lu, "Ning fu fei Goujian qie bu pei wei Qin Gui" (The Nanjing government is not Goujian and doesn't even merit being referred to as Qin Gui), *Wenming zhi lu* 17 (1935): 45–46.

46. Lin Guanghan, "Wo wei Goujian, ren fei Fuchai" (We are Goujian, but the other side isn't Fuchai), *Xibei xiangdao* 9 (1936): 3–8; see also Cohen, *Speaking to History*, 259 n. 103. Edited by a Communist, Cong Dezi, *Xibei xiangdao* was published every ten days under the auspices of the Xi'an army headquarters of Zhang Xueliang and Yang Hucheng, two Nationalist commanders who favored immediate resistance against Japan. In the wake of the Xi'an Incident of December 1936, in which both Zhang and Yang played key roles, the Nationalists shut down the paper (Zhao Jiabi, "Zufu: Guan Jigang" [My grandfather: Guan Jigang], January 18, 2003, http://gzs2.tougao.com/yhgm458/list.asp?id=64).

47. Jerome Bruner, *Making Stories: Law, Literature, Life* (Cambridge, Mass.: Harvard University Press, 2002), 7, 34–35, 60.

48. Gardner, *Leading Minds*, 13–14, 45–49.

49. Yang Tianshi discusses Chiang's diplomatic démarches in the years immediately following the Mukden Incident in "Lugouqiao shibian qian Jiang Jieshi de dui-Ri moulüe," 12–17.

50. See Yang Tianshi's discussion in ibid., 23–26; the need for concealing military preparations against Japan is also noted in Chiang, *China's Destiny*, 128.

51. Yang, "Lugouqiao shibian qian Jiang Jieshi de dui-Ri moulüe," 26–27.

52. For the Nationalist perspective, see, for example, Liu Zhen, *Guochi shigang* (An outline history of national humiliation) (Taibei: Zhengzhong shuju, 1974), 313, 330–31; and Cohen, *Speaking to History*, 260 n. 1.

53. Nancy Bernkopf Tucker, *Patterns in the Dust: Chinese–American Relations and the Recognition Controversy, 1949–1950* (New York: Columbia University Press, 1983), 198. See also Ralph N. Clough, *Island China* (Cambridge, Mass.: Harvard University Press, 1978), 96–98.

54. See, for example, the following two speeches by Chiang Kai-shek: "Fuzhi de shiming yu mudi" (My mission and goals on being reinstated in my post), March 13, 1950, in *Xian zongtong Jiang gong quanji*, 2:1959; "Guomin gemingjun jiangshi xuechi fuchou zhi dao" (The path to erasing humiliation and taking revenge followed by the officers and men of the national revolutionary army), November 1950, in ibid., 2:2078.

55. Chiang Kai-shek repeatedly admonished his compatriots to examine the reasons for the humiliating loss of the mainland and, mindful of their past mistakes, to strive to atone for them and make amends (Cohen, *Speaking to History*, 261 n. 3).

56. Ralph N. Clough, "United States China Policy" (1959), reprinted in Franz Schurmann and Orville Schell, eds., *The China Reader: Communist China* (New York: Vintage, 1967), 311.

57. Ralph N. Clough, "Taiwan Under Nationalist Rule, 1949–1982," in Roderick MacFarquhar and John K. Fairbank, eds., *The Cambridge History of China*, vol. 15: *The People's Republic, Part 2: Revolutions Within the Chinese Revolution, 1966–1982* (Cambridge: Cambridge University Press, 1991), 815–40.

58. The October 10, 1963, message is reprinted in James C. Hsiung et al., eds., *Contemporary Republic of China: The Taiwan Experience, 1950–1980* (New York: Praeger, 1981), 399–402. For similar themes in Taiwan newspaper editorials, see Cohen, *Speaking to History*, 261 n. 7.

59. Examples of titles incorporating the phrase *fuguo* are cited in Cohen, *Speaking to History*, 261–62 n. 10.

60. Colin Mackerras argues that theater may well have been a factor in the Communists' victory in the civil war ("Theater and the Masses," in Colin Mackerras, ed., *Chinese Theater: From Its Origins to the Present Day* [Honolulu: University of Hawai'i Press, 1983], 159).

61. Nancy Guy, *Peking Opera and Politics in Taiwan* (Urbana: University of Illinois Press, 2005), 5; see also 4, 9, 43, 66, 74, 82.

62. Quoted with permission from David Der-wei Wang, "1905, 1955, 2005," unpublished paper (1906). The ROC Ministry of Defense's involvement with Peking opera was especially strong prior to the mid-1960s but remained active after that time as well (Guy, *Peking Opera and Politics in Taiwan*, 9, 62, 69).

63. Chen Wenquan, *Goujian yu Xi Shi* (Goujian and Xi Shi) (Taibei: Xin shiji juyi, 1959); Tan Zhijun, *Goujian fuguo* (Goujian recovers his country), in *Zhonghua xiju ji* (Collection of Chinese plays), 10 vols. (Taibei: Zhongguo xiju yishu zhongxin, 1970–1971), 3:1–153; Zhang Daxia, *Goujian fuguo* (Taibei: Liming wenhua shiye gongsi, 1982). According to Zhang Daxia, an authority on Chinese opera, many other operas prior to his had also used the title *Goujian fuguo* (Cohen, *Speaking to History*, 101).

64. Tan, *Goujian fuguo*, 152; Chen, *Goujian yu Xi Shi*, 112.

65. The adulation of Chiang was ubiquitous in post-1950 Taiwan, and it began early in life, with primary school pupils exposed to it year after year in their Chinese (*guoyu*) primers. For examples, see Cohen, *Speaking to History*, 265 n. 46.

66. Biographical information on Huang can be found in Li Shuangqing's preface to *Zhonghua shixue lunji: Huang Dashou xiansheng qi zhi rongqing lunwen ji* (Essays on Chinese history: Essays in honor of Mr. Huang Dashou on his seventieth birthday) (Taibei: Liming, 1991), 1–46.

67. Huang's fullest account of his extensive activities promoting the Goujian story is in "Goujian," in *Zhonghua weiren gushi* (Stories of great Chinese) (Taibei: Huanqiu shuju, 1975), 56 n. 7. See also the introduction to Huang Dashou, *Zhongxing shihua* (Historical accounts of national resurgence) (Taibei: Shijie, 1955), 3 (front matter). "Goujian mie Wu" is the first of the seven items in *Zhongxing shihua*, 1–30.

68. "Cheng Tianfang xiansheng xu" (The preface of Mr. Cheng Tianfang), in Huang, *Zhongxing shihua*, 2.

69. Huang, "Fuyin qianji" (Introduction), in ibid., 3.

70. Michael Szonyi, *Cold War Island: Quemoy on the Front Line* (Cambridge: University of Cambridge Press, 2008), 113–16.

71. Huang, "Goujian mie Wu," 30.

72. Apart from Huang Jilu and Cheng Tianfang, noted earlier, Wang Yunwu, who served in numerous important posts first on the mainland and later in Taiwan, wrote a preface to Shen Gangbo et al., eds., *Minzu yingxiong ji geming xianlie zhuanji* (Biographies of national heroes and revolutionary martyrs), 2 vols. (Taibei: Zhengzhong shuju, 1966), in which Huang's piece "Goujian" appeared.

73. Hung-mao Tien, *The Great Transition: Political and Social Change in the Republic of China* (Stanford, Calif.: Hoover Institution Press, 1989), 195–97, 211–12.

74. For Huang's activities in this regard, see the appendix to *Zhonghua weiren gushi*, 341–86, and Cohen, *Speaking to History*, 110–14.

75. Lan Hong, *Woxin changdan* (Sleeping on brushwood and tasting gall) (Taibei: Dongguang chubanshe, 1976). The government's imprimatur was equally explicit in a biography of Goujian (*Goujian zhuan*) compiled and published by the General Political Department of the Ministry of National Defense in 1952, which I haven't been able to examine.

76. See the book's back cover for particulars.

77. Lan, *Woxin changdan*, 57, 60.

78. Ibid., 64.

79. Immanuel C. Y. Hsü, *The Rise of Modern China*, 6th ed. (New York: Oxford University Press, 2000), 911; also Clough, *Island China*, 61–62.

80. Doubtless there were additional items relating to the story published after the 1980s in magazines and journals. But I would expect the story's coverage in such publications to follow the same trends—both quantitative and qualitative—as found in book-length literature. This reasoning applies equally to publicity given the story in nonprint media.

81. Detailed information on the five works can be found in Cohen, *Speaking to History*, 130–33.

82. This kind of identification, borrowed from the Soviet Union under Stalin, could be used either to criticize or to praise a leading political figure. It was widely practiced in the historical dramas of the late 1950s in the PRC, according to Rudolf Wagner ("'In Guise of a Congratulation': Political Symbolism in Zhou Xinfang's Play *Hai Rui Submits His Memorial*," in Jonathan Unger, ed., *Using the Past to Serve the Present: Historiography and Politics in Contemporary China* [Armonk, N.Y.: M. E. Sharpe, 1993], 71). My clear impression is that the linkage can be extended beyond written literary works to the functioning of stories in political society generally in China.

83. Zhiqing [pseud.], "Buwang guochi de Goujian" (Goujian, who didn't forget our national humiliation), *Minzhong xunkan* 4, nos. 16–17 (1934): 18–19.

84. Xiao Jun's two-volume novel *Wu Yue chunqiu shihua* (A story from the annals of Wu and Yue), although written in the 1950s, was not published until 1980 (Harbin, China: Heilongjiang Renmin); Bai Hua's play *Wu wang jin ge Yue wang jian* (The golden spear of the king of Wu and the sword of the king of Yue) first appeared in *Shiyue* 2 (1983): 65–95, 64.

85. These works are discussed in Cohen, *Speaking to History*, 220–21, 225–26, 283–84 n. 60.

86. The combined effect of these two developments on promotion of the Goujian story is discussed in ibid., 220–24.

4. THE ENIGMA OF THE APPEAL OF JOAN
OF ARC IN WARTIME FRANCE

1. Wang Zhi and Tang Feng, "Ye tan woxin changdan" (More on sleeping on brushwood and tasting gall), *Dangjian yu rencai* 10–11 (2002): 53, quoted in Paul A. Cohen, *Speaking to History: The Story of King Goujian in Twentieth-Century China* (Berkeley: University of California Press, 2009), 213. For a somewhat different take on the value of "sleeping on brushwood and tasting gall" as a strategy for dealing with rejection in one's search for the ideal job, see Sun Hongming, "Qiuzhi zhong de 'woxin changdan'" ("Sleeping on brushwood and tasting gall" in job hunting), *Siwei yu zhihui* 11 (2001): 21.

2. On Hua Mulan, see Joan Judge, *The Precious Raft of History: The Past, the West, and the Woman Question in China* (Stanford, Calif.: Stanford University Press, 2008), passim. Hua Mulan was also an important symbol of resistance during the later Sino-Japanese War. For a comparison of her and Joan of Arc as female warriors, see Chang-tai Hung, "Female Symbols of Resistance in Chinese Wartime Spoken Drama," *Modern China* 15, no. 2 (1989): 171–74.

3. For one early-twentieth-century Chinese writer (Mei Zhu), it was precisely Joan of Arc's defiance of feminine norms that was the source of her renown. She never could have led the French against the English if she had been bound by the strict rules of gender separation and filial piety that were customary in China (Judge, *The Precious Raft of History*, 168). Joan of Arc was also held up as a model in other non-Western countries: a number of Chinese biographies of her were translated from Japanese accounts, which began to appear as early as 1866 (ibid., 166, 280 n. 108); and for accounts of Joan of Arc in Egypt, see Marilyn Booth, "The Egyptian Lives of Jeanne d'Arc," in Lila Abu-Lughod, ed., *Remaking Women: Feminism and Modernity in the Middle East* (Princeton, N.J.: Princeton University Press, 1998), 171–211. Significantly in terms of the argument I advance in this book, Booth, in trying to account for Joan of Arc's great popularity in Egypt between 1879 and 1939, suggests that her "persona, rewritten in Egypt by editors, regular magazine contributors, and readers writing in, could symbolize identities of immediate import to competing agendas and local struggles of the time. Jeanne could represent the anti-imperialist activist in the service of a nation in formation; the devout believer who puts personal faith into action on behalf of the nation; the peasant as crucial in the national struggle; the young woman as having to reconcile duty to nation with duty to family. In fact, Jeanne's encapsulation of the very struggle between different loyalties and identities, rather than simply her ability to represent those loyalties, is a key to Jeanne's popularity" (172).

4. For an extensive list of examples of Joan-inspired works, see "Cultural Depictions of Joan of Arc," *Wikipedia*, http://en.wikipedia.org/wiki/Cultural_depictions_of_Joan_of_Arc (accessed May 12, 2011).

5. John Flower, *Joan of Arc: Icon of Modern Culture* (Hastings, U.K.: Helm Information, 2008), 88. See Shakespeare's play *Henry VI, Part One* (1592), Southey's poem *Joan of Arc* (1795), Shaw's play *Saint Joan* (opened in 1923, first published in 1924), Brecht's play *Die Heilige Johanna der Schlachthöfe* (Saint Joan of the stockyards, 1932), Schiller's play *Die Jungfrau von Orleans* (The maid of Orléans, 1801) and his poem *Das Mädchen von Orleans* (The girl of Orléans, 1801), Yoshikazu's three-volume comic strip (*manga*) *Joan* (1995–1996), Twain's novel *Personal Recollections of Joan of Arc* (1895), Anderson's play *Joan of Lorraine* (1947), DeMille's film *Joan the Woman* (1916), Verdi's opera *Giovanna d'Arco* (Joan of Arc, 1845), Tchaikovsky's opera *The Maid of Orléans* (1881), and Panfilov's film *Nachalo* (The beginning, 1970). With regard to films in particular, Flower states that directors in no fewer than eight countries have produced feature, documentary, educational, and television films relating to the story of Joan of Arc (197). One of the finest of these films is the Danish director Carl Dreyer's *The Passion of Joan of Arc*, made in 1928 and discussed in Flower, *Joan of Arc*, 201–5.

6. Flower, *Joan of Arc*, 95, 143, 181–82, 199; Claude Grimal, "Appendix: The American Maid," in Flower, *Joan of Arc*, 260–61. See also William Shakespeare, *First Part of King Henry VI*, in *The Complete Works of William Shakespeare* (London: Spring Books, 1975), 474–500; Sumiko Higashi, *Cecil B. DeMille and American Culture: The Silent Era* (Berkeley: University of California Press, 1994), which gives detailed consideration to DeMille's film in chapter 5 (the quoted phrases are from 122, 140); and Kevin J. Harty, "Jeanne au Cinéma," in Bonnie Wheeler and Charles T. Wood, eds., *Fresh Verdicts on Joan of Arc* (New York: Garland, 1996), 241–43.

7. For an incisive and psychologically perceptive portrayal of Joan in all of her contradictoriness, see the long preface (dated 1924) with which Bernard Shaw introduces *Saint Joan: A Chronicle Play in Six Scenes and an Epilogue* (1951; reprint, Baltimore: Penguin, 1974), 7–48.

8. Mary Gordon, *Joan of Arc: A Life* (New York: Lipper/Viking, 2000), xxi.

9. For the ensuing account of Joan of Arc's story, I am indebted to Marina Warner, *Joan of Arc: The Image of Female Heroism* (Berkeley: University of California Press, 1981); Flower, *Joan of Arc*; and above all Larissa Juliet Taylor, *The Virgin Warrior: The Life and Death of Joan of Arc* (New Haven, Conn.: Yale University Press, 2009). Taylor, in an appendix to her book (192–200), furnishes a critical assessment of the major sources on Joan of Arc's life and career, which include—in addition to the written record of her trial and the nullification proceedings—numerous chronicles, letters, account books, contemporary poems, military manuals, and "theological treatises about her actions in the context of divine inspiration and gender" (200).

10. For an excellent picture of the complicated political arrangements characterizing France in the first half of the fifteenth century, see Warner, *Joan of Arc*, chap. 2.

11. Taylor, *The Virgin Warrior*, 17.

12. Willard R. Trask, comp. and trans., *Joan of Arc: In Her Own Words* (New York: Turtle Point Press, 1996), 5–7; see also Flower, *Joan of Arc*, 9–11.

13. Taylor, *The Virgin Warrior*, 45.

14. Quoted in ibid., 48.

15. Quoted in ibid., 49.

16. Warner, *Joan of* Arc, 64–65, 164; Taylor, *The Virgin Warrior*, 51–54, 61–66 (quotation from 66).

17. During the nullification proceedings in 1456, Joan's confessor reported that she had told him on the eve of the battle that "[t]omorrow blood will flow on my body from a wound above my breast." At her trial in 1431, Joan insisted that she had indeed known this beforehand (Warner, *Joan of Arc*, 109–10). Taylor asserts that others besides Joan's confessor also knew of the prediction and conjectures that Joan and her soldiers may have planned a ruse in advance of the battle to confirm English fears of her invincibility (*The Virgin Warrior*, 70–72).

18. Taylor, *The Virgin Warrior*, 84 (I have changed Taylor's spelling from "Reims" to "Rheims"); Warner, *Joan of Arc*, 70. For a slightly different chronology, in which the fighting in mid-June takes place *after* Joan visited Charles and persuaded him to go with her and his army to Rheims, see Flower, *Joan of Arc*, 22–23.

19. Taylor, *The Virgin Warrior*, 86; see also Warner, *Joan of Arc*, 70.

20. As given in Jules Quicherat, *Procès de condemnation et de réhabilitation de Jeanne d'Arc dite la Pucelle*, 5 vols. (Paris: Jules Renouard, 1841–1849), 5:186, quoted in Warner, *Joan of Arc*, 72.

21. Vita Sackville-West, *Saint Joan of Arc* (New York: Doubleday, 1936), 225, quoted in Flower, *Joan of Arc*, 24.

22. Taylor, *The Virgin Warrior*, 102. Warner, in apparent contrast to Taylor, asserts that the taking of Paris was "part of the plan she [Joan] claimed to have received from God" (*Joan of Arc*, 73).

23. Quoted in Taylor, *The Virgin Warrior*, 118.

24. Warner notes that, "[a]fter Orleans and Rheims, Joan failed to conjure the wonders to which her side had become accustomed" and then details the downhill course that ensued (*Joan of Arc*, 77–78).

It is fascinating to compare the trajectory of Joan of Arc's career after the sacred script received from her voices was consummated with the course of another—and very different—historical event after *its* sacred script ran out. I refer to the rebellion of the Heavenly Kingdom of Great Peace in the middle of the nineteenth century in China, commonly known as the Taiping Rebellion (1851–1864). Its founder and leader, Hong Xiuquan, fell ill in 1837 and had a vision in which he was taken up to heaven, where he was admitted into the presence of the Old Father, who complained that human beings had turned away from him and willingly placed themselves in the service of demons. There was a reference in the vision to Hong's Elder Brother, who at an earlier time performed miracles and remitted the sins of mankind; there were also references to Hong himself as the Younger Brother. Some years later, Hong's vision was given a Christian interpretation, the main protagonists being identified as God, Jesus Christ, and Satan. Hong came to believe that the Manchus, the then rulers of China under the Qing dynasty, were demons to be exterminated and that God would, through his emissary Hong Xiuquan (his Chinese son), free the Chinese people from the foreign (Manchu) yoke under which they lived. When the Taiping army reached Nanjing in March 1853 after winning a string of battles against the Manchus, Hong Xiuquan referred to the city as the "New Jerusalem," and the Taipings renamed it Tianjing, the "Heavenly Capital." But then something happened that was plainly suggestive of Joan of Arc's experience. God's instructions contained in Hong's vision had promised the overthrow of the demons once the Heavenly Kingdom was brought into existence, and for a time, as the Taipings fought the Manchus successfully against all odds (as Joan also had done in the first phase of her fighting against the English), the vision seemed to be confirmed by reality. But there was an element of ambiguity in both sacred scripts. Once the script ran out, the fundamental problem—the English for Joan of Arc and the French, the Manchus for Hong Xiuquan and the Taipings—remained unresolved, and in the absence of further heavenly guidance things began to fall apart. Following the coronation of Charles VII, sharp differences among strategic options emerged among the French, ending in serious setbacks at the hands of the English and their Burgundian allies; in the Taiping case, after the establishment of the rebel capital in Nanjing, the movement was severely weakened by dissension within the leadership, culminating eventually in the Manchu recapture of the rebel capital and defeat of the Taiping cause.

The preceding discussion relies heavily on the detailed and intricate analysis by Rudolf Wagner in his eye-opening monograph *Reenacting the Heavenly Vision: The Role of Religion in the Taiping Rebellion* (Berkeley: Institute of East Asian Studies, University of California, 1982). For Hong's explicit identification of the Taiping Heavenly Capital as the New Jerusalem, see his written commentary on the relevant passage in the Book of Revelation, quoted in Jonathan D. Spence, *God's Chinese Son: The Taiping Heavenly Kingdom of Hong Xiuquan* (New York: Norton, 1996), 295.

25. The great importance of male clothing to Joan's identity and its key role in her trial are dealt with at length in Warner, *Joan of Arc*, chap. 7; see also Taylor, *The Virgin Warrior*, 155–56, 160–62.

26. Quoted in Flower, *Joan of Arc*, 34.

27. Taylor, *The Virgin Warrior*, 163–66.

28. Ibid., 169–71.

29. Ibid., 181–82.

30. The observance of May 8—the anniversary of the date of the raising of the siege of Orléans and Joan of Arc's feast day—was suspended during the French Revolution. Napoleon, with a view to resolving tensions with the church, authorized the resumption of the practice in 1803. "United, the French Nation has never been conquered," he declared. "The Illustriousness of Joan of Arc has proved that there is no miracle that cannot be accomplished by the genius of the French when the National Independence is threatened" (quoted in Warner, *Joan of Arc*, 256).

31. Taylor, *The Virgin Warrior*, 183; Flower, *Joan of Arc*, 120; Warner, *Joan of Arc*, 240, 265–66. In the final volume of *Histoire de France* (1844), Jules Michelet enthusiastically identified Joan of Arc with the French nation; Jules Quicherat's scholarly compilation of the transcripts from Joan's trial and exoneration proceedings, *Procès de condemnation et de rehabilitation de Jeanne d'Arc dite la Pucelle*, appeared in the 1840s (see note 20).

32. The problems Guitton raises in regard to Joan's voices are discussed in Timothy Wilson-Smith, *Joan of Arc: Maid, Myth, and History* (Stroud, U.K.: Sutton, 2006), 213. The neuroscientist David Eagleman, although granting that it is "impossible to retrospectively diagnose with certainty," believes that Joan displayed a number of symptoms, including her voices, that "are certainly consistent with temporal lobe epilepsy." He adds: "When brain activity is kindled in the right spot, people hear voices" (*Incognito: The Secret Lives of the Brain* [New York: Pantheon, 2011], 207–8, 251 n. 11).

33. Barry Schwartz, "The Reconstruction of Abraham Lincoln," in David Middleton and Derek Edwards, eds., *Collective Remembering* (Newbury Park, Calif.: Sage, 1990), 86.

34. See, for example, the images of Joan in female dress in plates 16, 21, 22, 25, 35, 36, 39, 42, and 43 in Warner, *Joan of Arc*; see also plates 15 and 17 in Taylor, *The Virgin Warrior*.

35. Warner, *Joan of Arc*, 237. Gerd Krumeich generalizes this characteristic of Joan of Arc by asserting that "for the collective memory of the French she has always been and will always remain 'la Sainte de la Défense Nationale'" ("The Cult of Joan of Arc Under the Vichy Régime," in Gerhard Hirschfeld and Patrick Marsh, eds., *Collaboration in France: Politics and Culture During the Nazi Occupation, 1940–1944* [Oxford: Berg, 1989], 102).

36. Gabriel Jacobs nicely limns these complexities in "The Role of Joan of Arc on the Stage of Occupied Paris," in Roderick Kedward and Roger Austin, eds., *Vichy France and the Resistance: Culture and Ideology* (London: Croom

Helm, 1985), 106–8.

37. Wilson-Smith, *Joan of Arc*, 207.

38. Marc Pierre, Marquis d'Argenson, *Pétain et le pétinisme: Essai de psychologie* (Paris: Éditions Créator, 1953), 104, quoted in Peter Novick, *The Resistance Versus Vichy: The Purge of Collaborators in Liberated France* (London: Chatto & Windus, 1968), 9.

39. The panegyric and the leaflet quoted in Krumeich, "The Cult of Joan of Arc Under the Vichy Régime," 98–100.

40. Martha Hanna, "Iconology and Ideology: Images of Joan of Arc in the Idiom of the Action française, 1908–1931," *French Historical Studies* 14, no. 2 (1985): 215–39.

41. A notorious clause in the Vichy draft constitution singled the Jews out as "a race that conducts itself as a distinct community that resists assimilation" (quoted in Mark Mazower, *Dark Continent: Europe's Twentieth Century* [New York: Vintage Books, 2000], 60). On the thoroughgoing anti-Semitism of the Pétainist regime, see Novick, *The Resistance Versus Vichy*, 9–10, 84.

42. Both articles quoted in Krumeich, "The Cult of Joan of Arc Under the Vichy Régime," 101.

43. Nick Atkin, "The Cult of Joan of Arc in French Schools, 1940–1944," in Kedward and Austin, *Vichy France and the Resistance*, 265–68.

44. Quoted in Flower, *Joan of Arc*, 73–74.

45. H. R. Kedward, *Occupied France: Collaboration and Resistance 1940–1944* (Oxford: Basil Blackwell, 1985), 30. For the lyrics of "Maréchal, nous voilà!" see http://2ndww.blogspot.com/2009/08/marechal-nous-voila_27.html (accessed June 4, 2011). The hymn ends with the words "For Pétain is France, France is Pétain!"—again evocative of Joan, who was widely regarded as France's patron saint ("la Sainte de la Patrie").

46. Quoted in Eric Jennings, " 'Reinventing Jeanne': The Iconology of Joan of Arc in Vichy Schoolbooks, 1940–44," *Journal of Contemporary History* 29, no. 4 (1994): 717–18.

47. Mazower, *Dark Continent*, 81–82, 103.

48. For the quotations and a discussion of this portrayal of Joan, see Jennings, " 'Reinventing Jeanne,' " 720–21.

49. Ibid., 721.

50. The scholar, Maria-Antoinetta Macciocchi, is quoted in ibid., 722, 733 n. 44.

51. Flower, *Joan of Arc*, 73.

52. Jennings, " 'Reinventing Jeanne,' " 722–25, 730.

53. The original cable, held at the Archives nationales, Centre d'archives d'outre-mer, is quoted in Jennings, " 'Reinventing Jeanne,' " 731 n. 9.

54. Ibid., 713.

55. The poster is reproduced and its text translated in Flower, *Joan of Arc*, 75.

56. Wilson-Smith, *Joan of Arc*, 208; see also Krumeich, "The Cult of Joan of Arc Under the Vichy Régime," 102.

57. Another Vichy luminary who presented the regime with problems was the poet and essayist Charles Péguy (1873–1914). Like Joan of Arc, Péguy was venerated equally by de Gaulle and Vichy. He wrote voluminously about Joan of Arc, whom he greatly admired, and was widely read in Vichy schools and youth camps—despite the fact that he had been a socialist and ardent supporter of Dreyfus (Jacobs, "The Role of Joan of Arc on the Stage of Occupied Paris," 112).

58. The Communist Edith Thomas said in 1947 that during the war Joan of Arc had been "on everyone's lips and in everyone's heart, on altars and on the stage, in speeches made by reactionary officers and in the whisperings of the Resistance" (quoted in Flower, *Joan of Arc*, 74).

59. Jean-Marie Guillon, "Talk Which Was Not Idle: Rumours in Wartime France," in Hanna Diamond and Simon Kitson, eds., *Vichy, Resistance, Liberation: New Perspectives on Wartime France* (Oxford: Berg, 2005), 82.

60. W. D. Halls, *The Youth of Vichy France* (Oxford: Clarendon Press, 1981), 51–52, 226. Halls also supplies a long list of other offenses committed by teachers and students against the Germans (53).

61. Wilson-Smith, *Joan of Arc*, 208.

62. Jonathan Fenby, *The General: Charles de Gaulle and the France He Saved* (New York: Skyhorse, 2012), 2.

63. Churchill quoted in Alexander Werth, *De Gaulle: A Political Biography* (New York: Simon and Schuster, 1966), 101, 160; Harriman quoted in Raoul Aglion, *Roosevelt and de Gaulle, Allies in Conflict: A Personal Memoir* (New York: Free Press, 1988), 150.

64. All quoted in Aglion, *Roosevelt and de Gaulle*, 151–52.

65. Novick, *The Resistance Versus Vichy*, 3.

66. Brian Crozier, *De Gaulle* (New York: Scribner's, 1973), 119–33, esp. 122–23, 133.

67. Wilson-Smith, *Joan of Arc*, 208–9; Flower, *Joan of Arc*, 75.

68. Charles de Gaulle, *The Complete Memoirs of Charles de Gaulle, 1940–1946*, trans. Jonathan Griffin and Richard Howard (New York: Da Capo Press, 1984), 93. The French Tricolor with a red Cross of Lorraine inserted in the middle of the central (white) stripe became the flag of France in exile during the war.

69. Speech titled "The Two Roads," July 2, 1940, in Charles de Gaulle, *The Speeches of General de Gaulle* (London: Oxford University Press, 1944), 9.

70. Speech titled "How to Observe the Festival of Jeanne d'Arc," May 10, 1941, in ibid., 63–64.

71. Speech titled "The Men of Vichy Have Surrendered Syria," May 19, 1941, in ibid., 65. De Gaulle here echoed the propaganda in the clandestine Resistance paper *Libération* on May 18, which reported that the demonstration had succeeded brilliantly, with Parisians pouring into the streets under the frightened eyes of Nazi soldiers who dared not intervene (Jacobs, "The Role of Joan of Arc on the Stage of Occupied Paris," 111).

72. Speech titled "France, Crushed, Looted, and Betrayed Is Once More Finding Her Feet," October 2, 1941, London, in de Gaulle, *The Speeches of General de Gaulle*, 76. Joan of Arc is linked to similar themes in London speeches of January 13, 1942 ("This Indivisible War"), April 30, 1942 ("A Call to France for the First of May"), and November 11, 1942 ("United We Fight for a United Country"), in ibid., 123, 137–38, 178–82.

73. Speech titled "We Have but One Passion: France!" June 18, 1942, London, in ibid., 145, 147.

74. Radio message titled "Well, We Were Right!" June 6, 1943, Algiers, in Charles de Gaulle, *La France n'a pas perdu la guerre: Discours et messages* (New York: Didier, 1944), 239–40.

75. Flower, *Joan of Arc*, 75.

76. Werth, *De Gaulle*, 139–43; Crozier, *De Gaulle*, 235–58.

77. Novick, *The Resistance Versus Vichy*, 60.

78. Patrick Marsh, "Jeanne d'Arc During the German Occupation," *Theatre Research International* 2 (February 1977): 139.

79. For details on these productions, see ibid., 139–42; Jacobs, "The Role of Joan of Arc on the Stage of Occupied Paris," 109–15; Flower, *Joan of Arc*, 158–59; Alan Riding, *And the Show Went On: Cultural Life in Nazi-Occupied Paris* (New York: Knopf, 2010), 214.

80. Quoted in Flower, *Joan of Arc*, 239.

81. Marsh, "Jeanne d'Arc During the German Occupation," 144.

82. Riding, *And the Show Went On*, 214. See also Simon Kitson, "Vichy Web: French Culture During the War," http://artsweb.bham.ac.uk/vichy/culture. htm#bibculture (accessed July 13, 2011). Kitson says that in a memoir published in July 1942 (*Les décombres* [The ruins]), Rebatet "underlined his desire to see a German victory in the war and presented a denunciation of Republican decadence, especially that of the Popular Front. He felt that this decadence had caused France to lose its virility."

83. This statement was originally reported in *Opéra*, December 19, 1945, and is quoted in Marsh, "Jeanne d'Arc During the German Occupation," 142.

84. Critics quoted in Jacobs, "The Role of Joan of Arc on the Stage of Occupied Paris," 115; Beauvoir quoted in Riding, *And the Show Went On*, 214.

85. Kitson, "Vichy Web."

86. Jacobs, "The Role of Joan of Arc on the Stage of Occupied Paris," 118.

87. Ibid., 115.

88. Ibid., 118. The Milice (French Militia) was a paramilitary force formed in January 1943 by Vichy with German help. It regularly resorted to torture and, because its members were French and spoke the language, was often more feared than the Gestapo by members of the Resistance. On its origins and evolution, see Paul J. Kingston, "The Ideologists: Vichy France, 1940–1944," in Hirschfeld and Marsh, *Collaboration in France*, 62–66. For Lemaître's vivid accounts of Inquisition torture, see Claude Vermorel, *Jeanne avec nous* (Paris: Éditions Balzac, 1942), 60–62, 149.

89. Vermorel, *Jeanne avec nous*, 153–55. I have made a few minor changes in the translation given in Flower, *Joan of Arc*, 160–61.

90. Vermorel, *Jeanne avec nous*, 115, my translation.

91. Flower, *Joan of Arc*, 49.

92. Wilson-Smith, *Joan of Arc*, 216, where the poll results are also given.

93. Ibid., 211–12.

94. One such exception took place in the year 2012, when the six hundredth anniversary of Joan of Arc's birth coincided with the French presidential elections. In preparation for the first round of the elections, Nicolas Sarkozy, anxious to siphon votes from his strongest competitor in the right-of-center camp, Marine Le Pen (daughter of Jean-Marie Le Pen and since January 2011 head of the National Front), made a concerted effort to appropriate from the Right Joan of Arc's symbolic power, even traveling to Domremy and Vaucouleurs to honor the memory of the French heroine ("France Proclaims 600th Anniversary of Joan of Arc," http://www.telegraph.co.uk/news/worldnews/europe/france/8996648/France-proclaims-600th-anniversary-of-Joan-of-Arc.html [accessed November 19, 2012]).

95. Wilson-Smith, *Joan of Arc*, 216–21. In *Modernizing Joan of Arc: Conceptions, Costumes, and Canonization* (Jefferson, N.C.: McFarland, 2008), Ellen Ecker Dolgin traces the evolution of gender concerns and how the image of Joan of Arc was adapted to them over time.

96. Translated and quoted in Cohen, *Speaking to History*, 52.

97. This point is made in Chang-tai Hung, *War and Popular Culture: Resistance in Modern China, 1937–1945* (Berkeley: University of California Press, 1994), 78.

98. Wilson-Smith, *Joan of Arc*, 221.

5. ARTFUL PROPAGANDA IN WORLD WAR II: EISENSTEIN'S *ALEXANDER NEVSKY* AND OLIVIER'S *HENRY V*

1. Quoted in Jay Leyda and Zina Voynow, *Eisenstein at Work* (London: Methuen, 1987), 97, footnote. Or, as one scholar has characterized the creation of *Nevsky*, "Drawing on an event that was little documented in historical records, Eisenstein was free to use his imagination" (Birgit Beumers, *A History of Russian Cinema* [Oxford: Berg, 2009], 98; see also Richard Taylor, "Red Stars, Positive Heroes, and Personality Cults," in Richard Taylor and Derek Spring, eds., *Stalinism and Soviet Cinema* [London: Routledge, 1993], 88; Evgeny Dobrenko, *Stalinist Cinema and the Production of History: Museum of the Revolution*, trans. Sarah Young [New Haven, Conn.: Yale University Press, 2008], 76).

2. The historical sources on Nevsky are discussed in Mari Isoaho, *The Image of Aleksandr Nevskiy in Medieval Russia: Warrior and Saint* (Leiden: Brill, 2006), 1–26, quotation from 12.

3. Dobrenko, *Stalinist Cinema and the Production of History*, 4. Dobrenko describes Eisenstein as having "moved towards a conscious mythologisation of history in *Bezhin Meadow* . . . and particularly in *Alexander Nevsky*" (49).

4. This account of the battles against the Swedes and the German Knights draws heavily on the detailed and highly critical treatment in John Fennell, *The Crisis of Medieval Russia, 1200–1304* (London: Longman, 1983), 102–5.

5. Ibid., 103, 105–6.

6. Ibid., 108, 109, 112, 121, 167; Walter G. Moss, *A History of Russia*, vol. 1: *To 1917*, 2nd ed. (London: Anthem, 2002), 75. The sources of Mongol military superiority in the Rus lands—possibly as many as 130,000 troops in 1237—are summarized in Moss, *A History of Russia*, 1:69.

7. Long before its subjugation by the Mongols, Kiev was sacked by the leader of Suzdalia in 1169. Although historians disagree on whether—and if so to what degree—Kiev lost its preeminence in Russia after this date, Vladimir now replaced Kiev as the seat of the grand prince, and by the early thirteenth century Kiev was finished as Russia's main city. See Martin Dimnik, "The Rus' Principalities (1125–1246)," in Maureen Perrie, ed., *The Cambridge History of Russia*, vol. 1: *From Early Rus' to 1689* (Cambridge: Cambridge University Press, 2006), 110–11; Nicholas V. Riasanovsky and Mark D. Steinberg, *A History of Russia*, vol. 1: *To 1855*, 7th ed. (New York: Oxford University Press, 2005), 36–37; Fennell, *The Crisis of Medieval Russia*, 6.

8. For a very different interpretation of these events, see Isoaho, *The Image of Aleksandr Nevskiy in Medieval Russia*, 93–96.

9. Fennell, *The Crisis of Medieval Russia*, 114.

10. Moss, *A History of Russia*, 1:75; for a fuller account of Nevsky's actions in Novgorod and Suzdalia, see Fennell, *The Crisis of Medieval Russia*, 106–19.

11. Donald Ostrowski, *Muscovy and the Mongols: Cross-Cultural Influences on the Steppe Frontier, 1304–1589* (Cambridge: Cambridge University Press, 1998), 18, 21.

12. Riasanovsky and Steinberg, *A History of Russia*, 1:75.

13. Fennell, *The Crisis of Medieval Russia*, 112–13. Ostrowski notes that the Russian Church had been under Mongol protection at least since the census of 1257, when it was exempted from taxation (*Muscovy and the Mongols*, 18).

14. Isoaho, *The Image of Aleksandr Nevskiy in Medieval Russia*, 1.

15. Ibid., 380.

16. Donald Ostrowski, "Dressing a Wolf in Sheep's Clothing: Toward Understanding the Composition of the *Life of Alexander Nevskii*," *Russian History* 40 (2013): 67.

17. Ibid., esp. 41–42, 45, 54–56. See also Donald Ostrowski, "Redating the *Life of Alexander Nevskii*," in Chester S. L. Dunning, Russell E. Martin, and Daniel Rowland, eds., *Festschrift for Robert O. Crummey* (Bloomington, Ind.: Slavica, 2008), 1–17.

18. Ostrowski, *Muscovy and the Mongols*, 23, 138, 141, 164, 246; see also Isoaho, *The Image of Aleksandr Nevskiy in Medieval Russia*, 316–18.

19. Isoaho, *The Image of Aleksandr Nevskiy in Medieval Russia*, 283.

20. Ibid., 313–15, quotation from 313.

21. Moss, *A History of Russia*, 1:239; "Nevsky Prospect," *Wikipedia*, http://en.wikipedia.org/wiki/Nevsky_Prospect (accessed November 5, 2012). Peter the Great erected the monastery Alexander Nevsky Lavra on the eastern end of the Nevsky Prospekt, a location he chose because he believed it to be the site of Nevsky's victory over the Swedes in 1240 ("Alexander Nevsky Lavra," http://www.historvius.com/alexander-nevsky-215 [accessed November 5, 2012]).

22. Mike O'Mahony, *Sergei Eisenstein* (London: Reaktion Books, 2008), 54–85, quotation from 84.

23. The two films (both of the late 1920s), *The Old and the New* and *October*, are discussed in ibid., 86–115.

24. Sergei Eisenstein, "The Boy from Riga (An Obedient Child)," in S. M. Eisenstein, *Selected Works*, vol. 4: *Beyond the Stars: The Memoirs of Sergei Eisenstein*, ed. Richard Taylor, trans. William Powell (London: British Film Institute, 1995), 16, 801 n. 1. This essay was written on May 5–7, 1946, while Eisenstein was in the Kremlin hospital.

25. O'Mahony, *Sergei Eisenstein*, 118–59.

26. The full text is in S. M. Eisenstein, *Selected Works*, vol. 3: *Writings, 1934–47*, ed. Richard Taylor, trans. William Powell (London: British Film Institute, 1996), 100–105.

27. O'Mahony, *Sergei Eisenstein*, 160. O'Mahony isn't the only writer to draw this conclusion. See also, for example, David Bordwell, *The Cinema of Eisenstein* (New York: Routledge, 2005), 256; Russell Merritt, "Recharging 'Alexander Nevsky': Tracking the Eisenstein–Prokofiev War Horse," *Film Quarterly* 48, no. 2 (1994–1995): 34.

28. Jay Leyda, *Kino: A History of the Russian and Soviet Film* (1960; reprint, New York: Collier Books, 1973), 348; Peter Kenez, "Soviet Cinema in the Age of Stalin," in Taylor and Spring, *Stalinism and Soviet Cinema*, 63; Bordwell, *The Cinema of Eisenstein*, 27.

29. Leyda and Voynow, *Eisenstein at Work*, 97; Bordwell, *The Cinema of Eisenstein*, 26–27; "Chronology of Eisenstein's Life and Works," in Sergei Eisenstein, *Immoral Memories: An Autobiography*, trans. Herbert Marshall (Boston: Houghton Mifflin, 1983), 270–74.

30. Sergei Eisenstein, "From the History of the Making of the Film *Alexander Nevsky*," in *Selected Works*, 3:106–7, 370 n. 6.

31. Herbert Marshall, preface, in Eisenstein, *Immoral Memories*, xiii.

32. On April 8, 1940, Eisenstein penned the following in his diary: "The most successful things that I have done have been commissioned by the Government—*The Year 1905* [i.e. *The Battleship Potemkin*—Eds.], *October*, *Nevsky*" (quoted in Leonid Kozlov, "The Artist and the Shadow of Ivan," in Taylor and Spring, *Stalinism and Soviet Cinema*, 111).

33. "My Subject Is Patriotism," written in 1938, is included in Eisenstein, *Selected Works*, 3:117–20.

34. The original *Alexander Nevsky* was a Mosfilm Studios production of 1938. I have used the Criterion Collection DVD (New York, 2001), which is in Russian but has newly translated English subtitles, new digital transfer, and extensive image and sound restoration. I have also consulted and used the translated screenplay, which contains some materials supplementary to the finished film, in Jay Leyda, ed., *Eisenstein: Three Films*, trans. Diana Matias (New York: Harper and Row, 1974), 91–143.

35. *Ivan the Terrible, Part I*, was released at the end of 1944; it presents Ivan as a patriotic national hero, like *Nevsky*, made to order for the wartime situation the Soviet Union faced and was much admired by Stalin (it was awarded a Stalin Prize). *Part II*, which depicts state terrorism in an ambivalent way, failed to get past the regime's censors and wasn't finally released until 1958, ten years after Eisenstein's death. For interesting information on Prokofiev's working methods in his collaboration with Eisenstein, see Simon Morrison, *The People's Artist: Prokofiev's Soviet Years* (Oxford: Oxford University Press, 2009), 221–33. "Even the highly disciplined Eisenstein," says Harlow Robinson, another of Prokofiev's biographers, "was amazed at Prokofiev's rate of creativity and punctuality." Robinson continues: "Prokofiev's uncanny ability

to understand and interpret musically the rhythm of a given scene, and to de-
lineate the rhythmic/emotional contrast between shots and scenes (montage)
amazed Eisenstein. 'Prokofiev's music is incredibly plastic; it never becomes
mere illustration,' he said. In Prokofiev, he and his cinematographer Edward
Tisse 'found the third companion in our crusade for the kind of sound cinema
we had been dreaming about'" (*Sergei Prokofiev: A Biography* [New York:
Viking, 1987], 351, 353).

36. Sergei Eisenstein, "Alexander Nevsky and the Rout of the Germans," in *Selected Works*, 3:112, 371 n. 2.

37. Dobrenko draws attention to the reference to "German aggressors" in the
captions (*Stalinist Cinema and the Production of History*, 71). In "Alexander
Nevsky and the Rout of the Germans," Eisenstein elaborates on the differences
between the "Tatars" and the Teutonic and Livonian Knights and why the latter were far more to be feared (3:113).

38. O'Mahony, *Sergei Eisenstein*, 163.

39. Although the English subtitles in the Criterion DVD use "rabbit" for "hare,"
I have stuck with the latter because all of the references I have seen to the
folktale use "hare."

40. Sergei Eisenstein, "*Alexander Nevsky*," in *Notes of a Film Director* (New
York: Dover, 1970), 41; see also Leyda and Voynow, *Eisenstein at Work*, 97.
Prokofiev, who visited the Mosfilm Studio a number of times during production, wrote the following in a letter of July 13, 1938: "Half of the film is taken
up with the Battle on the Ice, which is being shot in the summer, the ice being
made out of asphalt painted white, glass, and white sand (snow powder).
I was at the filming several times; it's turning out great. Only the horses are
behaving badly: the 'ice' constantly needs to be cleaned" (quoted in Morrison,
The People's Artist, 224).

41. Eisenstein wrote a lengthy account of how he hit upon the idea of having a
favorite Russian folktale—as narrated, for good measure, by an ordinary representative of the artisan class—ignite in Alexander's mind the best strategic
plan for routing the Germans ("True Ways of Invention," in *Notes of a Film
Director*, 43–48).

42. Although a long roster of scholars, including such skeptics as John Fennell,
mention that the battle was fought on the ice, "none of them," according
to Donald Ostrowski, "says anything about the ice breaking up or anyone's
drowning." In fact, the idea of "the knights falling through the ice as they fled"
appears to have been invented by Eisenstein himself, with inspiration from the
Battle in Heaven in Milton's *Paradise Lost* ("Alexander Nevskii's 'Battle on
the Ice': The Creation of a Legend," *Russian History/Histoire Russe* 33, nos.
2–4 [2006]: 289–312, quoted phrases from 307, 309). As an indication of the
legend's staying power, in April 2012 a reenactment of the Battle on the Ice

was staged in Russia on the 770th anniversary of its alleged occurrence (see a photograph of the reenactment at http://newsline.photoshelter.com/image/ I0000anVg11BFr3E [accessed November 6, 2012]).

43. O'Mahony, *Sergei Eisenstein*, 167.

44. Eisenstein, "Alexander Nevsky and the Rout of the Germans," 3:116.

45. For the final scenes in the earlier version, see Leyda, *Eisenstein*, 182–86.

46. Dobrenko, *Stalinist Cinema and the Production of History*, 73; see also Bordwell, *The Cinema of Eisenstein*, 223. Russell Merritt raises questions concerning the evidence for Stalin's direct role in modifying the film's ending ("Recharging 'Alexander Nevsky,'" 39, 46 n. 6); see also Morrison, *The People's Artist*, 221; O'Mahony, *Sergei Eisenstein*, 161; Barry P. Scherr, "*Alexander Nevsky*: Film Without a Hero," in Al LaValley and Barry P. Scherr, eds., *Eisenstein at 100: A Reconsideration* (New Brunswick, N.J.: Rutgers University Press, 2001), 209–10.

47. Eisenstein, "True Ways of Invention," 47.

48. Bordwell, *The Cinema of Eisenstein*, 212; Dobrenko, *Stalinist Cinema and the Production of History*, 74; Beumers, *A History of Russian Cinema*, 98.

49. Morrison, *The People's Artist*, 222.

50. O'Mahony, *Sergei Eisenstein*, 168–69.

51. Maya Turovskaya, "The 1930s and 1940s: Cinema in Context," in Taylor and Spring, *Stalinism and Soviet Cinema*, 50; Kenez, "Soviet Cinema in the Age of Stalin," 56; Bordwell, *The Cinema of Eisenstein*, 27; O'Mahony, *Sergei Eisenstein*, 162; Ronald Bergan, *Eisenstein: A Life in Conflict* (Woodstock, N.Y.: Overlook Press, 1999), 304.

52. Nina Tumarkin, *The Living and the Dead: The Rise and Fall of the Cult of World War II in Russia* (New York: Basic Books, 1994), 61–63, Stalin quotation on 63.

53. When released in the United States in spring 1939, *Alexander Nevsky* was hailed in *Life* magazine with a two-page picture spread and greeted in the *New York Times* and elsewhere with rave reviews (J. Hoberman, "Alexander Nevsky," posted April 23, 2001, http://www.criterion.com/current/posts/8-alexander-nevsky).

54. Morrison, *The People's Artist*, 233. On the cantata, see Robinson, *Sergei Prokofiev*, 357.

55. Hoberman, "Alexander Nevsky."

56. In 2008, Russians voted Nevsky their most popular historical figure. It was only fitting, wrote Radio Free Europe/Radio Liberty in its blog of December 29, 2008, "that in an increasingly xenophobic Russia, a militant Christian saint uniting Russians against foreign invaders becomes the greatest national symbol." The vote was sponsored by a Russian state television channel. Stalin appears to have led initially in the vote, which was so embarrassing to the channel that

it encouraged Russians to vote for other national heroes. Although, in the end, Nevsky came in first, Stalin still placed third (Radio Free Europe, "Alexander Nevsky: A Fitting Hero for Today's Russia," http://www.rferl.org/content/ Alexander_Nevsky_A_Fitting_Hero_For_Todays_Russia__/1364743.html [accessed November 6, 2012]).

57. This connection has been widely noted. See especially Ian Christie, "Censorship, Culture, and Codpieces: Eisenstein's Influence in Britain During the 1930s and 1940s," in LaValley and Scherr, *Eisenstein at 100*, 113–16.

58. Michael Anderegg, *Cinematic Shakespeare* (Lanham, Md.: Rowman & Littlefield, 2004), 41. Other writers have also commented on the importance of *Henry V* for the postwar revival of the British film industry in the face of American competition. See Russell Jackson, *Shakespeare Films in the Making: Vision, Production, and Reception* (Cambridge: Cambridge University Press, 2007), 93; Foster Hirsch, *Laurence Olivier* (Boston: Twayne, 1979), 76; Jerry Vermilye, *The Complete Films of Laurence Olivier* (New York: Citadel Press, 1992), 117–18.

59. For information on Olivier's participation in the war effort and the quoted speech, see Anthony Holden, *Laurence Olivier* (New York: Atheneum, 1988), 169, 172–73.

60. Ibid., 169.

61. Quoted in Thomas Kiernan, *Sir Larry: The Life of Laurence Olivier* (New York: Times Books, 1981), 206.

62. Terry Coleman, *Olivier* (New York: Henry Holt, 2005), 146. Some will be surprised to learn that regular high-definition television service was introduced in Britain in 1936. Its early history is recounted in Asa Briggs, *The BBC: The First Fifty Years* (Oxford: Oxford University Press, 1985), 155–71.

63. Quotation from Coleman, *Olivier*, 146; see also Kiernan, *Sir Larry*, 204–5. Still an Italian citizen, del Giudice had been interned at the start of the war but was released "on the condition that he devote his energies, talents and financial resources to making wartime propaganda and morale-boosting feature films" (Kiernan, *Sir Larry*, 204). For a slightly different account of Bower's 1942 radio broadcast and del Giudice's part in launching the film production, see Holden, *Laurence Olivier*, 173–74.

64. Vermilye, *Complete Films of Laurence Olivier*, 112; Laurence Olivier, *On Acting* (New York: Simon and Schuster, 1986), 267.

65. Quoted in Kiernan, *Sir Larry*, 205.

66. The words were Carol Reed's, quoted in Holden, *Laurence Olivier*, 174.

67. Kiernan, *Sir Larry*, 205, 207–8; Coleman, *Olivier*, 159; Holden, *Laurence Olivier*, 181. The Inland Revenue was not at all amused by the tax-free nature of the payment and sued Olivier, although unsuccessfully (Richard Norton-Taylor, "How Olivier Staged a Tax Coup," *The Guardian*, March 1, 2006).

68. Ian Mortimer, *1415: Henry V's Year of Glory* (London: Bodley Head, 2009), 1.

69. Several scholars have questioned the reliability of the stories of Henry's riotous youth. See, for example, Felipe Fernandez-Armesto, "The Myth of Henry V," http://www.bbc.co.uk/history/british/middle_ages/henry_v_01.shtml (accessed November 9, 2012).

70. See the discussion in Janet Clare, *"Art Made Tongue-Tied by Authority": Elizabethan and Jacobean Dramatic Censorship* (Manchester, U.K.: Manchester University Press, 1990), 76–79.

71. Mortimer, *1415*, 36–38, 547, quotation from 38. For questions about the nature of the Lollard rising and the claim that Oldcastle initiated and led it, see Annabel Patterson, "Sir John Oldcastle as Symbol of Reformation Historiography," in Donna B. Hamilton and Richard Strier, eds., *Religion, Literature, and Politics in Post-Reformation England, 1540–1688* (Cambridge: Cambridge University Press, 1996), 6–26; and "Henry V of England," *Wikipedia*, http://en.wikipedia.org/wiki/Henry_V_of_England (accessed November 9, 2012).

72. For an illuminating discussion of the issues surrounding the killing of prisoners in the medieval Christian setting and the circumstances that appear to have prompted the historical Henry to give such an order, see John Keegan, *The Face of Battle: A Study of Agincourt, Waterloo, and the Somme* (New York: Viking, 1976), 108–12; see also Clifford J. Rogers, "The Battle of Agincourt," in L. J. Andrew Villalon and Donald J. Kagay, eds., *The Hundred Years War (Part II): Different Vistas* (Leiden: Brill, 2008), 99–103.

73. "Henry V of England." For other accounts of the famine conditions prevailing in Rouen at the time of the siege, see Larissa Taylor, *The Virgin Warrior: The Life and Death of Joan of Arc* (New Haven, Conn.: Yale University Press, 2009), 124–25; Robin Neillands, *The Hundred Years War*, rev. ed. (London: Routledge, 2001), 227; and "Siege of Rouen," *Wikipedia*, http://en.wikipedia.org/wiki/Siege_of_Rouen (accessed November 10, 2012). According to the article "Siege of Rouen," "[O]n Christmas day 1418, King Henry allowed two priests to give food to the starving people, but the day soon ended and the people went back to dying miserably in the ditch."

74. For the various numbers of combatants given in a wide range of fifteenth-century chronicle sources, see Anne Curry, *The Battle of Agincourt: Sources and Interpretations* (Woodbridge, U.K.: Boydell Press, 2000), 12. John Keegan states that there is general agreement that by the start of the battle Henry V's army had shrunk to about 5,000 or 6,000 archers and 1,000 men-at-arms, and the count on the French side ranged from 10,000 to 200,000 (*The Face of Battle*, 87), the latter a higher figure than the highest given by Curry, which is 150,000. In more recent scholarship, Curry estimates the size of the English army at around 9,000 and the French at roughly 12,000 (*Agincourt: A New History* [Stroud, U.K.: Tempus, 2005], 187, 192). Juliet Barker puts the English

army at 6,000 more or less; although she views it as "impossible to give [for the French] even an estimated number with any certainty," she believes it to have been far greater than Curry's estimate (*Agincourt: The King, the Campaign, the Battle* [London: Little, Brown, 2005], xvi, 274, 416 n. 24, quotation from 274).

75. Keegan, *The Face of Battle*, 78.

76. Taylor, *The Virgin Warrior*, xxiv.

77. Mortimer, *1415*, 536. See also Fernandez-Armesto, "The Myth of Henry V."

78. Rogers, "The Battle of Agincourt," 103. The most significant of the French errors, according to Rogers, "was the faulty deployment for battle, which was the root cause of the disordered state in which the French men-at-arms found themselves when they hit the English line" (103).

79. Keegan, *The Face of Battle*, 86.

80. Quoted in Michael Munn, *Lord Larry: The Secret Life of Laurence Olivier, a Personal and Intimate Portrait* (London: Robson Books, 2007), 129–30. See also the analysis in Hirsch, *Laurence Olivier*, 63–76.

81. Munn, *Lord Larry*, 130.

82. Munn, *Lord Larry*, 132; Vermilye, *Complete Films of Laurence Olivier*, 116.

83. Del Giudice quoted in Coleman, *Olivier*, 154; see also Holden, *Laurence Olivier*, 176. Olivier expressed his warm appreciation of del Giudice's contribution: "Filippo Del Giudice—bless him—was the moving force behind the project. . . . [H]e kept all financial worries from me and left me with complete artistic control, including every bit of casting" (*On Acting*, 270).

84. Quoted in Jackson, *Shakespeare Films in the Making*, 93.

85. My summation of the film *Henry V* is based on the Criterion Collection DVD (New York, 1999) and the screenplay *Henry V by William Shakespeare, Produced and Directed by Laurence Olivier*, ed. Andrew Sinclair, with an introduction by Laurence Olivier (London: Lorrimer, 1984) (hereafter *Henry V* screenplay). When required, I have used the text of the original Shakespeare play, *Henry V*, in William Shakespeare, *Major Plays and the Sonnets*, ed. G. B. Harrison (New York: Harcourt, Brace, 1948), 455–92 (hereafter *Henry V* play).

86. *Henry V* screenplay, 3–16; *Henry V* play, 455–60. See also Hirsch, *Laurence Olivier*, 70.

87. *Henry V* screenplay, 17–23; *Henry V* play, 460–62.

88. *Henry V* screenplay, 24.

89. Ibid., 25; William Shakespeare, *Henry IV, Part Two*, in *Major Plays and the Sonnets*, 415.

90. *Henry V* screenplay, 28–29.

91. Ibid., 29–34.

92. Ibid., 34–48.

93. Ibid., 49–53.

94. Ibid., 54–63.

95. Keegan, *The Face of Battle*, 90, 95–96.

96. *Henry V* screenplay, 63–69.

97. Ibid., 69–77.

98. Ibid., 81–91. I've changed the spelling of "Katharine" in the screenplay to "Catherine" for the sake of consistency with the spelling of the princess's name elsewhere in this book.

99. Quoted in Max Hastings, *Winston's War: Churchill, 1940–1945* (New York: Knopf, 2010), 393. The spirit of King's action, Hastings suggests, "would have warmed the prime minister's heart" (393). The lines from the play are in *Henry V* play, 468.

100. Angus Calder gives these figures in *The People's War: Britain, 1939–45* (London: Jonathan Cape, 1969), 562–63; Jackson gives substantially lower casualty numbers in *Shakespeare Films in the Making*, 114.

101. *Henry V* play, 464, 470, 473.

102. The order to kill the prisoners ("Then every soldier kill his prisoners") is given at the end of act IV, scene VI, and is further alluded to in the next scene ("Besides, we'll cut the throats of those we have, / And not a man of them that we shall take / Shall taste our mercy" [ibid., 483–84]). The final speech of the Chorus is in ibid., 492.

103. Quoted in John Colville, *The Fringes of Power: Downing Street Diaries, 1939–1955*, 2 vols. (London: Scepter, 1987), 2:162.

104. Douglas Brode, *Shakespeare in the Movies: From the Silent Era to "Shakespeare in Love"* (New York: Oxford University Press, 2000), 80; see also Hirsch, *Laurence Olivier*, 71–72.

105. Other adaptations of *Nevsky* in *Henry V* are demonstrated pictorially, through paired stills from the two films, in Jeff (Second Reel)'s blog, "Olivier's *Henry V* and Eisenstein's *Nevsky*," http://www.second-reel.com/annex/choruslines/olivier-nevsky.shtml (accessed March 20, 2013). Thanks to Nina Tumarkin for calling this blog to my attention.

106. Brode, *Shakespeare in the Movies*, 81–82.

107. Olivier, *On Acting*, 274.

108. Holden, *Laurence Olivier*, 177.

109. At the time of the film's release, a party of Free French sailors stationed in Britain are said to have walked out of the theater in protest (Ton Hoenselaars, "Recycling the Renaissance in World War II: E. W. & M. M. Robson Review Laurence Olivier's *Henry V*," in Ton Hoenselaars and Arthur F. Kinney, eds., *Challenging Humanism: Essays in Honor of Dominic Baker-Smith* [Newark: University of Delaware Press, 2005], 278).

110. Anderegg, *Cinematic Shakespeare*, 40.

111. The historian Simon Schama, who was born in London in 1945, asserts in a recent article that Olivier's *Henry V* still spoke to the English ten years after the war's end ("His Story, Our Story," *Financial Times*, June 9, 2012, http://www.ft.com/cms/s/2/534deef2-aeff-11e1-a8a7-00144feabdco.html). Thanks to Chris Munn for calling this article to my attention.

112. William Walton to Roy Douglas, May 1943, in Michael Hayes, ed., *The Selected Letters of William Walton* (London: Faber and Faber, 2002), 145.

113. Quoted in Michael Kennedy, *Portrait of Walton* (Oxford: Oxford University Press, 1989), 125. Walton appears to have agreed with Olivier. At some point early in the production, he was shown the film without sound. When he later saw it in its completed form, he said to Olivier: "Well, my boy, I'm very glad you showed it to me, because I must tell you I did think it was terribly dull without the music!" (quoted in ibid., 126). Olivier and Walton went on to collaborate on two other Shakespeare films, *Hamlet* (1948) and *Richard III* (1955).

114. Holden, *Laurence Olivier*, 179–80; Vermilye, *Complete Films of Laurence Olivier*, 116–17.

115. James Agee, review of *Henry V*, *Time* magazine, April 8, 1946, reprinted in James Agee, *Agee on Film: Reviews and Comments by James Agee* (New York: McDowell, Obolensky, 1958), 365.

116. Arthur Miller, *Timebends: A Life* (New York: Grove Press, 1987), 348.

117. John Flower, *Joan of Arc: Icon of Modern Culture* (Hastings, U.K.: Helm Information, 2008), 178 (quotation about *L'Alouette*); Claude Grimal, "Appendix: The American Maid," in Flower, *Joan of Arc*, 261–62; Lillian Hellman, *The Lark* (New York: Random House, 1956). Anouilh's plays were not particularly successful in America, the "first run of any length on Broadway" being Hellman's rendering of *L'Alouette*, which, apart from its timely political message, certainly owed part of its popularity to an all-star cast consisting of Julie Harris (who played Joan), Boris Karloff, and Christopher Plummer (Stewart H. Benedict, "Anouilh in America," *Modern Language Journal* 45, no. 8 [1961]: 342). Henry W. Knepler argues that the box-office success of Hellman's adaptation ("as much of a triumph in New York as a historical play is ever likely to be there"), compared to the reception of Christopher Fry's translation done earlier—which served as the basis for a London production that didn't last through the season—was due to the fact that it was simply better ("The Lark, Translation vs. Adaptation: A Case History," in Mark W. Estrin, ed., *Critical Essays on Lillian Hellman* [Boston: Hall, 1989], 64–71).

118. Alan Cowell, "In War and Hardship, Relishing a Taste of Nostalgia," *New York Times*, September 21, 2009; Claire O'Boyle, "Dame Vera Lynn's Rallying Call for Support for Troops in Afghanistan," September 1, 2009, http://www.mirror.co.uk/news/top-stories/2009/09/01/today-s-brave-troops-should-be-as-much-in-our-thoughts-as-heroes-of-70-years-ago-115875-21639076/;

Stephanie Kennedy, "At 92 Vera Lynn Charms Again," September 1, 2009, http://www.abc.net.au/am/content/2009/s2672719.htm.

119. This is exactly what happened also with the Academy Award–winning film *Yankee Doodle Dandy*, which depicted the life and music of George M. Cohan and starred James Cagney in the lead role. The film was released in June 1942, only months after Pearl Harbor, and includes President Roosevelt's presentation of the Congressional Gold Medal to Cohan for his contributions to morale during World War I, in particular through such songs as "Over There" and "You're a Grand Old Flag." Although Cohan actually received the medal from FDR in 1936, in the film the presentation takes place in the early stages of World War II, collapsing the patriotic mood of 1917 and that of 1942 into one. *Yankee Doodle Dandy*, directed by Michael Curtiz (whose *Casablanca* premiered later in 1942), was a huge box-office triumph, grossing more for Warner Brothers than any of its prior films ("*Yankee Doodle Dandy*," *Wikipedia*, http://en.wikipedia.org/wiki/Yankee_Doodle_Dandy [accessed July 6, 2012]).

120. Agee, review of *Henry V*, in *Agee on Film*, 365.

121. Quoted in Vermilye, *Complete Films of Laurence Olivier*, 118.

122. Quoted in Holden, *Laurence Olivier*, 181.

CONCLUSION

1. Jonathan Gottschall supplies numerous examples of the "power of story" (by which he generally means fiction) in the shaping of historical reality in *The Storytelling Animal: How Stories Make Us Human* (Boston: Houghton Mifflin Harcourt, 2012), 139–55.

2. Simon Schama, "His Story, Our Story," *Financial Times*, June 9, 2012, http://www.ft.com/cms/s/2/534deef2-aeff-11e1-a8a7-00144feabdc0.html.

3. See, in this connection, Gordon S. Wood's biting critique of what he considers to be Jill Lepore's failure to appreciate the importance of popular memory to American (or any other) society in her book *The Whites of Their Eyes: The Tea Party's Revolution and the Battle Over American History* (Princeton, N.J.: Princeton University Press, 2010) ("No Thanks for the Memories," *New York Review of Books*, January 13, 2011, 40–42).

4. For a moving essay on the lasting meaning of the Wounded Knee massacre for the Lakota, prompted by the danger that the site may soon pass into private hands, see Joseph Brings Plenty, "Save Wounded Knee," *New York Times*, April 12, 2013.

5. Vamik D. Volkan, "Chosen Trauma, the Political Ideology of Entitlement and Violence," paper presented at the "Berlin Meeting," June 10, 2004, http://www.vamikvolkan.com/Chosen-Trauma,-the-Political-Ideology-of-Entitlement-and-Violence.php (accessed October 31, 2011), emphasis in original; see also

Vamik D. Volkan, "Large-Group Identity and Chosen Trauma," *Psychoanalysis Downunder*, no. 6 (December 2005), http://psychoanalysis.mylithio.com/downunder/backissues/6/427/large_group_vv.

6. The same word for *story* and *history* is used in other languages as well (Jacques Le Goff, *History and Memory*, trans. Steven Rendall and Elizabeth Claman [New York: Columbia University Press, 1992], 102, 119–20).

7. See, for example, Terrence L. Gargiulo, *Making Stories: A Practical Guide for Organizational Leaders and Human Resource Specialists* (Westport, Conn.: Quorum Books, 2002), 36.

8. In a critique of President Obama's failure to communicate adequately to the American public the story of what he wants for America, Drew Westen wrote: "The stories our leaders tell us matter, probably almost as much as the stories our parents tell us as children, because they orient us to what is, what could be, and what should be; to the worldviews they hold and to the values they hold sacred" ("What Happened to Obama?" *New York Times*, August 7, 2011).

9. F. Michael Connelly and D. Jean Clandinin, "Stories of Experience and Narrative Inquiry," *Educational Researcher* 19, no. 5 (1990): 2.

10. The medical student is Valerie Gribben, whose article "Practicing Medicine Can Be Grimm Work" appeared in the *New York Times*, July 1, 2011; the historian of science is Anne Harrington, whose recent book *The Cure Within* is summarized in Erin O'Donnell, "Does Thinking Make It So?" *Harvard Magazine*, January–February 2009, 13. For more on the role of storytelling in improving people's emotional health, see James W. Pennebaker and Janel D. Seagal, "Forming a Story: The Health Benefits of Narrative," *Journal of Clinical Psychology* 55, no. 10 (1999): 1243–54, and Pauline W. Chen, "When Patients Share Their Stories, Health May Improve," http://www.nytimes.com/2011/02/10/health/views/10chen.html (accessed March 12, 2012). The Columbia ad is in the *New Yorker*, January 19, 2009, 11; on Columbia's Program in Narrative Medicine, see also Jerome Bruner, *Making Stories: Law, Literature, Life* (Cambridge, Mass.: Harvard University Press, 2002), 105–6.

11. See, for example, Bruner, *Making Stories*, esp. chap. 2.

12. For such scrutiny, see Yiannis Gabriel, ed., *Myths, Stories, and Organizations: Premodern Narratives for Our Times* (Oxford: Oxford University Press, 2004); for practical advice on the use of stories in business, see Gargiulo, *Making Stories*.

13. David Eagleman, *Incognito: The Secret Lives of the Brain* (New York: Pantheon Books, 2011), 137.

14. Dr. Michael S. Gazzaniga's research in brain science is described in Benedict Carey, "Decoding the Brain's Cacophony," *New York Times*, October 31, 2011. The distinguished psychologist Daniel Kahneman writes of the "remembering self's" working procedure that "it composes stories and keeps them

for future reference" (*Thinking, Fast and Slow* [New York: Farrar, Straus and Giroux, 2011], 387).

15. See Bruner, *Making Stories*, 27, and the discussion in the preface to this book.

16. "Those genetic lines that did not find their infants cute," Eagleman writes, "no longer exist, because their young were not properly cared for" (*Incognito*, 99).

17. One of the most informative and persuasive accounts of storytelling's role in the earliest evolution of *Homo sapiens sapiens* is Michelle Scalise Sugiyama, "Narrative Theory and Function: Why Evolution Matters," *Philosophy and Literature* 25, no. 2 (2001): 233–50. "The universality of narrative," according to Scalise Sugiyama, "suggests that those individuals who were able (or better able) to tell and process stories enjoyed a reproductive advantage over those who were less skilled or incapable of doing so, thereby passing on this ability to subsequent generations" (235). Also of interest are some of the essays in Jonathan Gottschall and David Sloan Wilson, eds., *The Literary Animal: Evolution and the Nature of Narrative* (Evanston, Ill.: Northwestern University Press, 2005).

18. Scalise Sugiyama, "Narrative Theory and Function," 234. David Bordwell and Kristin Thompson describe narrative as "a chain of events in cause–effect relationship occurring in time and space" (*Film Art: An Introduction*, 4th ed. [New York: McGraw-Hill, 1993], 65).

19. Tamotsu Shibutani, *Improvised News: A Sociological Study of Rumor* (Indianapolis: Bobbs-Merrill, 1966), cited in S. A. Smith, "Talking Toads and Chinless Ghosts: The Politics of 'Superstitious' Rumors in the People's Republic of China, 1961–1965," *American Historical Review* 111, no. 2 (2006): 408.

20. On the rumor of well poisoning during the Boxer period, see Paul A. Cohen, *History in Three Keys: The Boxers as Event, Experience, and Myth* (New York: Columbia University Press, 1997), 167–72; on the rumors generated by the Great Leap famine, see Smith, "Talking Toads and Chinless Ghosts," 405–27.

21. Avishai Margalit, *The Ethics of Memory* (Cambridge, Mass.: Harvard University Press, 2002), 95. See also Jan Assmann, "Collective Memory and Cultural Identity," trans. John Czaplicka, *New German Critique* 65 (Spring–Summer 1995): 125–33.

22. Ernest Renan, *What Is a Nation? Qu'est-ce qu' une nation?* trans. Wanda Romer Taylor (Toronto: Tapir Press, 1996), 47. Kwame Anthony Appiah discusses Renan's ideas in his review of Margalit's book, *New York Review of Books*, March 13, 2003, 35–37. See also Joep Leerssen, *National Thought in Europe: A Cultural History* (Amsterdam: Amsterdam University Press, 2006), 227–31.

23. J. M. Coetzee has Susan Barton, a character in his novel *Foe*, ask at one point: "Is that the secret meaning of the word *story*, do you think: a storing-place of memories?" ([New York: Penguin, 1987], 59).

24. Bruner, *Making Stories*, 25.

25. Gottschall, *The Storytelling Animal*, 177; see also 28, 197.

26. Mark Elvin, *Changing Stories in the Chinese World* (Stanford, Calif.: Stanford University Press, 1997), 5.

27. Benedict Anderson, *Imagined Communities: Reflections on the Origin and Spread of Nationalism*, rev. ed. (London: Verso, 1991), 5–7.

28. Ger Duijzings, *Religion and the Politics of Identity in Kosovo* (New York: Columbia University Press, 2000), 193.

29. Such writers include the cognitive psychologist Roger C. Schank (*Tell Me a Story: Narrative and Intelligence* [Evanston, Ill.: Northwestern University Press, 1990]), the philosopher David Carr (*Time, Narrative, and History* [Bloomington: Indiana University Press, 1986]), and the educational theorists F. Michael Connelly and D. Jean Clandinin ("Stories of Experience and Narrative Inquiry").

30. Margalit, *The Ethics of Memory*, 99.

31. This was how the Israel Ministry of Foreign Affairs framed it at the close of the twentieth century. See "Masada—Symbol of Jewish Freedom," August 17, 1999, http://www.mfa.gov.il/MFA/MFAArchive/1990_1999/1999/8/Masada+-+Symbol+of+Jewish+Freedom.htm.

32. Chartier's remarks, made in a paper delivered at the International Congress of Historical Sciences in Montreal in 1995, are quoted in Georg G. Iggers, *Historiography in the Twentieth Century: From Scientific Objectivity to the Postmodern Challenge* (Hanover, N.H.: Wesleyan University Press, University Press of New England, 1997), 12.

33. Iggers, *Historiography in the Twentieth Century*, 119; see also 12–13, 145. My own understanding of the relationship among historical reconstruction, reality, and truth is spelled out in *History in Three Keys*, esp. 3–13.

34. For a historian's effort at cataloging some of the many meanings and functions of memory, see Geoffrey Cubitt's introduction to *History and Memory* (Manchester, U.K.: Manchester University Press, 2007), 1–25.

35. As Gottschall puts it, "Our memories are not precise records of what actually happened. They are reconstructions of what happened, and many of the details—small and large—are unreliable" (*The Storytelling Animal*, 169). He cites many examples of the untrustworthiness of memory (156–76).

36. David Lowenthal, *Possessed by the Past: The Heritage Crusade and the Spoils of History* (New York: Free Press, 1996), 162–63.

37. Plumb, Nora, Lowenthal, and Bailyn's comments on the distinction between history and memory in this paragraph and the following one are drawn from Wood's important review of Lepore's *The Whites of Their Eyes* ("No Thanks for the Memories," 41–42). For a clear and useful account of the history/memory

issue, see also Pierre Nora, "Between Memory and History: *Les Lieux de Mé-moire,*" *Representations* 26 (Spring 1989): 7–24.

38. Jonathan Safran Foer, "Why a Haggadah?" *New York Times*, April 1, 2012.

39. For example, I recently read two wonderful works of historical fiction by the psychiatrist Irvin D. Yalom: *The Spinoza Problem: A Novel* (New York: Basic Books, 2012) and *When Nietzsche Wept: A Novel of Obsession* (New York: Basic Books, 1992). Yalom, unlike many authors of historical novels, includes a note at the end of each work telling the reader what parts and which characters in his novels are based on historical reality and what parts and which characters are fabricated. These notes are helpful but also deceptive because by fictionalizing the environment within which the nonfiction aspects of the works operate, he unavoidably ends up fictionalizing those nonfiction aspects as well.

40. Barry Schwartz, "The Reconstruction of Abraham Lincoln," in David Middleton and Derek Edwards, eds., *Collective Remembering* (Newbury Park, Calif.: Sage, 1990), 81–107, quotation from 103. Although following Maurice Halbwachs up to a point, Schwartz goes beyond Halbwachs's extreme presentism, arguing that alongside the transformations that the image of Lincoln has undergone, certain basic American traits and values have persisted unchanged through time. For a fuller account of Schwartz's views, see his article "The Social Context of Commemoration: A Study in Collective Memory," *Social Forces* 61, no. 2 (1982): 374–402; see also the discussion of his position in Lewis A. Coser, "Introduction: Maurice Halbwachs 1877–1945," in Maurice Halbwachs, *On Collective Memory*, trans. and ed. Lewis A. Coser (Chicago: University of Chicago Press, 1992), 26–27, 30.

41. Ken Burns, "A Conflict's Acoustic Shadows," *New York Times*, April 12, 2011. See also the account of changing perceptions of the Civil War in Harvard University president Drew Faust's lecture "Telling War Stories: Reflections of a Civil War Historian," delivered at the Cambridge Public Library in Cambridge, Massachusetts, January 10, 2012, reported in Katie Koch, "The Civil War's Allures, and Horrors," *Harvard Gazette*, January 12, 2012; and Andrew Delbanco's review of David W. Blight's *American Oracle: The Civil War in the Civil Rights Era* (Cambridge, Mass.: Harvard University Press, 2011) in " 'The Central Event of Our Past': Still Murky," *New York Review of Books*, February 9, 2012, 19–21.

42. David Lowenthal, *The Past Is a Foreign Country* (Cambridge: Cambridge University Press, 1985). The title of Lowenthal's book is drawn from the opening line of L. P. Hartley's novel *The Go-Between* (London: Hamish Hamilton, 1953): "The past is a foreign country; they do things differently there."

43. Quoted in Wood, "No Thanks for the Memories," 42.

44. J. H. Plumb, *The Death of the Past* (1969; reprint, New York: Palgrave Macmillan, 2004), 106–7. Plumb makes a similar comment in regard to Edward Gibbon, who in the second half of the eighteenth century, in Plumb's view, "raised the writing of history to a new level": Gibbon "sought a detached and truthful past, free from preconception or the idea of inherent purpose. Yet his detachment was infused with a warm and generous attitude to mankind in spite of its immeasurable follies and iniquities" (129–30).

INDEX

www.ingramcontent.com/pod-product-compliance
Ingram Content Group UK Ltd.
Pitfield, Milton Keynes, MK11 3LW, UK
UKHW030858190225
455302UK00004B/253